GANGBUSTERS

HOW A STREET-TOUGH

ELITE HOMICIDE UNIT

GANGBUSTERS

TOOK DOWN NEW YORK'S

MOST DANGEROUS GANG

MICHAEL STONE

D O U B L E D A Y

New York London Toronto Sydney Auckland

PUBLISHED BY DOUBLEDAY
a division of Random House, Inc.
1540 Broadway, New York, New York 10036

DOUBLEDAY and the portrayal of an anchor with a dolphin
are trademarks of Doubleday, a division of Random House, Inc.

Book design by Richard Oriolo
Map by Jeffrey L. Ward

Library of Congress Cataloging-in-Publication Data:

Stone, Michael, 1948–
Gangbusters / Michael Stone.
p. cm.
Includes index.
1. Gangs—New York (N.Y.)—Case studies. I. Title.
HV6439.U7 .N4685 2000
364.1'06'6097471—dc21
00-022662

1   3   5   7   9   10   8   6   4   2

For Missy, who taught me how to love

ACKNOWLEDGMENTS

THIS BOOK could not be written without the cooperation of the Manhattan District Attorney's office. My thanks to Robert Morgenthau, who allowed me full access to the Homicide Investigation Unit and never tried to influence what I wrote, and to Barbara Jones, whose counsel and trust were integral to the conception of this project.

I'm also indebted to the members, past and present, of the Homicide Investigation Unit and to the many men and women who played a part in the Wild Cowboys case. Virtually all of them spoke to me without hesitation, and were unstinting with their time and their efforts to remember details, some of which were extremely painful. They include, but are not limited to: Jessica DeGrazia, William Hoyt, Ed Stancyzk, Walter Arsenault, Ellen Corcella, the Hon. Fernando Camacho, Dan Brownell, the Hon. Gregory Carro, Deborah Hickey, Luke Rettler, Steve Fitzgerald, Terry Quinn, Steve Michard, Jose Flores, Angel Garcia, Robert Tarwacki, Nixon Fredrick, Garry Dugan, Mark Tebbens, Pat Lafferty, Andrew Rosenzweig, Joe Pernice, Gerry Dimuro, Charles Rorke, Eddie Benitez, Kevin Bryant, Barry Kluger, Ed Freedenthal, Don Hill, Linda Nelson, Lori Grifa, the Hon. Leslie Crocker Snyder, Alex Calabrese, Teresa Matushaj, Rocco DeSantis, the Cruz–Morales family, and the Cargill family, whose wisdom and candor are nearly as great as the loss they suffered at the hands of the Cowboys.

I am further indebted to Ron Goldstock, Paul Schectman, Warren Murray, Charles Blakey, Arthur Eisenberg, Richard Emery, Gerald Lefcourt, Richard Esposito, William Bratton, John Maple, John Miller,

Mike Giulian, and John Timoney for their valuable insight into the legal system and New York's law enforcement community.

On a personal note, my thanks to the many friends, family, and colleagues whose generous advice and support over the years led to the writing of this book, among them: Judith Daniels, Clay Felker, Richard Babcock, Peter Foges and Gully Wells, Anna, John Heilperin, Charles Bennett, Virginia White, Irik and Anne Marie Sevin, and the women in my life; my mother and daughters, Billie, Fiona, Sabrina, and Natasha Stone; my wife and love Pamela Balfour; and Elaine Kaufman, Dora Flowers and Alberta Brown.

Finally, my special thanks to my agent, Mark Reiter, without whose drive this book would still be an idea; to Linda Steinman, who worked tirelessly on the legal aspects of the manuscript; and to my editor, Roger Scholl, whose extraordinary craft and dedication is responsible for whatever good is contained in these pages.

—Michael Stone
New York, 2000

CONTENTS

LIST OF CHARACTERS

Robert Morgenthau—the District Attorney of New York County (Manhattan).

Barbara Jones—the Manhattan DA's First Assistant, she served as Morgenthau's Chief of Staff.

Nancy Ryan—the Chief of Trial Division under Morgenthau, she founded the Asian Gang unit and supervised HIU.

Walter Arsenault—Chief of HIU.

Dan Rather—an Assistant District Attorney in HIU, he was the prosecutor in charge of the Wild Cowboy investigation.

Dan Brownell—an Assistant District Attorney in HIU, he was the lead prosecutor in the Wild Cowboy trial.

Terry Quinn—HIU's Investigative Chief.

Garry Dugan—an NYPD detective assigned to Manhattan North Homicide, he later joined HIU as a senior investigator.

Mark Tebbens—an NYPD detective assigned to the 40th Precinct squad, he was the primary police investigator on the Double and Quad cases, and was later posted to HIU.

Luke Rettler—the Chief of Asian Gang unit, he shared offices with HIU.

Rob Johnson—the District Attorney of Bronx County.

Barry Kluger—the Bronx DA's Executive Assistant, he served as Johnson's Chief of Staff.

Ed Freedenthal—the Bronx DA's Chief of Narcotics Investigations, he was Don Hill's supervisor.

Don Hill—an Assistant District Attorney in the Bronx's Narcotics Investigations unit, he was the prosecutor in charge of the Quad case. Later he represented the Bronx in the joint investigation and prosecution of the Wild Cowboys.

Linda Nelson—a Bronx prosecutor, she assisted Don Hill in the Wild Cowboy case.

Lori Grifa—a Brooklyn prosecutor assigned to the Michael Cruz attempted murder case, she represented her office on the Wild Cowboy task force.

Charles Rorke—an NYPD lieutenant, he commanded the No. 3 HIDTA team.

Eddie Benitez—an NYPD detective assigned to HIDTA, he was the field officer in charge of the Wild Cowboy narcotics investigation.

Leslie Crocker Snyder—an Acting NYS Supreme Court Justice, she presided over the Wild Cowboy trial.

Lenin "Lenny" Sepulveda—the leader of the Wild Cowboys.

Nelson "the Whack" Sepulveda—Lenny's brother and second-in-command.

Wilfredo "Platano" De Los Angeles—the Cowboys' chief enforcer.

Jose "Pasqualito" Llaca—a high-ranking Cowboy who at various times served as Lenny's enforcer and partner.

Daniel "Fat Danny" Rincon—a high-ranking Cowboy, who, along with Pasqualito, managed the gang's Orange-Top affiliate.

Victor Mercedes—Fat Danny's half brother and partner.

Stanley Tukes—a Cowboy manager/enforcer and a shooter in the Quad.

Rennie Harris—a Cowboy manager/enforcer and a shooter in the Quad.

Linwood Collins—a Cowboy manager/enforcer and a shooter in the Quad.

Daniel "Shorty" Gonzales—a Cowboy manager/enforcer and a shooter in the Quad.

Rafael "Tezo" Perez—Lenny's right-hand man.

Santiago "Yayo" Polanco—the leader of the Coke Is It and Basedballs organizations, he was the first major crack marketer in Washington Heights and Lenny's mentor.

Rafael "Rafi" Martinez—the leader of the Gheri Curls, a major wholesale cocaine gang.

Jose "El Feo" Reyes—a major drug wholesaler and Lenny's chief ally and supplier.

Francisco "Freddy Krueger" Medina—El Feo's chief enforcer.

Raymond Polanco—a Brooklyn-based gun trafficker, he was Lenny's ally and a co-conspirator in the Cargill shooting.

Franklyn "Gus" Cuevas—former head of the Bad, Bad Boys, he became a major drug dealer. At first closely allied with Lenny, he eventually went to war with the Cowboys.

Manny Garcia—a Cuevas soldier shot and paralyzed by Freddy Krueger and Platano.

Gilbert Compusano—a Cuevas soldier, thought to have betrayed his boss.

Manny Guerrero—a Cuevas soldier shot and wounded by Pasqualito.

Elizabeth Morales—the matriarch of the Cruz–Morales family, and a witness against the Cowboys.

Michael Cruz—a witness against the Cowboys, shot by Pasqualito and Lenny.

Iris Cruz—a witness against the Cowboys.

Joey Morales—a witness against the Cowboys.

Janice Bruington—a shooting victim in the Quad and a witness against the Cowboys.

Freddie Sendra—a former Cowboy manager and a witness against the gang.

Frankie Robles—Pasqualito's sidekick, he became a cooperator and testified against the Cowboys.

Louise McBride—a resident of 348 Beekman, she pitched for the Cowboys and let her apartment to them as a stash house. Later she testified against them.

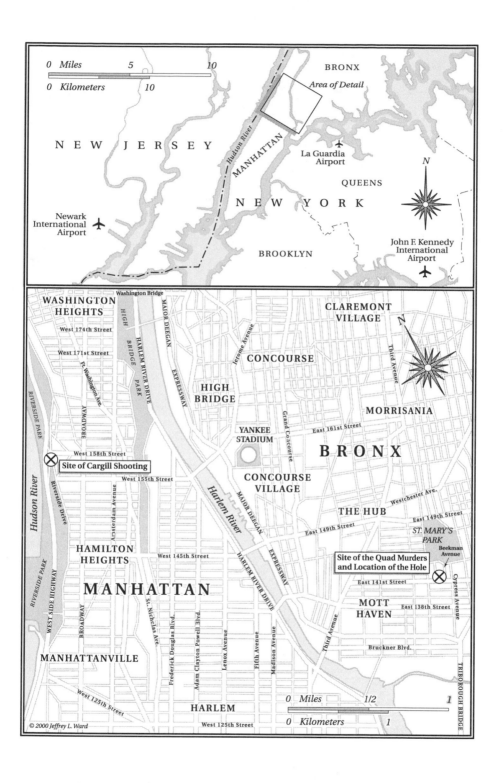

GANGBUSTERS

1

DEATH ON THE HIGHWAY

MAY 1991

NINETEEN-YEAR-OLD David Cargill's spirits were high in the early morning hours of May 19. Just back from his sophomore year at aeronautical college in Florida, the blond six-footer had gone to a party with several of his Tarrytown friends in nearby Elmsford, a small, blue-collar town thirty minutes north of New York City. Around midnight he called his mother—he always phoned his mother when he was going to be home late—and told her he was going to a club across the river in Nyack. Instead, he went to a bar in Tarrytown, and at about 2 A.M., along with former high school hockey teammates John Raguzzi and Kevin Kryzeminski, drove his Nissan pickup truck into Manhattan to cruise around. Cargill had installed a large new amplifier in the cab that afternoon, and he was eager to try it out on the open road.

Although Cargill had four older sisters—all working or in college, all married and having children or about to be—David was the star of the family. "I called him my sunshine boy," his sister Mary Anne would say of him. "He had these beautiful green eyes and he was just this beautiful kid—tall and muscular. He looked like he could have walked off the pages of *GQ*." But David's charm went beyond his looks. A bright, captivating child, he had grown into a strapping teenager, the captain of his hockey team, the most popular among his crowd. He was always having friends over, and they injected a note of mischief and wildness into the frilly precincts of the Cargill household.

But David was no angel. A gifted student in his early years—he scored a 96 on his math Regents—he had coasted through high school, devoting his energies to sports, socializing, and flying small planes on weekends with his father. More troubling was his taste for daredeviltry. David drove too fast; he drank and roughhoused with his buddies; and he bucked his parents' efforts to restrain him. A few years back, he nearly traded punches with his father during an argument over a pair of tattered jeans. "He was a tough teenager," his father, Innes Cargill, would say of him. "He pushed everything to the limit."

But during his junior year in high school David seemed to find himself. He became serious about his flying, began to focus on his schoolwork, and that spring got into all the colleges he applied to. He continued to err on the side of adventure—he would always be high-spirited and impulsive—but he wasn't reckless. He didn't drink and drive, he didn't use drugs. And even at his most rebellious stage, he had been good-hearted, respectful to older people, and surprisingly solicitous toward his two-year-old niece. He certainly didn't deserve to die.

The amp in the car was still blasting a couple of hours later as Cargill and his friends began the drive back to Tarrytown, a leafy river town about twenty-five miles north, on the West Side Highway. It was a cold, clear night, there was hardly any traffic on the road, and Cargill had his foot down hard against the accelerator. So Raguzzi, perched on the speaker in the back of the cab, was surprised when he saw the headlights gaining on them in the rearview mirror. At first he thought it was the police. But moments later he looked over at the passing lane and saw a beat-up burgundy sedan pull alongside, its passenger window wide open. He sensed something bad about to happen.

Suddenly he heard popping noises and felt his eyes fill up with liquid—Cargill's blood, as it turned out. "I went down for about fifteen seconds," he recalls. "I thought they'd thrown firecrackers at us." The truck began fishtailing across the road and he heard Kryzeminski say, "Dave, stop fucking around." He got his eyes cleared and saw Cargill slumped against Kryzeminski's shoulder, and Kryzeminski trying to get at the brake with his hand. Raguzzi grabbed the wheel and together the boys managed to pull the truck onto the off-ramp at 158th Street. Then, while Kryzeminski ran for help, Raguzzi tried to lift Cargill out of the driver's seat.

Raguzzi hadn't noticed the shattered windows, or the fact that there was blood and flesh smeared on almost every surface of the car. He had seen only the small hole where a bullet had entered the left side of David's neck. But when he reached behind his friend's head and felt the gaping exit wound, he realized what had happened. "I'd never seen anyone dead," he would say later. "But I knew when I flipped him over, that was it."

GARRY DUGAN was the kind of detective other detectives would want on the job if a friend or family member were the victim of a crime. Methodical, meticulous, relentless, the twenty-three-year NYPD veteran didn't solve cases so much as he exhausted them—running down obscure leads, keeping copious files, exhuming old crimes, and sparking new inquiries. At times his deliberate style rankled his bosses, who were charged with clearing cases quickly and cutting down on overtime. But no one was better at extracting statements from recalcitrant suspects or witnesses, wearing them down, as one former partner put it, the way water wears down rock.

Dugan worked at Manhattan North Homicide, an elite squad of investigators assembled some five years back at the start of the city's crack epidemic. Ostensibly, its mission was to help harried precinct detectives clear the soaring number of unsolved murder cases in drug-ridden uptown neighborhoods, mainly Harlem and Washington Heights. In fact, the unit was called in whenever a high-profile crime occurred in Manhattan. David Cargill's shooting qualified on both counts.

That morning Dugan had been doing his turnaround—consecutive night and day tours—and rather than make the ninety-minute commute to his home upstate, he'd slept over at his old station house in the Three-Four, the clove-shaped precinct that covered Inwood and most of the Heights at the upper end of Manhattan. He'd risen at seven, showered and dressed in the basement locker room, then called his unit to get the day's schedule. "You better get down to the Three-Oh," his sometimes partner Maria Bertini told him. "Looks like we've got a fresh one."

Bertini filled him in on what she knew about the case while Dugan signed in. "Male/white, 19, DOA at Harlem Hospital . . ." He recorded the details automatically, flagging the one that stood out. What the hell were three white boys doing up in the Heights at that hour? "Any other witnesses?" he asked.

"Just the two," Bertini said. She didn't sound sanguine about the case and he understood why. No leads, no suspects, no known motive.

"I'll be right down," he said.

The Three-Oh straddled the Heights at its lower end and bordered the Three-Four at 155th Street, about a mile due south from where Dugan had spent the night. He picked up a car from the lot behind the precinct and headed down Broadway, the main shopping thoroughfare in the Heights. It was a brisk spring morning. A low sun ducked in and out of the buildings on his left, producing a jazzy rhythm of light and shade. There weren't many people in the street, not much traffic. A few businesses were beginning to open—diners, doughnut shops—and the bodega workers were hosing down sidewalks and putting out fresh produce on stalls: mangos, bananas, plantains, bell peppers, and blood-red persimmons. A small crowd had gathered in front of the Three Star diner on 179th Street, waiting for the charter buses from the terminal around the corner to take them to Atlantic City; and a trail of church-goers, elderly black women in twos and threes, their hair shiny in the sunlight, formed in the direction of Reverend Ike's United Church, a converted movie palace between 175th and 176th streets.

Dugan knew the Heights better than the small rustic village where he lived with his wife and two teenage daughters. He had worked these streets as a uniformed cop for four years before transfer-ring to plainclothes, and even now most of his cases kept him in the neighborhood. It was one of the most violent in the city. He turned west into 177th Street—the bells of Incarnation Church on St. Nick's sounding low and resonant like a dirge—and drove three blocks over to the Hudson, then south onto the highway where the shooting had oc-curred. When he got to the river a sharp, brackish smell blew through the musty squad car. On his right the water was like slate and the sun flashed off the windows of the buildings on the far shore. He passed the exit for the Three-Oh and continued to 96th Street, then doubled back, driving slowly, looking for signs of the shooting—tire marks, shattered glass, yellow plastic tape to mark the crime scene. There were none.

For the second time that morning Dugan felt a twinge of con-cern. Good investigations, he knew, proceed from good crime scenes. Of course, a drive-by on the highway wasn't likely to furnish much physical evidence. But the absence of any signs of violence at all—that and the brilliantly unfolding spring day—had taken him by surprise and added to his sense that Cargill's murder was an aberration, an ex-traordinary event that would not yield easily to detection.

He turned off the highway at 158th Street—where Cargill's friends had exited a few hours before—and again headed down

Broadway, passing the Church of the Intercession, hunkering on its Gothic haunches, and Trinity Cemetery on either side of the avenue. Broadway widened here and the uneven rows of headstones were just visible over the stone retaining walls girding the sidewalks. It struck him that he was driving through a churchyard on his way to a murder investigation and he thought about the people buried there, the strata of earlier immigrants—Germans, Irish, Jews, Greeks, and West Indians—whose graves marked the changing character of the neighborhood. Now it was the Dominicans' turn. They had been pouring into the Heights—a million strong by some estimates—renewing the old cycle of poverty and striving. But the factory and waterfront jobs that had fueled the livelihoods of earlier generations were gone, replaced in large measure by the drug trade. The Dominican Republic had become a way station for Colombian cocaine importers during the late 1970s and the 1980s and Dominican wholesalers had forged links with their countrymen in the Heights. Dugan saw evidence of these links on nearly every block along his way—in the beeper stores and the wire and travel agencies that served as conduits for coca dollars; in the pool halls and empty-shelved bodegas that sold powder under the counter; in the silvered fronts of restaurants and nightclubs that catered to cash-laden dealers. Dugan knew that many, perhaps most of the shops he was passing had been bought and stocked with drug profits. And he knew the price those profits exacted from the community. In 1965, just a few years before he joined the force, there had been one homicide in the Three-Four. Last year there had been 113—113 murders, 113 bodies, almost all of them young men, fifty, sixty years from a natural death. But they wouldn't be buried here, he thought as he left the graveyard. The Dominicans sent their dead back home, their dead and their dollars, sometimes in the same casket.

CARGILL'S FRIENDS were able to give Dugan a partial description of the shooter's car, and Kevin Kryzeminski, sitting beside Cargill, had caught a glimpse of their assailants—two dark-skinned males in their twenties, possibly Hispanic. But neither young man had an explanation for what triggered the shooting. Instead they described a Saturday night of youthful high jinks—a beer party in Elmsford, a brief visit to a bar in neighboring Tarrytown, and then the thirty-minute ride to the city. They had driven to Manhattan in search of women and had cruised the grid of gloomy streets opposite the *Intrepid*, a refurbished World War II aircraft carrier docked along the highway. "What kind of women?" Dugan asked John Raguzzi, the young man who had ridden in the back of the cab.

Dugan, despite being tall and solidly built, with a builder's callused hands, was surprisingly mild in appearance. With his blue eyes, trim mustache, and a tam of fine white hair, he might have been mistaken, in his natty blue summer suit, for a bank manager or an insurance salesman or even a priest, if you overlooked the lay collar. Dugan was aware of the way people perceived him—his colleagues used to call him Father Dugan—and he encouraged that view. He was unfailingly polite, and spoke softly with just the hint of a brogue.

"Hookers," Raguzzi said, sitting across from Dugan at a folding table in one of the cinder-block cubicles banking the squad room. He was a good-looking kid, with a medium build, short black hair, and the shadow of a beard. He was still wearing his clothes from the night before—jeans, sneakers, a plaid short-sleeved shirt. He rested his hands on the table, lacing and unlacing his fingers while he spoke.

"Did you want to get laid?" Dugan asked him.

"No, we wanted a blow job."

"Did you get your blow job?"

"No."

"Did you get laid?"

"No."

"Did you stop or talk to any of the girls?"

"No, there were too many cops around," Raguzzi said. "We didn't want any trouble, so we decided to head back."

"Did anyone follow you?"

"No, I don't think so."

"Are you telling me that you were just driving on the highway and someone came alongside and shot at you for no reason?" Dugan asked.

"Yes, that's exactly what I'm telling you," Raguzzi said.

Outside in the squad room, Dugan huddled with Jerry Dimuro, the young precinct detective assigned to the case. Short and stocky with an energetic way about him, Dimuro had partnered with Dugan on several homicides since making detective two years ago and the two got on well. They had been working in tandem all morning, Dimuro questioning one witness while Dugan interviewed the other. "Do you believe what these guys are telling you?" Dugan asked him.

"Naw, they're leaving something out."

Given the location and the time of the shooting, Dugan felt certain that drugs were involved—a robbery, a bad transaction, a prior debt. But the young men denied that they'd had any dealings with drugs; indeed they denied that anything remarkable at all had occurred prior to the shooting. "Did you take a physics course at your high school?" Dugan asked Kryzeminski, after listening to his account several times.

"Yeah."

"Do you remember the part about every action causes a reaction?"

"Yeah, I remember that."

"Well, what you're describing to me is the reaction. There had to be something that caused that reaction. I want to know what that was."

He questioned the young men repeatedly, comparing their stories with each other, and with their own earlier versions. He built up a series of pictures in his mind, a kind of movie of the night's events, then homed in on the details—the route Cargill took after leaving the highway, the lighting conditions on the *Intrepid*—searching for an inconsistency that would signal a lie or an omission.

But their stories held and Kryzeminski was becoming impatient, rolling his eyes and drumming the table with his fingers.

Dugan rose purposefully from his chair. "Calm down," he told Kryzeminski, his voice low and even. "You're going to be here with me a long time. You can either love me or hate me and right now I don't particularly care which. 'Cause I'm not happy with your story. Look, can you think of anything, anything at all out of the ordinary that happened last night?"

Kryzeminski started to shake his head, then stopped. "Well, we almost had an accident getting onto the highway," he said.

Dugan sat down again. "Tell me about it."

Kryzeminski explained that on the way home, Cargill may have run a red light, cutting off another motorist on the ramp that leads to the elevated section of the highway at 57th Street. The other vehicle was a white sports car, possibly a BMW or Mercedes. But the incident had been minor—so minor that Raguzzi, crammed into the back of the cab, would later say he hadn't registered the event. The vehicles, after all, hadn't made contact. There had been no exchange between Cargill and the other driver, no gestures or threats. Moreover, the car that Cargill cut off was not the same car from which the shots had been fired.

Dugan was skeptical. He'd heard of similar kinds of shootings on California's freeways. But that kind of thing didn't happen in New York. Still, he didn't discount anything. He went over Kryzeminski's story several more times, then checked back with Raguzzi.

By midafternoon, Dugan felt he had gotten all he could from the young men. He still thought they were holding back and he hadn't finished questioning them. But he wanted their parents to speak to them overnight and he broached the idea to the Cargills as they were about to leave for the morgue. He had met them earlier that morning, a graying, somewhat rumpled couple huddled at the back of the squad room. A scientist, Innes Cargill had a flat, farmer's face and wide-set inquisitive eyes—a legacy, perhaps, of years spent hunched over a microscope—and his wife, Dugan noticed, was still wrapped in her coat, though it was warm and humid in the precinct. He had offered them his condolences and parsed their appearance with a policeman's eye: middle-aged, middle-class, not flashy, no conspicuous jewelry.

Later, he interviewed them at length about their son. He had liked them at once. Although they were in shock, dazed and deflated like survivors emerging from a wreck, they had held their feelings in check and tried to answer his questions thoughtfully. No, they didn't think David used drugs. He had always seemed to be against them, was scheduled to take a test for his pilot's license the very next day. Still, they left room in their replies for doubt and reassessment. They didn't try to control the investigation like so many of the victims' parents he interviewed. They weren't trying to hide things about their child, to sanitize or exculpate him or themselves. They just wanted to know what had happened, to understand who and what had killed their son and why he had been murdered. And finally that was what was so frustrating about the whole business. Dugan could not tell them. He could offer neither Cargill nor his wife an explanation, much less justice; and he could see that the mystery at the heart of the case was adding to their misery, infecting their grief and turning it inward.

At the end of his tour, Dugan picked up his car and headed home. It was nearly seven and a low, golden light had settled over the city. He took the highway at 125th Street, again retracing Cargill's route from the night before, this time matching the eyewitnesses' descriptions of events to the actual setting. He drove slowly in the center lane, imagining Cargill at the wheel, the blare of the speakers damping the noise from the road, the dark form of the shooter's car sharking into his peripheral vision, and then the popping of automatic gunfire, the last sounds he would ever hear. The case was dead in the water, Dugan thought. There wasn't any physical evidence to speak of. Raguzzi and

Kryzeminski had provided little helpful information, not even a partial plate number. And without a motive or some precipitating action, the vital link between crime and criminal was missing. The killer could have been anyone.

But something else was troubling the detective and it had nothing to do with solving the murder. During his twenty-three years in the Department, Dugan had investigated his share of incomprehensible crimes. He had known men bludgeoned and stabbed to death for the change in their pockets. A few years ago he had assisted in the investigation of a series of unprovoked shootings, the work of a Dominican gang who had targeted Yeshiva students up in Inwood Park just because they looked different. And then there was his most recent case—a grueling six-month investigation into the rape and ritual murder of a 13-year-old Colombian girl, Paola Illera, abducted on her way home from an East Harlem school. (That case had been especially frustrating for Dugan. As ordered by the squad commander, he'd worked around the clock, without success, and then had been sanctioned for racking up too much overtime.) But even these brutal acts had been caused by something—greed, bias, perversity, obsession. Random murder, the spontaneous, reasonless generation of violence, was new to Dugan's experience and it contradicted his most deeply held assumptions about criminal behavior. After five years working homicides, murder still disgusted Dugan—all murders, not just the murders of the innocent—but this killing scared him.

DUGAN COULDN'T have known that the Cargill case would embroil him in one of the biggest homicide investigations in New York City history, a case that would come to rule his life over the next four years. In fact, the investigation started slowly, with Dugan and Dimuro chasing the wispiest of leads: They interviewed Cargill's friends and fellow partygoers in Tarrytown, canvassed the prostitutes in the area around the *Intrepid*, and searched through motor vehicle and auto dealership records trying to find the cars Kryzeminski had described to them. All without success. Then, in July, Dugan traced a handgun that an off-duty cop had recovered near the site of the shooting to an illegal firearms dealer living in the same Florida town where Cargill had attended college. Speculating that the weapon may have played a role in Cargill's murder, Dugan called Anne Cargill to ask if David had owned a gun.

The Cargills were not coping well with their son's death. Over the course of the summer, they had phoned Dugan and Dimuro on an almost daily basis and Anne in particular involved herself in the minutiae of the investigation. The detectives always took time to respond to their calls—Dugan even visited them several times in Tarrytown—but they had little progress to report, and the frustration wore on both parents.

When they'd come here from Scotland some twenty-five years ago, the Cargills had two babies and no savings; but they wanted the opportunities the United States offered them, and they believed that if they worked hard, they could build a good life for their family. Innes Cargill parlayed a postdoc at Columbia into a career as a research chemist, and in 1987 started his own pharmaceutical testing firm. Anne Cargill taught school, and devoted herself to bringing up her children. Both she and Innes were the kind of parents who rose at 5 A.M. to drive their teenage daughters to swim practice. And they wouldn't hesitate to show up at a party or a dance club if one of their kids overstayed their curfew.

Their efforts seemed to have been rewarded. As their fortunes rose, they'd moved to the suburbs, settling in their own home on a tree-lined street in Tarrytown. Their children attended good schools, growing up happy and drug-free. And David, after a few troubling years, seemed headed for stability and success. So the bullet that slammed into his neck in the early morning hours of May 16 not only claimed his life; it also pierced the very certainties, the core beliefs around which Innes and Anne Cargill structured their lives. How, they now asked themselves, could all those years of industry and careful planning be wiped out by one apparently random act during the course of a single night? What was the point of good schools and safe communities if they couldn't even protect the life of their child?

At first both parents had been preoccupied with the practical details of burying their son. They couldn't wait to get his body back from the police, though for very different reasons. The suddenness and senselessness of David's death had left his father traumatized, like an amputee who dreams that his limbs are still intact. Reason told him David was gone, but the feeling part of his brain couldn't grasp the fact of his son's death. "It was very important to see him," Innes remembered. "I just had to touch his body, even though it felt so cold and rubbery, to run my fingers through his hair."

If Innes was seeking closure, Anne wanted nothing less than to bring David back to life. A former schoolteacher with a master's degree in education, she had curtailed her career to raise her son at home. "I had always been very hands-on with David, getting him out of scrapes, talking to his teachers, helping him with school projects," she recalled. "I felt if I could just get to see him now, I could make everything all right. They had shown us a photo of him at the morgue, but that wasn't real enough. I had to touch him all over, to close and open his eyes, to make it *not* real. I felt if I just prayed hard enough, I could bring him back. It was a long time before I realized he was gone forever."

Anne didn't confide her thoughts to anyone and busied herself instead with arrangements for David's funeral. But at least Anne was functioning, and she seemed well as long as she was able to do things for David. After the funeral, though, she sank into a long, deepening depression. "I was okay for about four days," she says. "Then I used to sit by myself. I didn't want to do anything. I just wanted to think about him—when he was a little boy, a trip we took to the Grand Canyon. I was desperately depressed. I didn't want to get out of bed. I didn't want to do anything. I just wanted everyone to leave me alone."

Her family forced her to see a psychiatrist. He prescribed

antidepressants, pain pills, migraine pills for the headaches she'd been having. "Which I immediately abused," she says. "The whole family was worried about me. But I didn't care. I didn't want to kill myself, but that's exactly what I was doing. I said to Innes, 'I just want to be with David.' "

It was around that time that Dugan, unaware of her precarious state, phoned Anne and queried her about the gun he had traced. She had seemed composed during the call, Dugan recalled. But later she seized on the idea that David had provoked his own death and became hysterical. She was hospitalized the next day.

Innes seemed to be adjusting better than his wife. He had been visiting David's grave two to three times a week—Anne couldn't bear to think of her son in the ground and stayed home—and he returned to work, administering the small, but profitable, company that he owned. But he also was experiencing problems. A teetotaler since the early 1970s, he fell off the wagon with a thud. "I went to work; it took me a day to do what I previously could do in two hours and I couldn't wait until five o'clock to get a drink. Beer, scotch—once I started, it was impossible to motivate myself to stop. The cycle went on for years. Some days I'd feel better, then I'd feel guilty about it. Why should I feel better?

"There was no way to tell from day to day how I'd feel. Most of the time I'd walk around with this feeling in the pit of my stomach—a gnawing feeling, an emptiness. Something was missing in my life, and I wouldn't know what it was and then I'd realize: It's David."

THE FIRST real break in the case didn't come until six months after the shooting, and as often happens, was unrelated to the exacting investigation that had preceded it. The traced gun, like all the other leads, went nowhere. Then, on November 27, Edwin Driscoll, an NYPD detective working with the FBI on an auto theft task force, phoned Dimuro at the Three-Oh squad and told him that the Feds had a CI (confidential informant) with knowledge of the highway shooting. He said that the informant had told FBI agents that Cargill had been murdered by drug dealers from Washington Heights, who killed for the fun of it, and had identified one of them by his street name: Platano. Cargill had cut the dealers off at the entrance to the highway, but the traffic incident was a pretext. The shooter, the leader of a brutal crack-trafficking gang, wanted to test-fire a gun that he had bought earlier in the evening.

Driscoll promised to try to set up a meeting with the informant, but later that afternoon when Dugan called back to expedite the process, FBI agent Jamie Cedeno, one of the informant's handlers, vetoed the request, claiming the risks of exposure were too high. "I'm not going to let you burn this guy," he told Dugan.

"Hey, nobody wants to burn your guy," Dugan told him. "The interview would be in the strictest confidence. Nobody would even know we're talking to him."

"I can't let you do that," Cedeno said, adding that he would be meeting the CI in two days and would ask him for more information then.

"What kind of crap is this?" Dugan asked Dimuro after Cedeno hung up.

CEDENO CALLED two days later, offering little new information. Dugan suggested a variety of compromises: Dugan and Dimuro would question the CI in Cedeno's presence; the CI could keep his name and all identifying details secret; or the CI and Cedeno could call the detectives from a secure location and Dugan would conduct the interview, if need be, over the phone. But Cedeno nixed them all, explaining that the gang was extremely violent and his informant was afraid that any leak would cost him his life. "Somewhere in the conversation you will ask him something about his identity or he will say something, and I'm not going to let that happen," he said. "Ask me the questions and I'll relay them to him."

Dugan was reluctant to do this. Interrogation is more art than science. The investigator needed a firm grasp of the details of a case in order to know what questions to ask, or to sense when a source was lying or perhaps even digging for information himself. It was clear to Dugan from what Cedeno had told him that his CI knew a lot more than he was saying—typically the case with informants—and it was also clear that Cedeno's priority was protecting his source. But Dugan was at an impasse. "Okay, let's play it your way," he said. "Ask him: Where does he know Platano from? Where did he meet him?"

"I can't do that."

"Why not?"

"Because that answer will reveal my CI's identity."

"What are we playing here? *What's My Line?*" Dugan was boiling. "We can't run a homicide investigation like this. These guys are a bunch of cold-blooded killers. They could kill others before we get them."

"Well, that's the chance we'll have to take," Cedeno said.

THREE WEEKS LATER, with Christmas just days away, the streets of Mott Haven were busy with traffic. But along Beekman Avenue—a two-block stretch of tenements in the heart of the South Bronx—there were hardly any signs of the holidays, unless you count the special low price Anthony "Amp" Green was running on his crack sales. The reed-thin drug dealer for the Yellow-Top gang, a foolish 17-year-old out to make a quick buck, was holding a fire sale of crack vials in the middle of another gang's—the Red-Top's—turf. He had been told to clear out—shots had even been fired over his head—but he just ignored the warnings.

On the cold night of December 16, two sedans rolled up to the narrow alleyway where Green did business. Sales were brisk; a dozen people clogged the cement corridor as hooded gunmen surrounded the spot. Two of them quickly pinned Green to a wall near the entrance to the alley and pumped six bullets into his legs and stomach. As Green crumpled to the ground, fatally wounded, as many as eight gunmen trained their weapons on his workers and customers, and in a scene of unimaginable horror, opened fire. For thirty seconds or more, chaos reigned as people clambered away from the lit-up guns, the building walls ringing with the stammer of automatic weapons.

Some were able to escape through a tear in the chain-link fence at the rear of the alley. Others were less lucky. One customer got cut down as he tried to scramble up a fire escape. Another, Cynthia Casado—a mother of three—was headed back to the street when she ran into a man who shot her in the head. She died on the spot, still clutching the yellow-topped vial of crack she had bought only moments before.

A slim, fortyish woman named Janice Bruington was on her way to visit her son and was passing the alley as the men started shooting. She had known the man who shot Amp Green since he was a small boy, but he didn't hesitate before whirling and firing at her as she fled the scene. She felt the bullet slam into her back and then her face hit the pavement. Wounded, she managed to roll under a parked car.

Manuel Vera was not as fortunate. The gunmen chased the harmless old crackhead sixty feet to the doorway of an adjoining building as he ran from the scene. Police would later find him there in a pool of blood, a necklace of crepe-paper Christmas decorations visible through the door. He'd been shot fourteen times.

By the time the gunmen returned to the sedans, and the cars had sped away, four people lay dead.

The case fell to Mark Tebbens, a 33-year-old precinct detective well known in the neighborhood. Standing six and a half feet, with the muscled arms and shoulders of a weight lifter, he was one of the few officers who commanded respect on Beekman Avenue. Not only was he big; he had what people in the street call heart—a kind of cold, fatalistic courage that values sinew and reputation above concerns over safety. Having grown up in a tough, diverse section of the Bronx, he had an innate grasp of his constituents and how to communicate with them. Moreover, they liked him. Boyishly handsome with an easy joking manner and an infectious laugh, he, like Dugan, dealt with people fairly and with respect—not just the working people but also the thieves and users and welfare moms, the people down on their luck who normally shun the police.

Tebbens quickly surmised the gist of what had happened. Amp Green had been killed by rival dealers who operated at the north end of the street. But Tebbens had a hard time grasping the additional carnage. Moreover, none of the victims other than Green were part of the Yellow-Top organization. Apparently, the shooters, members of the Red-Top crew, intended to send the block a message: We not only kill our competitors, but anyone who does business with them.

As Tebbens began investigating the case, he quickly realized that it had the markings of a double homicide he'd been assigned to in his second year on the squad, in 1989. In fact, he had locked up two of the Red-Top gang for the murders. One of them—a burly, garrulous Dominican known as Pasqualito—arrogantly told Tebbens that all the witnesses would either recant or disappear and that he would be back on the street inside a year. He was wrong—but only by a couple of months.

Although his sources gave him his first suspect within hours of the shooting—a local thug named Stanley Tukes—Tebbens knew that Tukes was a hired gun, incapable of planning, much less carrying out, an operation like the Quad, as the case was being called. Several eyewitnesses mentioned another gunman, but referred to him only as Darkman or the Dominican. Such was the fear of the Red-Top gang on Beekman Avenue that none of Tebbens' informants—some of them hardened criminals themselves—dared name the gunman in question, much less offer to testify against him in court.

Shortly after the incident, however, Jamie Cedeno, the FBI agent who had been in contact with Dugan and Dimuro a month earlier, came to Tebbens with information about the shooters. He told

Tebbens they belonged to a gang called Lenny's Boys, and quickly out-lined the organization's Dominican hierarchy, who lived across the river from the Bronx in Washington Heights. Much of what the agent told him, Tebbens already knew—the names of the gang's leaders: Lenny Sepulveda, who was then serving a nine-month jail sentence for gun possession, and his second-in-command and older brother Nelson. But the agent also talked about someone who sounded like he could be Darkman. A brutal killer, he was the gang's top enforcer and was said to be one of the leaders in the shooting in the Quad. The agent told Tebbens that he should contact a detective in Manhattan named Dugan. They were both, he said, looking at the same player.

Darkman was known on the street as Platano.

2

THE HOMICIDE

INVESTIGATION UNIT

1 9 9 2

THE CRIMINAL COURTS building rises seventeen stories above Centre Street in lower Manhattan. Built in 1940 over slums that spawned the city's first gangs, it houses the DA's offices and the county jail—familiarly known as the Tombs—as well as the courts. With its massive limestone towers and setback casement windows, it bears an impregnable, sharp-eyed look—justice not blind, but wary.

Most mornings that winter, Walter Arsenault, newly appointed chief of the Homicide Investigation Unit, HIU, arrived at his desk before dawn and found it littered with excrement—piles of bullet-sized mouse turds, like spent cartridges at a drive-by. Arsenault, a veteran prosecutor in the Manhattan DA's office, had been complaining to

Maintenance about the rodent problem for more than a year, and for just as long, Maintenance had been denying there was one. No problem, no need to fix it. After a while some of the investigators in his unit began laying traps, photographing their quarry with the office's crime scene camera, and Arsenault presented Maintenance with a pasteboard mock-up of their work—lurid snapshots of dead mice, each corpse neatly labeled with cause of death: blunt-force trauma, poison, asphyxiation. Maintenance was unmoved.

After fourteen years of government service, Arsenault was happy just to tweak the bureaucracy now and then. Besides, he already had too much on his desk to worry about mice. Head of a twelve-man task force of prosecutors and police that targeted the city's most dangerous killers, he was about to try a double-murder case, he was supervising several other big investigations, and mounting administrative chores depleted what little oxygen remained in his day. Law enforcement, Arsenault had long ago discovered, was an exercise in triage. It was easy to ignore a few small mice when you spent the bulk of your days prosecuting animals like Kenneth Bernard. Bernard, the defendant in Arsenault's upcoming murder trial, was a crack dealer who'd shot his client's brains out while she was giving him a blow job. Now there was a rat.

At 39, Walter Arsenault had been catching and convicting brutal killers all his adult life, and many felt there was no one better at it. A gifted trial lawyer, equally at home in the courts and on the streets, he'd spent six years in New Jersey at the Bergen County prosecutor's office, rising to head their Trial Division before he was 30. Later, after transferring to Manhattan in 1984, he led a four-year campaign against Harlem's Jamaican crack crews that reduced gang-related murders from about forty per year to nearly none. Now, as the chief of HIU, Arsenault directed New York's only dedicated drug gang unit, and in those dreary first few months of 1992, he was one of local law enforcement's few bright stories. Little did he know, though, that HIU's already strained machinery was about to be tested by the biggest, and one of the longest, investigations and prosecutions in its storied history: a multiborough case that would include both the Cargill shooting and the quadruple murders on Beekman Avenue.

Arsenault's corner office was a cool, dim cave at the rear of the unit. Although he had windows overlooking Chinatown with a view east to the Brooklyn Bridge, he blacked them out to shield his informants—the offices of Probation and Parole faced his across an air shaft—and ran the air conditioner year-round in protest against the building's antiquated and imperious heating system. The cluttered room contained shelved rows of souvenir police hats, a wall full of mug shots and crime scene photos, and, beneath his desk, a box overflowing with sweaty running clothes. He jogged from five to ten miles during his lunch hour. The early part of his mornings he spent hunched over his computer, updating his files from eye-high stacks of arrest reports and correspondence.

Arsenault was at the center of a network of gang specialists who tracked the movements of some 20,000 Jamaican drug traffickers worldwide. Until a few years ago, the Jamaican gangs—or posses as they called themselves—were shadowy, anonymous groups who moved with impunity from country to country, and even from city to city. One of Arsenault's first innovations after joining HIU was to coordinate his Jamaican initiative with police and prosecutors from Harlem to Hong Kong to the back alleys of Kingston, where the mention of Arsenault's name was said to inspire trembling.

For all of that, he was mild-looking, with a cherubic face, a bowl-cut curtain of lank brown hair, and goggle-sized glasses that at unflattering moments made him look nerdy, almost froggish. In fact, nothing could have been further from the truth. He'd been an athlete in school—soccer, hockey, lacrosse—and he'd kept his defenseman's squat build, thick through the legs and torso, tough to knock off balance.

It was easy to underestimate Arsenault, and many did. Padding through HIU's bunkerlike quarters in baggy jeans, a rumpled blue oxford shirt, and beat-up moccasins—his uniform out of court—he affected a scruffy undergraduate air, an indifference to the protocols of rank. Lori Grifa, a young Brooklyn prosecutor who worked closely with the unit, mistook him for a junior assistant the first time she saw him, and even after they were introduced, he was so "un-self-important" and Puckishly amusing, she had trouble squaring him with his title or reputation. Steve Fitzgerald, another young assistant who later joined HIU, recalls that he was so taken aback by Arsenault's informality during his interview that he thought someone was playing a joke on him—until Arsenault began to explain the details of HIU's operation. Then Fitzgerald's opinion changed dramatically.

It was often like that. He was so intense in his approach to things, yet personally so private and self-effacing, that at times there seemed to be two Arsenaults: one smart, authoritative, and entertaining; the other a little lost and out of sync—the soldier off the battlefield, a chemist away from his lab. In truth, he had a highly selective focus. The usual civilian pursuits—art, music, theater, television, restaurants, fashion, politics, most sports, making money, and material possessions of any kind—left him cold and mute. He had no social aspirations and no social graces, no talent for small talk or what is sometimes politely called polite conversation. People who met him outside the boundaries of his obsessions—his work, his family, his lifelong passion for ice hockey—came away with a fuzzy recollection, if they remembered him at all.

But he snapped into focus in a courtroom. Holding forth in a navy suit, his hair brushed back off his high forehead, his voice rich with candor and conviction, he was formidable. Even more so in small strategy sessions or alone with a colleague in his office, when he could relax and give full vent to his enthusiasms. He was a natural storyteller with an earthy sense of humor and a taste for hyperbole. Mostly, though, he was a historian. He had a computerlike mind, an ability to process huge amounts of information instantly, then spit them back—names, dates, the minutiae of cases that investigators had forgotten in their entirety. Grifa recalls showing him a mug shot at their first meeting, one Errol Williams, a small-time Jamaican hit man she had just convicted on murder charges. Arsenault glanced at the photo, then ticked off the subject's pedigree—his street names, gang affiliations, running mates, criminal history—right down to the neighborhood in Kingston where he'd been born. Grifa was stunned. She'd spent two months investigating Williams prior to his trial, and in the span of minutes, Arsenault, a prosecutor from another borough, had told her things about him she'd never guessed at. And that was not an isolated instance. Police and prosecutors would frequently come to Arsenault for help with some sketchy gang-related case and leave his office dazzled, convinced they had been in the presence of genius.

THE OLDER of two boys, Arsenault grew up in Hasbrouck Heights, a suburban idyll twenty minutes by bus from Manhattan. His father, George Arsenault, a U.S. Customs inspector for thirty-nine years, was scrupulous, stiff-necked, and outspoken. The son of Irish and French-Canadian immigrants, he weathered the Depression and World War II, and emerged, like so many of his generation, with a can-do optimism, an unshakable faith in himself and the future that he passed on to his sons. Walter was a quiet, even-tempered youngster, but he never backed down from an argument or a fight, no matter how much older or bigger his adversary. "When Walter felt he was right," George Arsenault says, "you couldn't move him left or right."

Even as a boy, he was an avid reader, devouring thick tomes—mostly history, but also literature, adventure, and science—at a single sitting. When his school sponsored a speed-reading course, 12-year-old Walter whipped through the test material so much faster than everybody else, indeed so much faster than the course's objective that his teacher accused him of faking—until Arsenault took a comprehension test and scored 100.

He had a peculiar, obsessive turn of mind. He would focus on a subject for a year or eighteen months at a time, learning everything he could from books, museums, movies, field trips, then lose interest and move on to the next thing. At eight he became an Egyptologist, trekking to the Museum of Natural History on weekends to view the mummies. Later he delved into the Civil War and dragged his parents to battlefields in Virginia and Maryland. Later still he took up karate and Japanese culture, followed by an excursion into World War II. In high school he read the *Iliad* repeatedly, which led him to Greek and Latin, archeology, and Schliemann's Cretan digs and the search for Troy.

He earned a scholarship to Johns Hopkins, where he continued his eclectic approach to education, majoring in the classics before quickly switching to the social and behavioral sciences. For a while he wanted to teach, and he had all but decided to join the Peace Corps when in his senior year he read *Tiger in the Court*, a memoir by Herbert Stern, the crusading U.S. Attorney who rooted out political corruption in North Jersey. Oddly, law was one of the few areas Arsenault had not dipped into at Johns Hopkins, but the rhythm and intensity of Stern's investigations reminded him of his own intellectual flights, the thrill of exploring hidden worlds, of unearthing core truths. More important, Stern was working on the side of the angels. His triumphs represented the power of the prosecutor to stand up to the world's bullies—not just individual felons but organized gangs like the Cosa Nostra and political conspiracies like that of the Kenneys of Hudson County, New Jersey, the ones who thought they were untouchable.

Arsenault never looked back. He attended law school at Rutgers, interned at Stern's old Camden office (Stern had been appointed to the bench by then), and joined the Bergen County prosecutor's office after graduating in 1978. Working as a local prosecutor turned out to be the best move Arsenault could have made. He discovered he liked laboring in the trenches, dealing with cops and street people, the long hours and constant pressure, the camaraderie.

Arsenault would seek out the most dangerous cases, then investigate the hell out of them. If he needed a corroborative witness or an informant, he'd go out to the neighborhoods himself. "He was without fear, ballsy as hell," Paul Polifrone, a veteran detective assigned to Arsenault, says. "He seemed to enjoy the prospect of confrontation. If he heard that someone was the baddest ass, he'd want to get right into his face, and he wouldn't back down. He could handle himself too. He didn't look it, but he was some kind of black belt. Still, I remember telling him, 'I don't care if you have ten black belts, you're not going to stop a bullet and you probably won't stop a knife.' "

Yet despite Arsenault's freewheeling antics in the street, he demonstrated a balanced approach to his cases, and he advanced quickly, ultimately moving to the Manhattan DA's office in 1984, before being plucked for assignment to HIU.

STREET INVESTIGATIONS, as Arsenault was quick to point out in explaining the success of HIU, rarely involve rocket science. Much more about common sense and doggedness, they require an ability to get along with all kinds of people, many of them skittish and unsavory. Arsenault still rode to the Harlem precincts at 3 A.M., when most potential cooperators seemed to get arrested, still spent hours every day talking to the army of informants he'd cultivated over the past four years. He had learned early that there were few secrets within the Jamaican community, and he bullshitted with everyone who came to his office—girlfriends, junkies, hustlers looking for a per diem, as well as convicted killers, who in different circumstances would not hesitate to pump a bullet into his head. Some of those he liked the best.

Ironically, it was the so-called good guys, his partners in law enforcement, with whom Arsenault was most likely to quarrel. His plainspokenness and pungent wit—qualities that served him well with juries and cops—worked against him when he had to deal with administrative issues. He was a reluctant manager at best, uncomfortable at second-guessing colleagues and heavy-handed, often tactless when he did. He distrusted authority, even his own, and so he acted from the zeal of conviction rather than the temperance of true leadership.

He was the same with higher-ups. He hated the turf building and credit grabbing that are a part of any bureaucracy, and he refused to play politics or humor those who did. He was often blunt with trial bureau chiefs who refused to hand over their gang-related cases, or with police commanders who denied there were gangs operating in their precincts—no problem, no need to fix it. Lately he'd learned to edit himself, but he'd made his share of enemies over the years and the frosty silence that replaced his normal candor was barely an improvement.

THE HOMICIDE Investigation Unit had been created in 1983 specifically to investigate and prosecute Manhattan's violent street gangs. By 1992, those gangs—mostly Dominicans, Jamaicans, Puerto Ricans, and American blacks who banded together to sell drugs—had become New York's No. 1 crime problem, the engine for its soaring homicide rate and a blight on its quality of life. Fueled by huge drug revenues and armed with automatic weapons, they commandeered chunks of the city's real estate—buildings, blocks, parks, entire neighborhoods—preying on the poor, co-opting the young, and intimidating or killing the defiant. They were also one of law enforcement's thorniest problems. Their layered conspiracies were virtually immune to the beat cop and squad detective. Special tactical units (TNTs) were good at busting street sellers and low-level managers, sometimes called Dixie cups because they were easily replaceable. But penetrating the top levels of those gangs entailed a dedicated, long-term investigation—and the police had neither the savvy nor the will to mount that kind of campaign.

Operating out of ramshackle offices in the Criminal Courts building, HIU not only initiated gang investigations but followed them through trial, a process that could easily take two years or more. It was also one of the few gang task forces in the country that was proactive. Most other units reacted to crises; HIU investigators linked up seemingly random murders and identified gang hierarchies before police knew they existed.

Every day, calls for counsel and intelligence poured in from London, Kingston, Boston, Baltimore—from sheriffs in West Virginia and Kansas whose towns had suddenly become infested with strange Jamaican posses. To other cities' dismay, the violent drug-trafficking gang had become one of New York's most notorious exports, and not by accident. New York City gangs discovered these new markets—where crack frequently sold for ten times the price in Spanish Harlem—when they went out of state to buy guns. (New York's gun laws were among the nation's toughest.) Whenever Arsenault traveled in the United States, he visited the gun shops whose names appeared on the firearms he confiscated off the streets of Washington Heights and the Lower East Side. His favorite was a store in Texas called Bob's Guns 'N Toys.

But HIU's mission was neither guns nor drugs. It was murder. In targeting the city's most active and elusive killers, they were the only unit that seemed able to slow the train of gang-related violence then racing through Harlem and the Heights.

Lately that violence had begun spilling out of the slums, inundating the city's justice system and menacing its toniest neighborhoods. In just the previous six years, New York's murder rate had risen more than 50 percent and the number of shootings, robberies, assaults, and carjackings had also soared. Swamped by so much serious crime, the New York police had all but given up on misdemeanor arrests and the streets teemed with an army of malefactors—beggars, scavengers, squeegee men, graffiti artists, vandals, public urinaters, jostlers, drug pushers, and purse snatchers—fostering the climate for still more violence. Meanwhile, the courts and prisons were filled to overflowing. Trial dockets lagged by a year or more, prosecutors were offering bargain plea agreements to reduce their caseloads, and some arrestees were walking simply because the system couldn't process their cases fast enough.

But numbers told only part of the story. More troubling was the quality of crimes being committed—wanton, senseless acts of which Cargill and the Quad were only the leading examples. What lawmen found so chilling was the casualness of the violence, the spate of shootings fueled neither by rage nor by any persuasive emotion. All over town young men, some as young as twelve, were spraying the streets with gunfire, resolving the slightest disputes with deadly finality. Murder itself seemed to have changed—the idea of it, what it meant to kill someone had become commonplace, commodified, an advertisement for itself.

The reasons for this new violence are still being debated. Clearly some ghetto neighborhoods became poorer, meaner places during the 1970s, breeding grounds for a host of pathologies from child abuse and teenage pregnancy to drug addiction and crime. For that, some experts blame the cultural upheavals of the 1960s that weakened traditional institutions, not least of all the police, whereas others point to government welfare policies that they feel undermined family structure among the poor. Others cite fair housing laws that inadvertently sped the exodus of the middle class from Harlem and other ghetto communities, leaving them underpopulated and disorganized. Still others trace their decline to the city's deteriorating manufacturing base, the factories and shipyards that once provided stable employment for many "at-risk" males.

But nothing catalyzed the city's convulsive violence during the 1970s and 1980s more than its expanding illicit drug trade. It created a vast criminal labor force, unmatched since prohibition, and an even larger population of addicts whose only means of supporting their habits were through crime. It attracted a dizzying, multiethnic array of importers who shattered the Mob's monopoly over the illegal drug supply and set rival distribution groups at war with one another. And the huge profits that rolled in only sharpened competition and fueled the deployment of costly, high-tech arsenals.

The first violent drug gangs appeared on the streets in Harlem in the early 1970s. Before then, the city's illegal narcotics market consisted almost exclusively of heroin and was dominated by the Mafia, who controlled the overseas supply and distributed the drug through a limited number of franchisees, mostly tough, experienced American black associates like Frank Matthews and Nicky Barnes. These "old hands" had hammered out their own territorial arrangements over the years and it was not unusual, for example, for several different heroin organizations to conduct sales peacefully out of the same Harlem hotel.

Later a number of other groups, chiefly the ethnic Chinese, challenged the Mob's hegemony over the supply side of the heroin market; and the emerging popularity of cocaine brought still more outfits into the mix. The Mob, reeling from federal drug prosecutions and their own internal strife over narcotics issues—many Mafia bosses didn't want to be associated with drug running—became one more player in a crowded market. But the competition for the consumer's dollar played out most fiercely in the street, where droves of sales organizations began cropping up. With no one body to regulate their business practices, the retailers took matters into their own hands and the modern-day violent drug-trafficking gang was born.

These groups, volatile and heavily armed, began selling narcotics out in the open—the drug market's equivalent of fast-food outlets—fueling the already ballooning demand and increasing competition for prized selling locations. From 1970 to 1980, the city's murder rate climbed by more than 60 percent.

Under the best circumstances, the introduction of drugs and drug gangs into slum neighborhoods would have had deadly consequences. But in New York the emergence of the narcotics market coincided with one of the most dispiriting periods in NYPD history. In 1968 a series of federal inquiries in the wake of widespread urban race riots exposed shocking levels of bias and brutality in many big-city police departments and concluded that the police, far from being the solution to the disorders, were part of the problem. Meanwhile, theories linking criminal behavior to social factors were misinterpreted—often by cops themselves—in ways that marginalized the Police Department's role in preventing or reducing crime. As a result, many officers, especially white police in minority precincts, hunkered down in station houses and radio cars, virtually abandoning the streets to drug dealers and other felons.

In New York, the 1972 Knapp Commission hearings further demoralized the police. Sparked by the disclosures of an honest cop named Frank Serpico, Knapp and other inquiries uncovered systemic corruption in the Department's Vice and Narcotics divisions. Then, two years later, the city's budget crisis triggered cutbacks that led to the resignation of many of the Department's most experienced men. Between 1974 and 1981, manpower declined sharply and, more troubling, average tenure fell from thirteen to five years.

But the PD was especially unprepared to meet the explosion in drug trafficking. Still reeling from the corruption scandals, the Department adopted regulations that effectively barred regular officers from making narcotics arrests. The spectacle of beat cops blandly making their rounds while crack dealers blatantly pushed their product further disheartened the force and shattered the public's already fragile confidence.

Special narcotics units were hardly more effective. Saddled with production goals, they specialized in so-called sweeps—saturating an area and arresting large numbers of fungible low-level street workers, mostly addicts themselves. But they rarely committed the time or resources necessary to capture the gang's hierarchy because in the Department's accounting system, the arrest of a gang's leader received the same statistical weight as the arrest of his lowest-ranking worker. So when the "buy-and-bust" units moved to a new neighbor-hood, the gangs simply re-formed around their old leadership—some-times with new workers, but often with the same ones. Flooding the system with hordes of small-time dealers choked the already overbur-dened courts and prisons, which disgorged them back onto the streets within days, if not hours.

Some narcotics units—often in tandem with the Feds—did conduct long, complex investigations. But they were generally inter-ested in weight, in making the big bust, and they focused on the indi-viduals and small groups at the wholesale level. Most violence, however, occurred at the retail or street level among the large, well-armed gangs battling one another for turf. But the way the Department was structured, Narcotics was given very little incentive to investigate violence. Whatever murders they solved were credited to Homicide, who, for similar reasons, had no interest in recovering drugs. As a result, there was very little communication, much less coordination, between the two divisions, even though they were frequently investi-gating the same people.

It was Jessica DeGrazia, Manhattan DA Robert Morgenthau's First assistant, who first recommended the establishment of a special homicide task force devoted solely to tackling gang crime. As a prose-cutor, DeGrazia had discovered firsthand how ill equipped the system was to deal with the new violence.

In 1980, after she won a conviction in a difficult murder case, the police offered DeGrazia three detectives to continue working with, and over the next three years the Trinity Project, as the program be-came known, locked up a number of previously untouchable killers, most of them connected to Harlem's increasingly violent drug gangs. DeGrazia learned that Harlem's criminal subculture, especially its drug trade, was a very small world. Everybody knew everybody else. Infor-mants developed in the course of one investigation were invariably helpful in the next. One case led to another.

In 1983, convinced that she knew how to slow down Harlem's

soaring homicide rate, DeGrazia worked up a proposal for a special unit, based on the Trinity program, that would proactively police gangs, and presented it to Morgenthau. As it turned out, Morgenthau had been looking for a vehicle to attack the violent drug gangs in upper Manhattan, an area of growing concern for the office. Recently a gang of Harlem-based heroin traffickers known as the Vigilantes had murdered Bobby Edmonds, a state witness in the upcoming trial of the group's top enforcer, Nathaniel Sweeper. Morgenthau wanted to hit them back hard; anything less than the swift capture and conviction of Edmonds' killers would be viewed by gangs all over Manhattan as an exploitable weakness.

As a result, that fall, Morgenthau appointed William Hoyt, a 43-year-old career prosecutor, to head a small task force called the Homicide Investigation Unit, and persuaded the Department to assign two detectives under him. Hoyt, an ex-marine, driven and demanding, was one of the office's top homicide prosecutors, and a skilled, imaginative investigator. He quickly made his mark by bringing down the Vigilantes. It was an auspicious beginning for the unit and in short order they added a second prosecutor and two more investigators.

I T W A S A B O U T that time that crack first hit the streets. A drug could not have been better designed to promote violence and disorder. Its cheap, intense high garnered a broad new market, most notably inner-city women, the wives and mothers who had provided a measure of stability to poor, vulnerable households. Once, these women had been deterred from using hard drugs by needles and the high price of heroin and powder cocaine. Now for a few bucks they could experience euphoria with the ease of lighting a cigarette. It was the ideal coffee break, the five-minute getaway, a perfect antidote to the humdrum of slum living. It was also highly addictive and the long-term costs of maintaining crack's short, peaky high turned out to be far greater than for other drugs.

Even more troubling was the pernicious, reinforcing relationship between crack use and crime. With more users committing exponentially more thefts, the market for stolen goods collapsed, accelerating the cycle of larceny and glut. A construction tool or car radio that once fetched $30 at a fence now barely brought $10; as a result, addicts had to steal three times as much to satisfy their habit. And whereas heroin has a soothing, narcotic effect that lasts for hours, crack often produces a speedy, paranoid psychosis. Not only were crackheads stealing more, but their crimes were more brazen and more likely to end in violence.

But it was the business of selling crack that ultimately shredded any semblance of safety or order in the streets. As disorganized and violent as the drug trade had become, the necessity of finding a good connection, especially among the older, more established heroin suppliers, and the high price of entry into the market—a kilo of heroin cost up to $200,000—acted as a brake against unfettered competition and ensured some measure of stability.

Crack exploded that stability. No one group could control its spread. An ounce of cocaine that could be bought on the street for $1,000 yielded 320 to 360 vials of crack—more if cut—that sold initially for $10 apiece in many locations. Anyone with a hot plate and a few hundred dollars could go into business and triple his money overnight. The old order—already shaken—crumbled completely.

Unlike "crude" heroin or cocaine, where the purity varied, a vial of crack in the South Bronx and a vial of crack in Harlem were essentially the same. Enterprising dealers quickly realized they weren't in the drug business, they were in the service or convenience business. More than ever, location counted, and the battle for turf broke out into open warfare.

Once the supplier had ruled the drug trade. You needed a good connection to do business, and if you had one, the addicts would find you, wherever you set up shop. Now the neighborhood toughs were king, the gangs with the most muscle, as long as they were willing to use it. Within months of crack's appearance gangs began shoring up their troops. Jamaican and Dominican gang leaders called up young men from their native villages, men without police records or known identities, to protect their interests and ease their expansion into other territories. The murder rate began to spiral. The police estimated in 1988 that one in three homicides in upper Manhattan was gang-related, but many investigators felt that the rate was at least double that. And even those numbers underestimated the true impact of the gangs.

With their vast incomes they drove the market for illegal guns and stolen cars. (Federal reporting laws made it imprudent for them to buy cars with cash.) Gang members moonlighted as stickup artists or let themselves out for contract murders. Worst was their impact on the young (whose status as minors shielded them from New York's draconian drug laws). In many neighborhoods the gangs functioned like a centrifuge, sucking in impressionable kids, arming them and schooling them in violence, then spewing them back into the streets. In the drug-ridden Three-Four, the murder rate had more than tripled from 35 in 1980 to 119 in 1991, *even* while the burglary rate had nearly halved during the same period.

THROUGH THE SPRING of 1988, Hoyt's tiny HIU unit had convicted seventeen gang members for twenty-one murders—a remarkable record given the difficulty of the cases and HIU's limited resources. But still a drop in the bucket. By Hoyt's own reckoning, there were at least sixty gangs selling drugs in upper Manhattan alone, and those gangs, according to police estimates, were responsible for five hundred or more murders in the four years since IIIU began operating.

Then in 1988, with the addition of Walter Arsenault, HIU began to change the way it tackled gang enforcement. Arsenault at the time was a 36-year-old senior counsel laboring in one of the office's six trial bureaus, chafing under the constraints of conventional casework. Before joining HIU he'd prosecuted several gang murders, and like

DeGrazia and Hoyt before him, each time he'd stumbled into a rat's nest of related crime. "There was all this stuff going on in the shadows of those cases—murders, robberies, drug operations," he recalls. "The defendants and the victims were at the center of Harlem's drug world, and at one time or another their lives intersected with most of the gangs and stickup groups in the area. We learned about one gang in the Black Park housing project which was employing off-duty Corrections officers to guard their sales spots. But the way the system was set up, the detectives who were assigned to my cases were authorized to work only on those particular cases, and there were no resources in the Trial Division to follow up on the leads. It was very frustrating. I had all this good information, but I didn't have the arms and legs to pursue it."

Arsenault's efforts to expand the scope of his investigations would have a profound effect on HIU.

WITHIN WEEKS of Arsenault's arrival at HIU, Hoyt enlisted him in a case that would change the way the unit prosecuted gang crime. Asking Arsenault into his office, he showed him a photograph of a severed head sitting like a soccer ball on Edgecombe Avenue, a busy Harlem thoroughfare that was the center of Jamaican life in Manhattan. The victim, Hoyt said, had been "jointed"—cut into pieces, starting with his fingers and toes, while still alive. Hoyt had information that the killers were members of a Jamaican crack crew. But the Jamaicans were an insular community, poorly understood by law enforcement, and that case and numerous other homicides in the area were still unsolved. Hoyt asked Arsenault to take them on.

Several days later, Arsenault escorted a BBC film crew to Edgecombe Avenue with Ray Brennan, a PD detective assigned to HIU. The first thing he noticed, apart from the crowds of shoppers thronging the sidewalks, was the brazen way the dealers did business. Again and again he saw them doing hand-to-hand sales in the open, counting their receipts in plain view. Nor did they scatter when the van approached, as almost any other gang would. Instead they held their ground, at most turning toward the building walls when the camera was pointed at them. Then the bricks started raining down from the rooftops. Several bounced off the van, leaving huge dents in the roof and sides, and terrifying the BBC reporter. "Don't they realize you're the police?" she asked Brennan.

"Sure they do," he replied. "That's the whole point."

In fact the police were powerless against the posses. When they showed up in force to clear the corner, they were outnumbered. "In 1988, 1989, the Spanglers were convinced that that was their corner and the police thought so to," Arsenault says. "The Department would never admit it, but a lot of cops from the Three-Oh used to tell me that they were under affirmative orders not to get out of their cars on Edgecombe Avenue."

Arsenault spent the next three months—a lifetime in law enforcement—studying his adversaries. Hoyt paired him with newly recruited Terry Quinn, a former police sergeant familiar with the area—he'd been Garry Dugan's boss at Manhattan North Homicide—and the two men scoured Harlem in search of informants. They had the cops in the Three-Oh and neighboring precincts call them whenever they arrested a Jamaican; they would drive over and pick up the case, often debriefing the suspect on the spot. They copied unsolved homicide case folders, took them home, and pored over them at night. They ordered up rap sheets and mug shots and put together photo albums. And they compiled lists of nicknames, real names, gang affiliations until finally the data began to blur and run together. "There was no scrap of information we weren't interested in," Arsenault recalls. "Most precinct detectives, when they debrief an informant, only want to hear about the case at hand. They don't have time for a lot of other stuff. But you couldn't tell us anything we didn't want to know, that wouldn't somehow fit in later on. A lot of times guys would come in still thinking about cooperating and we'd tell them some obscure detail about themselves that we'd picked up along the way—where they were born, who their girlfriend was three years ago—and they'd be awestruck. Then they'd tell us everything because they thought we knew it anyway."

Their first break in the investigation came from a jailhouse informant named Rohan Smith (a pseudonym). A veteran of the posse wars, Smith was built like a fireplug, with a big coal-colored head as bald as prison barbers could make him. "Rohan was the franchise CI," Arsenault recalls. "He'd been around forever and knew everyone and everything. The first time he came into my office, he said to me, 'I know who you are and I'm going to tell you everything you want to know, but I want some things from you too.' So I asked him what he wanted and he said, 'I been in jail for two months, mon, I want a blow job,' and I kind of looked him over and told him, 'Sorry, you're not my type.' Well, he thought that was about the most hysterical thing he'd ever heard and we became friends and he ended up telling me everything I wanted to know and more."

Jovial and smart, Smith spent days at a clip in Arsenault's office educating the prosecutor about the history and lore of the posses in Kingston and New York. He explained how the gangs correlated with certain neighborhoods back in Kingston—the Spanglers were from Matthews (pronounced Match-ez) Lane, the Dunkirk Boys from Franklintown—and how they had aligned themselves with the political parties there in exchange for protection and patronage, much as the Irish, Italian, and Jewish gangs did in old New York. He said the politicians had armed the gangs with U.S. and Cuban weapons during the turbulent 1960s, turning long-standing, but relatively nonviolent rivalries into bloody vendettas.

The posses exported some of that violence to New York and other cities. But the splinter crews managed to coexist peacefully until crack came along. The Jamaicans were the first groups to market crack in the city, Smith said, and for a while everyone made "wild money."

But the competition over sales spots reignited long-simmering tensions among the posses and the murder rate exploded.

The Spanglers were the largest and most violent of the posses, boasting a membership of 200 to 300, at least ten times bigger than any gang HIU had encountered in the past. The Spanglers, Smith said, "owned" the corner of 145th and Edgecombe and the blocks on either side. But numerous other groups controlled locations in Harlem as well—Two Mile Posse, the Cocaine Cowboys, the Dunkirk Boys among them. Smith described the major players in each gang, their rank, pedigree, sidelines—who were the shooters, stickup artists, and suppliers. Gradually a picture of gang life on Edgecombe Avenue emerged, and Arsenault began to see the complexity and enormity of what he was up against.

Arsenault and Quinn drew up a list of all the known posse members in upper Manhattan, ranked them from most to least dangerous, and started building cases against them. "It was just a wish list, really," Arsenault says. "At first we went after the Spanglers, but it was all linked. We'd bring someone in to talk about an old Spangler homicide and he'd tell us about four other murders that happened the week before in London, Dallas, Los Angeles, and Baltimore. We had no idea what we'd find. The Spangler investigation led us to the Cocaine Cowboys, which led to Two Mile, which led to the Dunkirk Boys. We just started going down the list, taking out targets of opportunity."

Their tactics were equally helter-skelter. Mainly, they'd find Jamaicans with drug cases against them, then use New York's tough drug laws to lever their cooperation against more violent associates. If they wanted someone badly, they'd use an undercover to buy them and turn them over to Immigration for deportation. Then if they tried to reenter the United States, as they inevitably did, they'd bust them again and send them away for five years. Arsenault wasn't particular about his methods. He used any tool to chip away at the gangs. He reached out to the Feds and to local authorities in other jurisdictions. Just one of his targets, a walking murder machine named Kirk Bruce who was suspected of killing 60 people in the United States, and roughly 200 in all, if you included his native Jamaica, was convicted on murder charges in Maryland thanks to witnesses supplied by Arsenault.

What distinguished their investigation from previous HIU cases was their determination to take out all the members of a gang, and then all the gangs in an area, to dismantle every bit of infrastructure so that new or hybrid groups couldn't re-form. The plan worked far beyond their expectations. Once Arsenault and Quinn had assembled a critical mass of informants and evidence, the posse members turned against one another and flocked to the unit to make deals for themselves. In 1989 HIU locked up the Spanglers' top five lieutenants. (The gang's leader fled to Jamaica and was killed by rivals shortly afterward.) In 1990, working with the Feds, the unit took down nearly 200 more gang members. By 1991 the posses either were in jail or had fled Manhattan.

ARSENAULT'S "whole gang" approach was a break from the past. The unit was changing in other ways as well. Hoyt had always run HIU as though it were a kind of independent authority. But HIU's heightened profile and the introduction of forceful personalities like Arsenault and Quinn raised issues of oversight and set Hoyt on a collision course with his supervisor, newly appointed Trial chief Nancy Ryan.

A graduate of Yale Law, Ryan, then in her late thirties, was known around the office as a brilliant and ambitious lawyer, a good friend and an implacable enemy. Tall and lithesome with aquiline features and straight-cut chestnut hair, she had joined the office in 1975, risen quickly, and founded the Asian Gang unit, a precursor and model for HIU. In fact, Ryan had been DeGrazia's first choice to head HIU, but she was then in the midst of an investigation into the Ghost Shadows, the largest and most violent of Chinatown's youth gangs, and she reluctantly declined.

Some office insiders felt that Ryan and Hoyt were bound to clash. Both were strong-willed and had a proprietary interest in HIU. Ryan wanted to create a new post at the unit—a kind of supervising investigator—and install James McVeety, a former police sergeant who had worked for her in the Asian Gang unit. Hoyt accepted the need for better supervision, but was a stickler for loyalty and perceived McVeety as Ryan's man. When Ryan hired him over Hoyt's objections, Hoyt abruptly resigned.

Ryan appointed Arsenault to succeed him, and expanded the unit, adding six new prosecutors and investigators. In response, Arsenault broadened its approach to gang removal. Wrestling with the Jamaican posses had convinced him that the best way to neutralize a violent gang was to pull it up by its roots, and he'd begun casting around for a legal strategy that would enable him to do that. By 1991 he'd found a way: rarely used state conspiracy laws that allowed prosecutors to target an entire gang at once. All Arsenault needed was the right case to try it out.

THE GHERI CURLS, so called because their members all wore the same permed hairstyle, were the latest incarnation of the violent drug-trafficking gang—well organized, well armed, and extremely violent. In the late 1980s the gang sold weight cocaine from a string of apartments on West 157th Street, but their true product was terror. Like an occupying army, their leaders, the five Martinez brothers, commuted to the block from expensive suburban homes in identically gold-painted cars. And they brought enforcers with them, imported from the Dominican Republic to protect their operation and threaten and brutalize residents who dared complain that *their* homes had been turned into an all-night drug market. When one of those residents, a retired city worker named Jose Reyes, ignored the gang's threats and began organizing tenants to go to the police in early 1990, a Gheri Curls triggerman tracked him to a crowded neighborhood park and shot him in the back of the head. Though dozens of people witnessed the execution and Reyes was a popular figure on the block, no one came forward.

A Three-Oh beat cop named James Gilmore—himself the target of death threats—had been trying for more than a year to get the Department to move against the Gheri Curls. Gilmore had a number of confidential sources in the neighborhood who gave him information about the gang's activities. But they were afraid to press charges against the gang because they felt that cops in the precinct were in league with the dealers. (In fact, authorities in 1994 indicted 33 officers from the Three-Oh on corruption charges, of which 28 were found guilty.) Narcotics failed to launch an investigation and the precinct did nothing, so Gilmore brought the case to HIU. Arsenault assigned it to an eager young prosecutor named Fernando Camacho.

THE GHERI CURLS became HIU's "first big modern case," in Arsenault's words, the culmination of its long learning curve and a template for future investigations. With Gilmore's help, Camacho, a chubby, baby-faced prosecutor with an engaging, excitable manner, amassed intelligence about the gang and used investigators to make numerous undercover buys into key gang members. He didn't want to just take the Gheri Curls down; he wanted to annihilate them.

In November 1991 he arrested the entire gang on drug conspiracy charges, enfolding Reyes' murder and other violent acts into the indictment. New York State's conspiracy laws were poorly understood by most prosecutors; their use marked a radical departure from the traditional homicide investigations that had been HIU's hallmark. But they allowed Camacho to get all the Gheri Curls off the street at once, leaving no one to retaliate against potential witnesses. With the streets clear, Gilmore's sources began to come forward and gang members began to cooperate against each other.

The "whole gang" approach paid another dividend. In the past

HIU's piecemeal arrests of gangs like the Spanglers and the Jamaican posses, though opportune, often diffused the larger story behind those investigations. Camacho's lightning strike against the Gheri Curls focused attention on the gang: their uniform hairstyles and gilded cars, their battles against the police and their reign of terror over a neighborhood. It was a compelling story and the media loved it, generating a windfall of publicity for the unit and, more important, for Morgenthau.

Not everyone was well disposed toward the unit, however. Many police chiefs, for example, felt that the DA should get out of the investigation business altogether and let the cops do their job. HIU's success only sharpened their resentments.

Moreover, there were tensions between the DA's special investigative units and the Trial Division, the mostly anonymous line assistants who catch 90 percent of the office's cases. That Morgenthau, having begun his career as a proactive U.S. Attorney, lavished attention and resources on big-case units like HIU did little to endear it to turf-conscious police commanders, or some of Morgenthau's own bureau chiefs.

But with Morgenthau basking in the reflected glow of HIU's success and Ryan running interference for them in Trial, HIU had equipment and support staff.

They would need those resources and more in the following year, as they launched an investigation into an even bigger case, the gang behind the Quad murders and the Cargill case.

3

THE WILD COWBOYS

JANUARY 1992

THROUGH JANUARY 1992, Walter Arsenault had only the sketchiest notion of who Lenny, Platano, and the Red-Top gang were. He'd been hearing about them for some time from Fernando Camacho, whose informants invariably named them among the most feared organizations in the city; and Terry Quinn had apprised him of conversations he'd been having lately with a precinct detective named Jerry Dimuro, the primary in the Cargill case. But other than an apparent connection between the Cargill shooting and the Quad murders in the Bronx, Arsenault had little hard information about the Red-Top operation.

More to the point, he didn't have the manpower to go after

them. Camacho was getting ready to take down the Gheri Curls. Ellen Corcella, a senior HIU prosecutor, was working on Black Park, the American black gang that employed Corrections officers as guards for their heroin operation in the eponymous Harlem housing project. And Camacho, a tireless rainmaker, had three other Washington Heights gangs in the pipeline.

Because of their limited resources, HIU depended on the police to investigate the early stages of their cases—to help identify the members of a gang, where they sold and stashed their drugs, who they'd reputedly killed. Over the years, Hoyt and then Arsenault and Quinn had developed an extensive network of so-called buffs—cops and detectives who loved their work and went beyond the routines of their job to try to root out the core sources of crime on their turf. HIU functioned as a kind of clubhouse for these buffs, who regularly stopped by the unit on their way to and from court to get information about targets or just gossip about the street. More important for Arsenault, they acted as emissaries for the unit, recommending them to police with tough gang-related cases. James Gilmore, the beat cop who sparked the Gheri Curls investigation, for example, had been referred to HIU by detectives in his precinct. Similarly, detectives in Jerry Dimuro's old Narcotics module would convince him to pay a visit to Terry Quinn.

Even then, getting the Department to cooperate was inevitably a tricky negotiation for Arsenault. The police were reluctant to cede control of their cases—even old, unsolved homicides, even though HIU always gave credit back to the primary detectives for the arrests they made. Typically, Arsenault had to sell the unit to the precinct commanders, many of whom had never heard of HIU, using the lure of publicity—guaranteed seats at the press conference when the indictments were brought down—to convince them to sign on.

Meanwhile, Mark Tebbens remained the lone detective investigating Red-Top. Although he had help from Manhattan detectives Garry Dugan and Jerry Dimuro, who were pursuing leads in the Cargill case, Tebbens, at best, hoped to pry loose the shooters responsible for the Quad murders in the Bronx. He knew that as long as Red-Top remained entrenched on Beekman Avenue, he would have a hard time finding witnesses to testify against them. But then Tebbens was used to adversity in his dealings with the gang.

T E B B E N S had first encountered the Red-Top gang two years before in one of his first cases in the Four-Oh, the public execution of two enemy drug dealers on Beekman Avenue by Red-Top gunmen that became known in police circles as the Double. It was a vicious, bloodthirsty affair. On September 3, 1989, Luis Angel "Chico" Rivera and Orlando "Tito" Berrios, drug dealers from another part of the Bronx, drove onto Beekman Avenue in a livery car with two cronies, Gee and Ant. They didn't realize they'd entered Red-Top turf, nor were they aware that the gang had targeted them for killing a friend of theirs several months ago. Chico was visiting his girlfriend, who lived nearby with their son. The four had stopped to greet a prison buddy of Chico's they'd chanced upon exiting a bodega at the south end of the street.

Moments after their arrival, they were spotted by Red-Top. It was a hot summer night, Labor Day weekend, and the streets were jammed with people playing music, drinking beer, hanging out. The gang, including Lenny, Pasqualito, and Victor Mercedes, quickly moved in on Chico and Tito. Mercedes, gun drawn, shouted at Rivera, "This is for my brother," and pumped a bullet into Chico's stomach.

Chaos ensued. Mercedes and Pasqualito shot Chico three more times, wounding him fatally as he tried to climb into the back of the waiting livery car, shooting the driver in the leg as he sped away. Ant and Gee, who had frozen like deer caught in headlights at Red-Top's approach, took off up Beekman Avenue, escaping into St. Mary's Park behind a fusillade of gunfire. Tito, who was wounded, ran around the corner onto 141st Street and then peeled off north on Cypress Avenue. People from the neighborhood watched in horror as Lenny, Pasqualito, and Mercedes raced after him down the middle of the street. On Cypress, Tito flagged down a green sedan that was making a U-turn, begging for help. When the driver waved him off, Chico dove through the passenger-side window, pleading for his life. Then the driver saw the advancing gang members and abandoned the car. Tito scrambled into the driver's seat, but by now his pursuers had surrounded the sedan. As he floored the accelerator, they fired into the car. Badly hit, Tito crashed into a van parked on the west side of the avenue. The shooters quickly regrouped around the vehicle, firing some thirteen bullets into Tito's shuddering body, nearly severing his left hand from his arm.

Tebbens had thrown himself into the investigation, and managed to build credible cases against both Pasqualito and Victor Mercedes. But though scores of people had witnessed the shootings, he was able to coax only a few to testify against the Red-Top enforcers. A year ago, he learned, Pasqualito had beaten the rap for a similar public homicide in St. Mary's Park after the witnesses in the case withdrew. When he was arrested for the Double, Pasqualito bragged to Tebbens that the same thing would happen again. Worried, Tebbens took special measures to insulate his witnesses from threats and inducements. Nonetheless, one by one they defected, and two years later the case was taken off the calendar, and Pasqualito and Mercedes were released.

ON A BITTER January night three weeks after the Quad homicides, Tebbens sat in a surveillance van on Beekman Avenue watching for the Red-Top enforcer, Platano, to appear. "This don't feel right," Chubby whispered. It was freezing inside the van. Mark Tebbens could see the ragged outline of Chubby's breath against the dim red glow of the cabin lights. A gang of street mopes circled the van. "They think you're the police or some stickup guys." Tebbens counted two or three in the passenger-side mirror poking at the side panels, working the door levers. But what got his attention was a lone black-jacketed figure sauntering deliberately toward them from across the street. He cupped his eyes and leaned his hooded face into the darkened windshield. Then he stepped back and lowered one of his hands to his waistband. "Gun," Tebbens thought.

"Yo, Tebbens, man, if they think we're rip-off guys, they're going to start shooting," Chubby said. "You better get your boys down here."

Chubby was Benjamin Green, the older brother of Anthony Green, the Quad's first victim. Chubby had turned up at the Four-Oh squad a few days earlier, saying that he wanted to help with the investigation. "I was going to take care of this myself," Green told Tebbens. "But my mom's already lost one son. She don't need to lose another." Short and skinny, Chubby was a smart, articulate street kid who seemed to know who was who on Beekman Avenue.

Tebbens had met with Detectives Dugan and Dimuro from Manhattan after the FBI agent brought Platano to his attention, and together the three investigators had decided to make the Red-Top enforcer their main target. Not only was he the common thread in their investigations—an eyewitness to the Cargill homicide, a shooter in the Quad—but he was clearly a psychotic killer, someone they wanted to get off the streets as quickly as possible.

Tracking down Platano hadn't been easy. None of the detectives knew his real name or what he looked like. Though Tebbens had several Quad witnesses who referred to one of the shooters as Darkman or the Dominican—the man Tebbens suspected was Platano—only one, Angel "Chico" Puentes (a pseudonym), an unreliable street hustler, was willing to identify him by name. So when Chubby told Tebbens he not only knew Platano but could point him out to the detective, Tebbens spent the next few days cobbling together an arrest plan and scrounging equipment.

According to Green, Platano transported drugs onto Beekman Avenue most nights about midnight. Tebbens knew he didn't want to take Platano near the gang's stronghold or in the open, where he might be able to escape or, worse, trigger a shoot-out. Instead, he set up surveillance with Chubby and another detective, Mike Calderon, in a van across the street from the delivery point, and stationed an apprehension team—six police, two unmarked cars—a few blocks away. The idea was to trap Platano in his car as he tried to exit the block.

Tebbens knew the gang would be wary of any strange vehicle on the block, especially in view of stepped-up police activity following the Quad. So he picked a beat-up van that looked dirty from the outside. He recruited a Latino officer, dressed in street clothes, to drive them to the spot, then leave as though he were visiting around the corner. And just in case things went awry, he'd put two sector cars on radio alert. But he hadn't reckoned on their being mistaken for another gang, nor was he prepared for the suddenness and ferocity of Red-Top's reaction. Within moments of the van's arrival, Red-Top's workers had swarmed over them.

The gunman backed away from the windshield and rounded the side of the van. Tebbens lifted his walkie-talkie and quietly called in the radio cars. Then he slid back behind the side-panel door, drew his gun, and braced for a shoot-out. "Come on, guys. We've got a shooter here," Tebbens whispered into the radio. He saw the side door latch jiggle back and forth and sensed the gunman's impatience. Any second now, he would try to force the lock, perhaps shoot it out. If he did, Tebbens decided he would try to catch him in the chest as he entered the van, while his eyes were still adjusting to the dark.

"Here they come!" Calderon whispered from the back of the van. Tebbens moved to his side, and through a crack in the door panels saw two sector cars cruising up the avenue as their antagonists dispersed into the dark folds of the neighborhood.

Surprisingly, once the patrol cars moved on, the gang seemed to lose interest in the van. Across the street the gang's headquarters, a five-story tenement at the north end of Beekman, rose like a fortress, commanding a clear view for blocks around. Crack sales were made from a covered walkway spanning the side alley, a gloomy corridor cut into the solid front of buildings crowding the street that Chubby called the Hole.

Green pointed out the gang members on the block, mostly young neighborhood toughs hired by Red-Top. The gang leaders themselves lived elsewhere, but they hung out on Cypress, the next street over, and made their presence felt on Beekman. While Lenny, Red-Top's leader, was in jail on gun charges, he ran things through his brother Nelson and trusted lieutenants like Platano. He called the block every day, according to Green, sometimes leaving instructions for the gang with a local family who let out their apartment as a kind of clubhouse.

Tebbens adjusted the periscope hidden in an air vent on the van's roof and scanned the block. It was past midnight and a chill wind gusted in from St. Mary's Park at the north end of the avenue; still, traffic flowed ceaselessly—stockbrokers from New Jersey and Westchester in their BMWs and Suburbans, gang-bangers from the Heights in their Hondas and hoop-dies, slowly circling the block, trailing salsa music and raw, rumbling exhaust. Tebbens had known for a while that there was a Red-Top crew selling crack out of the alleyway at 348 Beekman; over time he had learned bits and pieces about the structure of their organization. But as Green continued his dissertation on the group's activities, Tebbens began to realize the true scope of the scene before him. What had seemed at first glance to be just a lively street scene was in fact a complex, highly structured drug market. The men nearest the alley were in constant radio communication with lookouts stationed on the rooftops, who screened customers as they came onto the block, steering them into the Hole or, when the line backed up, to a vacant lot across the street. Youngsters on mountain bikes—seemingly at play— ran errands for the older crew members, bringing coffee and sandwiches and beer from a bodega at the south end of Beekman and providing another level of intelligence, while women, their faces framed by squares of tenement light, called down to the men huddled on stoops or around cars. At times the whole neighborhood seemed to pulse to the rhythms of the Hole, the steady beat of sales, the thrum of incipient violence.

"That's him," Green said.

Tebbens watched as a black Chevy Caprice, its windows tinted, pulled into Beekman from the park road and stopped in front of 348, almost directly across from the van. Tebbens thought he recognized the car. Platano emerged from the driver's seat, dressed in black jeans and a puffed-out black army jacket over body armor. He was smaller than Tebbens had imagined him, and his expression under the arc light was grim. Suddenly the detective remembered why his car had seemed familiar. A month before he'd seen Anti-Crime chasing a black Caprice down Beekman Avenue—the target of an attempted gun search—and joined the pursuit through Mott Haven's narrow side streets and onto the Queens-Bronx Expressway. Tebbens had watched helplessly as the sedan threaded traffic at speeds over 100 mph and, without slowing, tore through an automatic tollbooth, splintering the wooden guard arm. Platano, he realized now, had been the driver. He alerted the backup team and told them to be ready. Platano's visit would be brief, Chubby had warned him. "Thirty seconds, no more."

Platano's effect on the block was electric. A group of men lounging near the entrance to 348 scattered at his approach. He was joined at the curb by his passenger, a tall, skinny youth dressed in identical black togs. Both men had drawn large-clip automatic guns—Mac-10s or Mac-11s, Tebbens guessed—and held them in plain view in front of them. Platano was carrying a large shopping bag full of what Tebbens supposed was crack. He moved slowly, looking left and right at almost every step. At the entrance they backed up against the building wall and checked the block a final time, their eyes resting briefly on the van. Then the tall, skinny kid—whom Chubby called Mask—peeled off and entered the building; Platano followed him in a moment later.

Tebbens used the seconds they were in 348 to move into the driver's seat and to radio the other cars again to be ready. He intended to pull out behind Platano and block him in case he tried to back up the street. Meanwhile the other cars would converge on Beekman from either side of the avenue, cutting him off and hemming him in. A third sector car would provide backup. He felt that if they could surround him in a contained space they had a good chance of bringing him down. Watching Platano—his intensity, the military precision of his movements—he felt he might try to shoot his way out.

Platano exited the building with his partner, paused briefly for a word with the location manager, a local tough Chubby knew as Linwood, then moved swiftly to the Caprice and started up the engine. "He's coming," Tebbens called into the transmitter, then started the van as Platano accelerated down Beekman. Tebbens pulled out after him. "Come on, guys," he said. "You better get over here. He's coming fast."

Tebbens was halfway down the block when he realized the backup wasn't going to make it. He floored the gas pedal, but the van had no juice. Where the hell was everybody? He saw the Caprice turn left into 141st Street where the arrest team should have been and shouted into his radio: "He's heading over to Cypress. He's going to take a right at the next block."

Tebbens rocked forward against the accelerator. The radio bristled. "We've got him, we've got him," someone was yelling, the squawk and breakup adding hysteria to already excited voices. Moments later he heard: "We're chasing him. We're in pursuit on Cypress," and Tebbens knew they'd lost him.

He rounded Beekman and saw one of the arrest cars slanted across 141st Street. Later he learned that the cops had improvised a roadblock and trapped Platano at the corner of Cypress Avenue. But when they went to arrest him, he backed into the car behind him, pushed it off at an angle, and sped away. A generation ago the cops would have fired on the fleeing car or at least tried to shoot out his tires—after all, Platano was the main suspect in a quadruple homicide—but new regulations governing the use of deadly force and discharging one's weapon prohibited the officers from firing even a warning shot.

Platano had disappeared once again into the night.

IN MANHATTAN, Dugan and Dimuro also set up surveillance at places where Platano was said to hang out, but without success. Nor were their informants any help. Dugan resumed the search for Platano's BMW. Drug dealers feel special about their cars. Dugan had known several who lived in hovels—flats without heat or furniture—who wouldn't dream of leaving their cars unattended. He concentrated at first on the precinct's garages, fanning out from the 600 block on West 171st Street, the gang's home base. But the car didn't show up and the attendants—usually a repository of information about neighborhood comings and goings—claimed to have no knowledge of Platano or the car.

Then, on a cold afternoon on January 6, his luck momentarily changed. Dugan and Dimuro had spent the day checking out lots and were driving back to the precinct, heading east along 174th Street in an unmarked squad car. At the Audubon Avenue intersection, Dugan suddenly spotted the BMW. "Don't make it obvious," he told Dimuro. "But check out the car on your left." Dimuro tilted his head sideways. There, parked in the second spot along the avenue, not more than thirty feet away, was a white BMW with a blue convertible top.

"Jesus," Dimuro said. "That's the car."

There were two men in it, their faces visible through the windshield. The driver matched the FBI's description of Platano.

Like Tebbens, Dugan was chary of taking Platano head-on. He turned left into Audubon and went around the block. Dugan was already reaching for his gun as they coasted in behind the BMW. Then he froze. The car was empty. Platano and his pal had snuck out the passenger-side door while they had been stalled in traffic.

Barely pausing, Dugan drove down the block to watch the car for the rest of their shift. Then Dimuro called Mark Tebbens in the Bronx to let him know they had Platano in their sights and to make sure his evidence was strong enough to justify an arrest. "Go ahead and grab him," Tebbens said.

Dugan and Tebbens had talked regularly since their first meeting at the Three-Oh, unusual for detectives working in different boroughs, and had developed an instant rapport. They shared the same kidding sense of humor, and Dugan's greater age and experience seemed to smooth the competitive edge that sometimes crops up between investigators. In time, they would adopt one another as mentor and mentee. But most important, they recognized a mutual appetite for hard work, that quality of perseverance that more than any other feature distinguishes good detectives from their mediocre counterparts.

MARK TEBBENS was ideally suited to be a street cop. A giant of a man, broad-shouldered and washboard trim, he projected confidence that he could handle himself in any situation. "Physical force isn't the most important thing on the job, until you need it," says Kevin Burke, who partnered with Tebbens during his early days in the Five-Two, a high-crime precinct in the North Bronx not far from where both men had grown up. "When the cops in our sector called in for backup and we'd pull up, they were always happy to see that big foot coming out of the car."

Burke and Tebbens worked steady midnights in Anti-Crime, a special plainclothes patrol unit that targeted street crimes from auto theft to illegal gun possession. They were so effective that even after the Department disbanded their unit in the wake of corruption scandals at similar plainclothes units around town, their CO kept them on duty and out of uniform, the only Anti-Crime cops on the midnight tour.

Tebbens not only knew who the bad guys were, he wanted to collar them all, according to Burke: "He had this intensity, this fire in his belly. We all start out that way, but after a few years most guys begin to burn out—the politicking, all the bullshit on the job. But Mark never lost that resolve. You could see it. He'd get that look like 'You can come with me or not, but I'm going to get this guy,' and you knew how it was going to end, that you were going to be out all night if that's what it took."

Tebbens was used to being on the outside. The son of an NYPD cop, he grew up in Wakefield, a working-class community in the northeast section of the Bronx. During the 1960s, Wakefield was a neighborhood in flux. Mainly Irish and Italian, but with expanding pockets of black and Hispanic families, the area broke down along ethnic and racial lines. Tebbens, whose father was white and whose mother was Puerto Rican, was caught in between, not wholly accepted by any one group.

There was tension at home as well. Mark's parents divorced when he was five; and his father, rarely around before the breakup, remained a shadowy figure throughout his childhood. Grace Tebbens tried to fill in the void, but she was forced to work two jobs after the separation, and was often absent herself. What's more, divorce was still taboo within the conservative Catholic precincts of Wakefield, and it added to the stigma of Mark's mixed parentage.

A big, sullen kid full of pent-up anger, he was expelled from Catholic school at five for disruptive behavior. Then at 11, he was removed from his local public school for fighting and transferred to PS 78, a tough minority school located in the nearby Edenwald projects. Mark had to fight for respect on a daily basis.

With his spotty school record and penchant for getting into scrapes, Mark was headed for serious trouble. What saved him was athletics. He loved sports, especially basketball. Well over six feet and nearly 250 pounds, he dwarfed the other players. Under the tutelage of the school's athletic director, the first in a series of coach-father figures, Mark developed the skills and work habits that enabled him to use his size and toughness to good advantage. By the time he was 14, he had made himself into one of the top players in the area, and was offered a full scholarship to attend Dalton, an elite private school on Manhattan's Upper East Side.

Nothing in his background, however, prepared him to compete with his new schoolmates academically or socially. Once again he was the outsider. They lived, many of them, in spacious apartments and brownstones in the city's toniest neighborhoods and vacationed in the Hamptons or Europe. Those who had summer jobs interned at top law firms and investment banks. Tebbens commuted to Dalton on the subway, and helped out after school—when he didn't have practice—at his uncle's ice-cream shop.

But Tebbens had endured too many disruptions to be intimidated by his new surroundings. He didn't try to pretend to be someone he wasn't; in fact, he regaled his classmates with tales of the street. He worked hard and muddled through the curriculum—and he played ball, winning the school's most valuable athlete award and earning a football scholarship from Northeastern.

But months before he was scheduled to leave for college, his mother, who worked as a store detective in Westchester, was hit by a car while chasing a shoplifter in the street. Critically injured, Grace Tebbens recovered, but her rehabilitation was slow and strained the family's finances. Tebbens' brother lacked Mark's drive and discipline, and had fallen in with a bad crowd and begun drinking heavily and using drugs.

Mark completed a year at Northeastern, but that summer he decided not to return to Boston, in order to help out at home. He found work at a number of security-related jobs, while continuing his education at John Jay, a Manhattan-based college specializing in criminal justice.

After taking up boxing—his father had offered to train him for the Golden Gloves, and after a year of hard work he'd made it to the semifinals—he took the NYPD exam, and entered the Academy. His father, interpreting Mark's choice as a betrayal, saw him only one more time, a year later at the funeral of Mark's brother, who died of a heroin overdose.

Tebbens got his detective's gold shield seven years later in 1989 and transferred to the Four-Oh in the Bronx. His strengths as a detective grew out of his experiences as a youth—crossing racial, ethnic, and class lines; learning to deal with all kinds of people. "Mark was my idea of a complete detective," HIU's Terry Quinn would later say. "He could do investigations, he knew how to interview. But he never lost touch with the street. A lot of detectives, a few years behind a desk, they get lazy and forget what it's like out there. But Mark always had good instincts."

IN MANY WAYS, Tebbens' style was the opposite of Dugan's. Tebbens, ten years younger, was a product of the street whose approach to cases was visceral and reflexive; he charged at suspects head-on, pawing them until he found an exploitable weakness. Dugan used a subtler and more methodical approach in his investigations, circling his adversaries, tracking them through careful observation, learning their histories through police, motor vehicle, and phone records, weaving intricate webs of evidence.

Still, Dugan admired Tebbens, his youthful raw energy and streetcraft, and Tebbens respected the older man's wisdom about investigations and the arcane politics of policing. But their different methods may have had less to do with age than background. Tebbens had grown up amid a jumble of classes, races, and ethnic groups; he was used to conflict, the scrum of confrontation and direct action. Dugan, on the other hand, was the product of a happy and homoge-

neous working-class childhood, a second-generation police officer and
the consummate insider, born into a large Irish-American clan with
roots in the city three generations deep.

Dugan's father, James, was a detective on the police force.
Slope-shouldered and potbellied with a round Irish face and brushed-
back white hair, he was a dead ringer for the 1970s sitcom character
Archie Bunker, at times comically hidebound. When Garry's older sister asked her father to teach her to drive, he refused, claiming that it
was not a proper role for a woman.

James Dugan had come of age during the Depression, and his
character had been even more firmly forged in the war. He faced life's
vagaries with stoicism and quiet, uncomplaining dignity. He revered
his wife, Alice, a devout Catholic as warm and expansive as he was but-
toned-down; and when she fought long battles against cancer and kid-
ney disease—though she survived into her fifties, she was hospitalized
for long stretches—Garry never heard his father utter a bitter word.

The last of three children, Garry grew up in Carroll Gardens, a
tidy working-class enclave in downtown Brooklyn, studded with three-
story painted-brick houses, with patches of lawn and hedgerows that
formed a single green line in summer. When Garry was 10 the family
moved to Staten Island, where his father had transferred to help form
the borough's first narcotics squad. Garry's days were tightly bound by
the regimens of school and church, and the routines of his mother's
lace-curtain domesticity.

Weekends and holidays, Garry helped his father with household repairs, learning his way around pipes, wiring, and Sheetrock. He
was clever with his hands and enjoyed the physical work and the slow,
methodical progress from plans to finished product. His moral education centered on the church, and he took his job as altar boy seriously,
learning Latin so he could participate in the services.

A feckless student, he preferred to spend his afternoons with
the girls from the nearby convent school, and he had no aptitude for

athletics. But he possessed judgment and uncanny discretion, a core of self-control that set him apart from his peers. Some of that restraint had been bred into him by his father; and some, no doubt, sprang from his religious training. Perhaps the largest part stemmed from his mother's bouts with illness, ordeals that tested her family's resolve and forced Garry early on to confront the prospect of loss and mortality. Whatever the source of his maturity, he was a leader in his circle of friends, steady and self-confident, someone others went to when they were in a jam.

Garry could not help noticing the powerful effect his father's gold shield had on other adults. Friends, neighbors, relatives came to him for counsel, and tradesmen were only too happy to offer his son a free seat in the local movie theater or a sandwich at the Automat. Although he studied dental technology at Brooklyn Community College, the mystique of the Police Department won out, and he decided to take the NYPD entrance exam. After entering the Academy, he married Lorraine Wiest, an education major, who lived near him in Staten Island, and took night courses at NYU, receiving a bachelor's degree in English literature in 1973. For a while he thought of going to law school, but the fact was he loved being a cop. After his first daughter was born the following year, he dropped the idea of law school for good.

His first assignment was to the 7th Precinct on Manhattan's Lower East Side, a melting pot for immigrants and the city's poor and elderly. Having lived his entire life in the clannish confines of church and parish, he might have been walking a beat in another country. His ears buzzed with the street cadences of Spanish, Russian, Yiddish, Arabic, and Urdu; and his senses reeled from the exotic sights and smells of a dozen different cultures and cuisines.

He spent the majority of those first years getting to know the people in this new land. He developed an inexhaustible curiosity about his neighborhood, and he had a knack for talking to the shop owners and residents on his beat—pleasant, practical, nonjudgmental—that invited their confidence. He picked up Spanish, the way he'd once studied Latin as an altar boy. He revisited crime victims and complainants in their homes and at their workplaces, and he stopped in at every shop and restaurant in his sector, learning about their histories, their families, their businesses.

Thanks to his many contacts, he was privy to a continuous stream of information about the neighborhood—who the troublemakers were, where they hung out, what they were up to. And he was diligent about collecting that information, collating lists of suspects, nicknames, addresses, known associates, license plate numbers. He was also a natural leader among his fellow officers, who elected him as their union representative and usually deferred to him in the field and at crime scenes.

In 1983, he transferred uptown to the Three-Four to shorten his commute to the home he and his wife bought four years earlier in upstate New York. The Three-Four was becoming New York's busiest precinct, the nexus of the city's cocaine and contract-murder markets. Most of the violence was directed at local drug dealers and the stickup artists who preyed on them. But some victims were bystanders and, occasionally, cops. One night in 1989 two Three-Four officers were shot dead in separate incidents, just hours apart.

Always among his precinct's arrest leaders, Dugan was one of the Department's most heavily decorated officers, demonstrating coolness and courage under fire on numerous occasions. In 1983, after foiling an armed robbery, Dugan finally accepted an appointment to the precinct's newly formed robbery unit. In short order, Dugan's team became one of New York's most effective at curbing the soaring robbery rate. Three years later, he was drafted into the Department's elite Manhattan North Homicide unit and promoted to detective.

The skills that made Dugan an outstanding street cop—a talent for dealing with people, an unusual ability to spot patterns of criminal activity—served him well as a detective. He was a meticulous investigator, a tireless collector of facts who constructed cases with the same patience and precision he had learned as a teenager working with his father on their house in Staten Island. "Garry would exhaust every lead, track down every witness; he was relentless," says Sylvester Leonard, a veteran lieutenant, who was chief of Dugan's robbery unit. "Garry had what all good detectives have: a passion for the work, a way of inhabiting a case and making it his own." But unlike other investigators, many of whom would become personally involved in their cases, often to the point of obsession, Dugan kept his feelings at a remove. His passion stemmed from his craft, the satisfaction he got from doing the job well. "He was the steadiest man in the unit," Leonard says. "You never had to worry about him taking shortcuts or not doing the right thing. He approached every case in the same way."

But Cargill wasn't like other cases.

METHODICAL AS EVER, Dugan called in to the precinct and put a tracer on the BMW, then settled in for a long stakeout. He was prepared to stay all night if necessary, and when Platano hadn't returned by midnight, Dugan phoned his squad and put in a request for overtime. But he wasn't optimistic. Overtime was arguably the most divisive issue on the force, pitting career-minded supervisors, charged with holding down expenses, against active police, whose numerous arrests generated long hours and extra pay. Always a source of tension, it was especially frustrating for investigators like Dugan in the early 1990s, when police bosses felt that the causes of crime were outside their control, and thus were reluctant to expend scarce resources on cases that didn't make headlines.

The problem went beyond that. Dugan had seen plenty of good officers jammed up, transferred from line duty to desk jobs because their bosses knew that a cop making arrests in the street not only taxed their budget but was more likely to trigger complaints of corruption and brutality. Yet cops who never made collars were left alone year after year. Precinct commanders were promoted for keeping the peace and not rocking the boat. The crime rate could shoot up during their tenure, but as long as there were no riots or major corruption scandals on their watch, they were thought to be doing a good job.

In fact, Dugan had never had a real problem over his activity. Though he routinely headed the list of his precinct's overtime earners, he was also among the leaders in arrests—and not the bullshit kind, but serious felonies. His supervisors knew they were getting good value with Dugan, and they backed him up to the chiefs who flagged his record. In cop talk, collars justify everything.

But in his last case—the highly publicized murder/rape of 13-year-old Paola Illera—Dugan had been unable to make an arrest, and his boss, a deputy inspector new to the command, failed to protect him when the chiefs questioned his overtime allotment. Instead, the inspector ordered an inquiry, and Internal Affairs, after poring over six months of records, uncovered a minor error in Dugan's memo book. As a result, Dugan was docked three vacation days, and prohibited through the next quarter from earning overtime.

Dugan hoped the bosses would be more farsighted tonight. After months of patient investigation and plenty of legwork, he and Dimuro had stumbled on one of the cars Kevin Kryzeminski had described to them the day after his friend's murder, and with it an opportunity to unlock two of the city's most nettlesome cases. At the very least, they had a chance to take one of the city's most fearsome killers off the street and preempt future acts of violence. How many, he couldn't begin to know. But Dugan was certain that lives would be saved.

When he called the squad, however, Dugan was told that his request had been denied. The squad sergeant told him he'd alert one of the sector cars to keep an eye on the BMW. Disappointed, Dugan went home. He didn't even feel right tracking Platano on his own time. The Department discouraged such actions. The Supreme Court had mandated that governments must pay employees overtime, even when unauthorized; and the NYPD automatically investigated any off-duty arrests. When he returned the next day, Platano's car was gone, as he knew it would be. What he didn't know was that in failing to lock up Platano—when Tebbens had an eyewitness ready to identify him as one of the shooters in the Quad—they had lost a chance to avert a gang war.

THE POLICE traced the BMW through its plate number to Felipe Capellan, a small-time hood with a Massachusetts address. Although Dugan was unable to locate him, he learned from his rap sheet that Capellan had an upcoming court date—March 25—in Manhattan.

It was Dugan's partner, Dimuro, who moved the case forward first. He had worked Narcotics before becoming a detective and he knew the kind of terror gangs like Red-Top exercised in the street, as well as how tough it was to build cases against their top people. Early on, he'd despaired of solving the case. Now that he knew some of the killers behind the murder, and had read the FBI reports, he was even more pessimistic.

A couple of detectives from Dimuro's old Narcotics unit told him about the Homicide Investigation Unit's work in cracking the Jamaicans and the Gheri Curls in the Three-Oh. As a result, Dimuro decided to look up Terry Quinn. "They told me that Quinn was a big pain in the ass, but that he gets results," Dimuro recalled. "I'd already heard about Quinn and I knew what he was doing with the posses on Edgecombe Avenue. So I figured: Who gives a shit about personalities? I'm a big pain in the ass myself."

Dimuro called Quinn several times about Cargill, giving him some of the details about the gang behind the shooting. Quinn expressed interest in the case, but counseled patience. HIU's investigators were busy helping Fernando Camacho prepare for the Gheri Curls trial. In the end, Dimuro decided an appeal in person might spark some action.

He found HIU tucked into a corner of the fifteenth floor.

Hunkered down behind anonymous, bulletproof glass doors, the unit had a functional, unfinished look—two spare office suites flanking the investigators' squad room, a large, loftlike space studded with cheap metal desks, carpeted by some scabrous, mud-colored material. It looked like an office out of Dimuro's own precinct, and he immediately felt at home. Only the carpeting seemed out of place, and that, Quinn later explained, was a gift from the Feds. A team of ATF agents who briefly shared space with the unit had installed the stuff in compliance with federal work rules.

Dimuro was apprehensive about meeting Quinn. If Arsenault was HIU's head, Quinn was its heart and sinew; the force who drove the unit through hard times, who gave it its toughness and credibility in the street.

Quinn grew up in the 1940s and 1950s in Williamsburg, a tough working-class section of Brooklyn, a paycheck away from the slums. His father, a bare-knuckle fighter during the Depression, sold insurance in the projects, and his older brother was a charismatic ruffian and racketeer; together they taught Terry the streets. He was one of those larger-than-life cops you'd expect to see in the movies—gritty, driven, with a big ego, fast with his hands and wits. A twenty-five-year veteran of the force, he had been one of the Department's go-to guys, someone they tapped when they needed a case solved and weren't particular how it got solved. And Quinn had rewarded his bosses with headline collars—the "Silver Bandit," a Greenwich Village stickup artist who had eluded the police for years; the Columbia Rapist, the superintendent's son who had raped and murdered a young Columbia student on the rooftop of one of his father's buildings in 1984. The publicity from those and other cases had earned Quinn his share of detractors, cops who felt that he was precipitous, self-serving, not a team player. But even his critics conceded he got the job done.

He rode his men hard, but he never asked them to do more than he was willing to do himself. He was often the first one through the door, and on several occasions he paid for it with serious injuries.

During one crack house raid in 1986, he pursued a perp through a trap door and tumbled headfirst down a steep ladder, effectively scalping himself and fracturing his skull. Though his wounds were severe—later at the hospital he would be given last rites—he still managed to hold on to his man until help arrived; and afterward, when the Department offered him disability with three-quarters pay, he turned them down flat and returned to his unit.

The older detectives in Dimuro's squad advised him not to approach Quinn, and Dimuro knew that Dugan wouldn't be pleased that he'd taken the case to the DA's office. However, as the primary on the case, Dimuro decided he needed to do something. "I had detectives calling me late at night at home telling me I was making a big mistake by going outside the squad, that Quinn had fucked them before and he would fuck me now," Dimuro recalled. "But I didn't see any alternative. I felt there was no way we were going to clear this case without help."

A graying middleweight in the final strides of his forties, Quinn had mellowed since his days in the Department. Of medium height and build, he had short, springy hair, a pleasant Irish face, pug nose, and impish blue eyes behind steel-framed glasses. But he'd stayed in shape and never lost that aura of physical threat. He still moved like a boxer, constantly in motion, dividing space efficiently, pinning you down when he wanted your attention; even his speech, larded with street slang and police jargon, had a kind of corporeality, the terse phrases, delivered in a brassy Brooklyn timbre, like fingers jabbing into your chest.

Quinn took Dimuro back to the unit's lunchroom—a small office with a fridge and a conference table banking the squad room—and gave him HIU's dog-and-pony. Dimuro already knew the broad strokes of the organization, but Quinn listed a few details that another lawman would appreciate: a back stairway that connected the unit directly to the "Bridge of Sighs"—the walkway that linked the Tombs to the courthouse—and enabled them to produce prison informants quickly and discreetly, as well as the fact that HIU tried most of their cases in front of Leslie Crocker Snyder, a special narcotics judge who understood complex gang investigations and remanded defendants who posed threats against witnesses.

After talking to Quinn, Dimuro was certain he'd made the right decision in involving HIU, and Quinn was definitely on board. Dimuro's only reservation was the amount of time Quinn said it would take HIU to do the investigation: three months just to get started, a year and a half before they made the first arrests. If Quinn was going to steal his case, Dimuro wished he'd hurry up and do it.

HAVING TALKED with Dimuro, Quinn brought in Fernando Camacho, HIU's Dominican gang expert, to bring him up to speed. The three men met for about an hour, and Walter Arsenault, back from a court hearing, joined them halfway through. Quinn and Camacho would recommend either taking on or turning down the case based on its viability and potential impact, but Arsenault would make the final decision.

Quinn did most of the talking, embellishing Dimuro's threadbare report, weaving the detective's bits of fact, rumor, and supposition into a chilling narrative. First he reviewed the Cargill case, naming Lenny as the shooter and placing Raymond Polanco, the Brooklyn gun dealer, and Platano in the car with him. All three, Quinn told Camacho, belonged to a Dominican gang whom he called the Wild Cowboys, whose principal members had been friends since childhood and together attended George Washington High School in the Heights. He told Camacho that they were involved in heavy drug dealing and gun sales and had committed numerous homicides in the Heights, the South Bronx, and Brooklyn.

The gang ran West 174th Street in the 500 numbers, Quinn told Camacho, and then went on to list a number of their other possible drug spots in Manhattan. He named two suspected dealers from Washington Heights, Reuben Perez and Jose Menor, who were said to be associated with the gang. He added that the Cowboys had recently extended their drug operation to the Bronx and were responsible for the quadruple homicide on Beekman Avenue in December.

Having sketched the broad strokes, Quinn filled in some details about the gang that Dimuro and Dugan had put together. Lenny, the gang's leader, was in jail for another five months on a gun charge. In his absence, Polanco and Platano were running the drug operations. Polanco, Quinn said, was a particularly nasty character: in addition to supplying gangs all over the city with guns, he had been involved in numerous shootings in Brooklyn and the Heights, both as the triggerman and as the target.

But Platano, Quinn went on, was the one all the others feared. Rumor had it that several years ago a crony accidentally shot him in the back of his head. He miraculously survived and returned to the street more violent than before. He recently bragged to informants that he'd been involved in twelve homicides since July, and it was said he liked to finish off his victims with a shot to the back of the head, a kind of bizarre signature that reenacted his own brush with death. Among his victims were a high school baseball star, paralyzed from the neck down by a barrage of gunfire; a young man shot merely for using the same street name as Platano; a woman in her twenties, stabbed to death for reasons unknown; and a 13-year-old girl, killed by a stray bullet as she exited a chicken store in the Bronx during a shoot-out between rival dealers.

Quinn's presentation of the Cowboys to Camacho had been an exercise in speculation, an attempt to stitch together a few threads of information provided by second- and third-hand sources. No one really knew Polanco's status vis-à-vis the Cowboys—he was a Brooklyn guy known for guns, not drugs—and Perez and Menor were even sketchier figures, the Guildenstern and Rosencrantz of the investigation, drawn from footnotes in an FBI report. Even the gang's name was a Quinn invention. On the street, they were known as Lenny's Boys or simply Red-Top. But in an interview with Dimuro, a teacher from

George Washington recounted telling Lenny and his pals they were "just a bunch of wild cowboys." With its echoes of frontier lawlessness, the epithet seemed ideally suited to their outfit, and carried a romantic imagery that Quinn knew would appeal to cops and reporters alike.

Like any good politician, Quinn had already begun packaging the case, in order to command the office's attention and resources. He had an ability, rare among his fellow detectives, to define investigative targets and, no less important, to sell them to the higher-ups who controlled his budget. Worried about jurisdiction, Quinn played up those parts of the investigation that established the Cowboys as a Manhattan gang. As a result, his written notes, summarizing the meeting, highlighted the Cargill homicide and made Polanco, a key player in that case, a member, even a leader, of the Cowboys. More important, he assumed the Cowboys' drug operation was based in Manhattan—an assumption that would have far-reaching effects for the investigation—and linked the gang to Perez and Menor, dealers who were known to operate in Washington Heights. By contrast, his report downplayed the Cowboys' activities in the Bronx and failed to mention the Quad at all.

Even before Quinn finished his presentation on the gang, however, Arsenault felt that they were going to be HIU's next big case. They were not only violent but arrogant. There were plenty of homicidal gangs operating in Manhattan in 1992, but Arsenault was looking for the ones that murdered flagrantly, who acted as though they were above the law and were perceived to be untouchable. The Cowboys were clearly that. What's more, Arsenault was not unmindful of the gang's link to Cargill and the Quad. It never hurt to have a big, sexy centerpiece murder to grab a jury's attention and hold it through a long, complicated trial.

Arsenault did have certain reservations. HIU's investigators were currently tied up—it would be six to eight months before Quinn was able to focus full-time on the gang, and Camacho, busy preparing for the Gheri Curls trial in the fall, would be unavailable for at least a year, probably longer. Moreover, Arsenault wasn't fooled by Quinn's presentation; he realized right away that most of the homicides that Quinn described had taken place in the Bronx, outside of HIU's Manhattan jurisdiction.

But given Arsenault's frame of mind, these impediments seemed more like foothills than real obstacles. "We were pumped up," he recalled. "We were finishing up the Spanglers and we'd just indicted the Gheri Curls on conspiracy charges. Nancy Ryan was then the most powerful person in the office after Morgenthau, and she loved us. We were going to be her next Jade Squad, the model for taking down violent drug-trafficking gangs worldwide. She'd got us two new prosecutors, and she was trying to get us new investigators with grants, and of course she was running interference for us on the eighth floor. With her on our side, it never occurred to us we couldn't do a joint investigation with the Bronx, or that we wouldn't have enough resources to do another big case, even one with forty or fifty defendants.

"Camacho had this idea of taking back the Heights block by block, just marching up Audubon and Broadway and taking down every gang along the way. The precinct detectives all said he was crazy, that there were too many crews, that they weren't organized in a way that you could take them down together. But privately I agreed with him. We were sending out a message: If you killed people in Manhattan, we were coming after you, and we were the biggest, toughest gang around."

Still, Arsenault kept quiet at the meeting. He preferred to let his senior people warm to an investigation in their own way. HIU's cases could run for years and required extraordinary dedication; he wanted to make sure his key players were fully on board before getting immersed in the process. Besides, he never had a problem motivating his investigators. His problem was stopping them from taking on too much.

Shortly after the meeting broke up, Ray Brennan, one of the unit's senior investigators, overheard Quinn talking to Arsenault about the Cargill homicide in the lunchroom. "That's one case you'll never solve," he said.

"If there was any question before whether we were doing the case, that capped it," Arsenault recalls. "Telling us we couldn't solve Cargill was like waving a red flag in front of a herd of charging bulls."

4

THE SEARCH FOR PLATANO

JANUARY 1992

WHILE DIMURO lobbied HIU to take over the Cargill-Cowboy investigation, Tebbens and Dugan continued their search for Platano. In mid-January, a week after his abortive stakeout on Beekman Avenue, Tebbens and three Bronx detectives drove down to the Palladium late one night. The Palladium was a stadium-sized dance club on East 14th Street created by former Studio 54 founders Steve Rubell and Ian Schrager, and a reputed Cowboy hangout.

Tebbens befriended the chief of security, an ex-cop who said he knew Platano. He told Tebbens he hadn't seen him that night but that Platano sometimes paid the doormen to take him around to a back entrance in order to avoid the lines and the metal detectors. Then he took Tebbens to a bar area featuring Latino music and pointed to a large, powerfully built Hispanic man with a fat, bushy mustache. "That's Frankie Cuevas," he said. "If Platano's in the club, he'll be drinking with him."

Tebbens walked over to the bar and stood a few places down from Cuevas. The muscular detective was used to dominating a room, but Cuevas nearly matched him in size. He was six feet, about 230, with stabbing black eyes. Wearing a sporty black suit, a white silk shirt with a spread collar, thick braided gold necklaces, knuckle-sized gold cuff links, and double rows of gold rings on the fingers of each hand, Frankie was not someone Tebbens was likely to forget.

It was after midnight, but the nightclub was crowded. At one end people were dancing, the women's dresses glinting red, green, and gold in the aquarium light of the dance floor. Still Cuevas manned his post at the bar, and throughout the evening a stream of flashily dressed men and women came up to pay their respects to him. Platano, however, was not among them, and after several hours Frankie left and Tebbens and his team called it a night.

MEANWHILE, in one of those flashes of coincidence and good detective work, Timmy Burke, an Anti-Crime cop in the Four-Oh, told Tebbens that he had arrested a guy some eighteen months back named Platano, who was a suspect in the murder of a Bronx dealer. There wasn't enough evidence to hold him and he had been released. But before letting him go, Burke had filled out a stop-and-frisk report, on which Platano's address was listed. Burke had spent a few weeks rummaging through the precinct's antiquated filing system for the form, but he'd at last located it.

According to the stop-and-frisk report, Platano's real name was Wilfredo De Los Angeles, and he lived at his mother's home in Washington Heights. Tebbens was elated; finally he had a bead on the shadowy figure that had eluded him for nearly a month, and Dugan and Dimuro for a good deal longer than that. That afternoon, Tebbens and another detective paid Platano's mother a visit.

Anna De Los Angeles turned out to be a petite, fortyish woman with a polite, demure manner. She wore a simple housedress when Tebbens called on her, with no makeup or ornamentation save a small gold crucifix. After Tebbens introduced himself, Mrs. De Los Angeles explained that she spoke little English; she went to fetch her daughter to translate.

Tebbens found himself looking into a modest, well-kept apartment. A crucifix and a picture of the Virgin Mother hung on the living-room wall facing him across the small entrance hall. There were more religious icons on shelves and tabletops. The only jarring note was the expensive furniture, new and garish under plastic covers, a present, no doubt, from Platano.

When Anna returned with her teenage daughter, Tebbens made up a story about his investigating an anonymous tip of child abuse in the building. Did she have any other family members living with her? Mrs. De Los Angeles told Tebbens she had an older son, Wilfredo, but that he lived away from home and rarely visited. She didn't know where he lived. Wilfredo had grown up in the area and attended nearby George Washington High School. It was as much as he could glean about Platano from the cover story he had used. On his way back to the Bronx, however, Tebbens stopped in at George Washington High and managed to get a yearbook photo of Platano. For the first time he had a sense of what Platano looked like. A routine motor vehicle check on De Los Angeles turned up a handful of unanswered summonses and at least four suspensions. But Platano's rap sheet was clean. Despite his reputation, he had never been arrested or spent a day in jail.

Two weeks later, on January 29, the FBI received a tip that Platano had scheduled his car for service in New Jersey and would be carrying drugs. Special Agent Harold Bickmore alerted the New Jersey State Police. They arrested Platano as he rode through Englewood, a sleepy commuter town twenty minutes west of Manhattan. Bickmore phoned Jerry Dimuro the next morning. He told Dimuro that Platano was being held at the Bergen County jail under the alias of Paul Santiago, pending arraignment. Dimuro called Dugan at the Three-Four and the two detectives hurriedly drove to the jail.

Dugan was taken aback when he caught his first glimpse of his deadly quarry. Flanked by Corrections officers, Platano looked like nothing more than a slight, scared young man with cropped hair and a slender, clean-shaven face. There was nothing intimidating about him. His head was bowed, his shoulders sloped, his hands and feet were small. "From all that I had heard, I expected a wild animal," Dugan recalled. "He walked toward us with these small, mincing steps as though he had ankle bracelets on, which he didn't, and his hands cuffed and extended in front of him like an altar boy." Dugan told him he and Dimuro were from New York, and that they had no interest in his business in New Jersey. It was Platano's first arrest, and he was obviously petrified, which Dugan took advantage of, explaining that New Jersey's drug laws were more stringent than New York's, that he might never see the light of day.

Since there were no interview facilities at the jail, Corrections officers had partitioned a small area in the main corridor and set up a folding table and chairs. Platano, wearing a bright orange prison jumpsuit, sat between Dugan and Dimuro, his back to the parade of prisoners marching to and from court. "The conditions were far from ideal," Dugan recalled. "To get a confession or any kind of statement, you need a private room, just you and the subject one-on-one, or two-on-one. Instead we were squeezed together in the center of the jail, one of those paper accordion dividers separating us from the other inmates. You could overhear everything going on outside in the corridor."

Platano seemed intent on convincing his interrogators they had the wrong man. As Dugan began the interview, he leaned forward, balling his hands on the table, pinching his uniform material from time to time, as if to say: What am I doing here in these clothes?

"Why do they call you Platano?" Dugan asked, to break the ice.

"It means green banana," he said. "I've had it since I was a kid."

"Did you give them your real name?"

Platano started. "No," he said.

"What is your real name?"

"Wilfredo De Los Angeles." At least Platano was being truthful to that extent.

Dugan first took Platano's pedigree—names and addresses of family members, girlfriends, a snapshot of his life to date.

"Are you employed?" Dugan asked.

"No. I used to work as a mechanic."

"Where?"

"Porfirio's," he said. "In the Bronx on Featherbed Lane."

"What kind of repairs did you do?"

"Engines," he answered vaguely. Dugan glanced at Platano's soft palms. It was clear he'd never done a day's work in his life.

"You know that we didn't come here to talk to you about the narcotics charge that they have you for," Dugan announced then. "Detective Dimuro is from the Three-Oh squad in Manhattan and I'm from the Manhattan North Homicide squad. We're here to talk to you about a homicide in New York. If you can help us, we can probably help you get out of this mess." The detectives then related the details they knew about Cargill's murder—the near fender bender on the on-ramp, the presence of Platano's white BMW, the shooter's burgundy sedan—in order to convince Platano that they already knew what had happened. "We know that you didn't shoot anybody," Dugan told him. "However, we know that you saw this."

Platano began to nod.

"The kid on the highway," Dimuro said.

"It wasn't me," Platano blurted out nervously. "It was Lenny." He looked quickly left and right to gauge the impact of his statement on the detectives. Clearly he'd resolved to give up Lenny in hopes that it would bring him a ticket out of jail.

"Who's Lenny?" Dugan asked him disingenuously.

A wave of confusion crossed Platano's features. Didn't the detectives already know about Lenny? They seemed to know everything else about the shooting. "He's the boss," Platano said.

"The boss of what?"

"Our boss. The boss of our location in the Bronx."

"Where in the Bronx?"

"Beekman Avenue."

"And you belong to that group?"

"Yeah, I'm part of it."

"Who else belongs to that group?"

Platano named Lenny's older brother, Nelson, and two others whom he placed in the car with Lenny on the night of the Cargill shooting: Fat Frankie and Raymond, who he said supplied the gang with guns.

"What do you do?" Dugan asked.

"I make deliveries," Platano answered.

When Dugan asked about his other duties, it quickly became clear that Platano wasn't going to implicate himself further. So the detectives focused on the details of his drug deliveries: what cars he used, the "clavos"—secret compartments—where he hid the drugs, his methods of delivery. "What's Lenny's last name?" he asked suddenly.

"I don't know."

"Where's he from?"

"Manhattan—171st Street, near Broadway."

"Who's he live with?"

"With his mother. And his older brother."

"Where did you meet him?"

"In the streets—near there."

Dugan and Dimuro asked him questions in rapid-fire sequence, not giving him time to think. He tried to limit his responses, but he was on a slippery slope, giving up more and more details in an effort to seem cooperative. Suddenly he folded his head into his arms and began to cry.

Dugan looked over at Dimuro, who rolled his eyes. Platano's tears seemed forced. Still, there was an element of genuine fear in his demeanor.

"If Lenny finds out I'm talking about him, he's going to kill me."

"Is he tougher than you?"

"Of course, he's the boss."

"Who else has he killed?"

Platano looked up at Dugan, his face set. "I'm only going to talk about this one thing," he said.

"Okay," Dugan said. "Let's talk more about it."

Over the course of two hours, Dugan and Dimuro quizzed Platano relentlessly about the night of May 19, making him describe each link in the chain of events leading to Cargill's murder. That Saturday night Lenny had taken a group of his top workers nightclubbing—a custom among gang leaders. Platano had gone out separately with his girlfriend, Christina Torres, and ran into Lenny after midnight at the Limelight. He stayed at the bar with Torres, while Lenny and his group drank $150 bottles of Cristal champagne at one of the tables. Later, as he was leaving, he ran into Lenny again in the parking lot. Lenny was getting into a red Monte Carlo, with Raymond Polanco, who was delivering an AK-47 that he had repaired for Lenny, and Fat Frankie, another drug dealer. Platano was driving. Lenny sat next to him.

Platano told Dugan and Dimuro that he headed up to the Heights along the West Side Highway with Torres. On the ramp, leading to the elevated portion of the road, Cargill's red truck, coming at an angle from 57th Street, veered into his lane and cut him off. Polanco, who had been behind Platano, pulled alongside him, and Lenny asked what had happened. Platano told them that the guy driving the truck was crazy. Polanco took off after him. Platano described a wild chase up the highway that ended after he passed the other two cars and saw flashes of gunfire in his rearview mirror. Later he heard that Lenny had "iced a gringo."

Dugan doubted some of the details of Platano's statement, but in the main, his version jibed with Dugan's understanding of the case. For the first time, the detective realized he knew what had happened on the night of Cargill's murder.

But in law enforcement, knowledge without proof is worthless. Even with Platano's detailed statement, Dugan could not arrest Lenny for the shooting. Prosecutors don't like to try homicides on the basis of one witness's account—especially a witness like Platano. And though Platano had been careful not to incriminate himself, any defense lawyer would claim that Platano was a co-conspirator in the crime; in state law, unlike federal law, testimony by an accomplice is insufficient for conviction.

Given what they had, Dugan and Dimuro couldn't even keep Platano off the street. Dugan contacted Tebbens to let him know that Platano was in custody. But already the witnesses in the Bronx who had named Platano as a shooter in the Quad had backed away from their original statements, undermining Tebbens' ability to get an arrest warrant. It was frustrating, but only too common in the case of gang crime. Everyone was terrified of retribution from the remaining Cowboys. Three days after his arrest in New Jersey, Platano walked on $45,000 bail.

5

JOINING FORCES

FEBRUARY 1992

DESPITE THE FACT that Platano had gone free, Dugan felt encouraged by his progress in the investigation. He now had his first solid
piece of evidence against Lenny, numerous leads for his investigation
of Platano, and the names of two more possible eyewitnesses in the
Cargill case: Fat Frankie, whoever he was, and Platano's girlfriend,
Christina Torres.

After interviewing Platano, Dugan and Dimuro got Torres' address and went to verify Platano's story with her. A heavyset, plain-
looking woman several months pregnant, Torres lived in a roomy but
nearly empty apartment in the Gun Hill section of the Bronx. Except for

a large aquarium in the hall and a bed and night tables in one of the rear rooms, the apartment was unfurnished.

It was immediately clear to the detectives that Torres had not been with Platano on the evening of Cargill's shooting. When Dugan questioned her about the incident, she looked genuinely puzzled. "What shooting?" she asked.

"Were you in Wilfredo's BMW on the West Side Highway any-time when there was a shooting involved?" Dugan asked her.

The phone rang before she could answer him. She picked up the receiver and spoke rapidly in Spanish. Dugan understood enough to recognize the caller as Platano, who seemed to be coaching her. "Well, were you there during the shooting?" he asked after she put the phone down.

"Yes, I was there."

"When did it happen?"

Torres looked blank.

"Do you remember what season it was? Was it summer, winter?"

The phone rang. Platano again. When Dugan heard her asking Platano what the weather had been, he lost interest in the interview. Clearly, Platano wanted Torres—someone he could trust would not talk to the Cowboys—to back up his story. Later, as Dimuro quizzed her about Cargill, Dugan inspected the room. He saw a stack of mail on the bed; the letters were addressed to Christina Maldonado—a family name?—on Manor Avenue at the other end of the Bronx.

After finishing with Torres, the detectives decided to check out the Maldonado residence as well. The apartment was located in a non-descript walk-up in the middle of a quiet residential block. But there was an unusual amount of activity on the corner, where Manor intersected with the main thoroughfare of Watson, despite the cold and the late hour. The detectives realized they were looking at a thriving drug market.

A doubter of coincidence, Dugan tried to make sense out of the events of the day. Platano's link to Torres indicated to him that Platano had business on the block. His first conclusion was that he had discovered another Cowboy sales spot. It also occurred to him that Platano might be moonlighting. As it turned out, neither assumption was true. But the intersection of Watson and Manor would play a significant role in the case.

AT HIU, prosecutor Fernando Camacho was eager to launch the Cowboy case, despite the fact he was in the midst of preparing for the Gheri Curls trial, and had three other cases already in the pipeline. Terry Quinn, as HIU's investigative chief, was a somewhat grouchier gatekeeper. Twenty-five years in the Department had sensitized him to the politics of policing, and the prospect of a long, resource-intensive investigation—with its logistical and jurisdictional tangles—always brought out the prickly side of his nature. After running some quick checks, however, Quinn, too, began lobbying Arsenault to take on the Cowboy investigation. "At the start of every investigation," Arsenault would tell people, "Terry'll give you a hundred reasons why we can't do this case, and then the next day you'll see him at his desk surrounded by the homicide folders and he'll be telling you: We have to do this case. He's like this punch-drunk fighter who tells you he'll never raise his fists in anger again, and then the bell rings and he comes out swinging."

Still, Arsenault recognized that there were substantial problems with the Cowboy case. First, many of the violent acts attributed to the gang, including the Quad, took place in the Bronx, outside of HIU's Manhattan jurisdiction. Quinn expected to uncover more murders in Manhattan, and Arsenault was pretty sure the unit could get clearance to investigate the Cowboys' Bronx drug activities; yet even then they could end up with the worst possible combination: a large, time-consuming drug conspiracy case with relatively few homicides.

Second, it became evident early on that the gang's crack operation was strictly retail. That made it unlikely that HIU's undercovers would be able to buy the Cowboys' leaders, as they did with gangs that sold wholesale like the Gheri Curls. In the wholesale world, the money was so great that the gang leaders couldn't help but involve themselves—they couldn't trust tens of thousands of dollars to a low-level flunky. Because the Cowboys sold retail—directly to individual users—HIU would have to deal with the gang's low-level street sellers, then try to flip them against the higher-ups. But the relatively small transactions—and correspondingly low penalties—would give investigators little leverage when negotiating with the dealers they arrested. What's more, those dealers—often junkies and street people themselves—made unreliable informants and unpersuasive witnesses.

The third and most immediate obstacle was the backlog of cases that jammed up the unit's investigators through the summer. It would be six to eight months before Quinn and his people could focus full-time on the Cowboys. And Arsenault knew Camacho would be busy for at least a year, probably more. Arsenault was pretty sure he could finesse the investigative shortfall. He knew, for instance, that Garry Dugan and Jerry Dimuro were already looking at the gang in connection with the Cargill shooting, and that by having that case assigned to HIU—an easy matter for Ryan to arrange—they would benefit automatically from their research. He'd also heard about Mark Tebbens in the Bronx, and was confident he'd share what he knew about the Cowboys with the unit. And by spring, Arsenault knew, he could enlist outside help—the Feds or a police Narcotics unit—to begin surveillance on the gang's drug operation. But he knew if he waited for Camacho to take over the reins of the investigation, the case might never get off the ground. So Arsenault asked him to hand off the investigation to a new prosecutor whom Ryan had brought up to the unit that winter. Reluctantly, Camacho agreed, and in a move that he would come to regret, Arsenault assigned Dan Rather to the case.

WHEN YOU FIRST met Dan Rather, you experienced a kind of double vision. With his square good looks, boyish earnestness, and gentle Texas accent, he was a dead ringer for his father—the famous CBS news anchor—when he was an up-and-coming CBS reporter. But the younger Rather adamantly discouraged the comparisons. He never talked about his father to his colleagues, or revealed much at all about his private life. Not that he was standoffish. He played basketball and softball in the office leagues, he shot pool and drank with his bureau mates after work, and he was especially popular among the younger assistants, who frequently sought his advice for their cases. But even in groups he was something of a loner—pensive, remote, a little wary, as though he were used to being under scrutiny. And perhaps in a way he *was* under scrutiny.

Many of Morgenthau's young litigators had prominent surnames—Kennedy, Cuomo, Vance, D'Amato. The prosecutor's office has always been a stepping-stone to public life, and Manhattan was the Harvard—part training ground, part finishing school—of big-city DAs. Typically, these young scions glided through their three-year tours, then moved on to other challenges in law and politics. But there was no indication that Rather was biding his time or looking for an easy ride. From his freshman year in 1985 he distinguished himself as one of the brightest and hardest-working among his class. He seemed to revel in being a prosecutor.

The elder of two children, Rather, 34, spent an itinerant childhood growing up all over Texas. He was by his own account a rowdy teenager, more interested in playing basketball and fighting with the local gangs than in going to school. He had calmed down when he moved East to attend college at Columbia, where he majored in philosophy. Later at Georgetown, the gritty imperatives of criminal law drew him to the bar. But he never lost his taste for ideas. "Dan was a legal eagle," Luke Rettler, at the time one of Rather's intimates, says. "He read all the journals, he liked comparing cases. A lot of DAs, myself included, have a much more fact-based approach. We're mainly interested in the law as it applies to our cases. But Dan wanted to know why certain laws were the way they were."

Rather also showed a real talent for investigation. He seemed to enjoy the challenge of large, complex cases, and he was passionate about the work. "I felt it was God's work, that there was no higher calling," he says. "I felt that if you really care about justice in poor communities, you needed to do violent-gang work."

After joining Morgenthau's office in 1985 out of law school, Rather rose to become a Criminal Court supervisor and homicide assistant before Nancy Ryan tapped him for HIU at the beginning of 1992. But despite her enthusiastic recommendation, Rather had his detractors. Some colleagues interpreted his aloofness as arrogance; others objected to his behavior on the basketball court, where he was a trash talker who always seemed to be on the edge of provoking a fight, an unnecessary quirk, in that he was a gifted player. But the most troubling rap against Rather was his dearth of big-trial experience. He had a reputation in the office for being a reluctant prosecutor, someone who overinvestigated his cases, then pled them out before they came to verdict. The fact is that most cases settle before trial, and the better a prosecutor prepares his case, the more likely his defendant will try to plead. Still, Rather was joining a homicide unit without ever having tried a homicide.

Rather saw the Cowboys as the case of a lifetime. Moreover, it seemed to dovetail with an investigation he had conducted before joining HIU involving a car theft ring that stole cars on consignment for big drug dealers allegedly based on West 171st and 174th streets.

Rather jumped into HIU's investigation of the Cowboy case by doing AGIS dumps—computer runs on NYPD arrest data—to find out who'd been collared on West 171st and 174th street during the past year. Surprisingly, relatively few names came up. Clearly the gang members weren't being arrested in their own neighborhood. But when Rather searched for people arrested citywide who lived on those blocks, the list of names expanded dramatically. What's more, many of them were being arrested in the 40th Precinct—the Mott Haven section of the Bronx, where the Quad occurred.

The case of a lifetime began slowly, however. With HIU's investigators jammed up through the summer of 1992, Rather did what he could on his own, pulling arrest folders, assembling photos and going over them with informants. But his most important move was in reaching out to NYPD detectives Garry Dugan and Mark Tebbens.

Dugan, for his part, was furious when he learned that Dimuro had taken the case to the DAs. Like many of his colleagues, he hated going outside the Police Department chain of command; too often, he knew, it meant ceding control of the investigation to the prosecutors. Moreover, he'd never heard of HIU. Nor did he see how the DA's office could help them at that embryonic stage of the investigation. In his experience, you went to a prosecutor only after you had solid evidence. Despite his skepticism, however, Dugan agreed to accompany Dimuro on a visit to meet Rather a few days later.

The visit was a revelation to Dugan. Rather began by assuring Dugan he wouldn't interfere with his investigation. For the moment he just wanted to act as a repository for intelligence on the Cowboys, to help coordinate Dugan's investigation with Tebbens' investigation in the Bronx. What particularly impressed Dugan was Rather's sweeping vision of the case. He made it clear that he intended to target the entire gang, not just Cargill's killers. What's more, he had a plan that would enable him to do it. First, he would identify the members of the gang and exhume all the old unsolved cases they could find that were connected to them. Next he would enlist the assistance of a special narcotics unit, either from the NYPD or from a federal agency like the ATF, to do a joint investigation into the Cowboys' drug operation. Then he would arrest selected lower- and mid-level members with knowledge of the gang's activities and attempt to "flip" them against the gang's leaders and most violent enforcers. Finally, when he had accumulated enough evidence, they intended to "take down" all the remaining Cowboys at once, so that there would be no one left to carry on the gang or to threaten witnesses.

But the linchpin of Rather's plan was his intention to make use of the state's conspiracy statutes, something he had discussed at length with Arsenault. Dugan had never heard of them. Rather explained that conspiracy laws, like the federal racketeering statutes known as RICO, allowed prosecutors to indict suspects strictly on the basis of their membership in a criminal organization. Defendants are normally tried for the commission of discrete, so-called substantive crimes—murder, assault, the sale or possession of drugs—and the evidence used to convict them must relate to those specific acts. But to obtain a conspiracy conviction against a member of the Cowboys, Rather needed only to prove that he had knowingly furthered the interests of the gang's drug operation—say, by loaning them a car, or buying the vials they used to package their crack, or paying the utility bill for one of their stash houses.

Dugan immediately saw the advantage in investigating and prosecuting that kind of case. It would be far easier to implicate the top-level Cowboys who insulated themselves from the gang's illegal activities and never touched the drugs or money or tied themselves to their enforcers. And the stiff penalties carried by a conspiracy conviction would give him leverage in "flipping" low-level gang members, arrested for otherwise minor crimes. But the best part of Rather's legal strategy was already familiar to him.

For years Dugan had been doing conspiracy-style investigations. Like the best detectives, he was an obsessive gatherer of information. He looked at a suspect's bank account, the cars he drove, where he'd been ticketed, the restaurants and clubs he patronized, his associates, whom he'd called when he'd been arrested, what schools he'd attended—the kind of information that might lead him to an informant and help him solve a case, but was often inadmissible in a courtroom. Suddenly, he realized, those details were not only relevant but vital to a prosecutor trying to demonstrate to a jury the existence and structure of a criminal organization, how it formed and operated. In the space of an hour's conversation, Rather had turned Dugan's investigative dross into evidentiary gold.

At the first meeting, Rather was somewhat vague about the

details of HIU's plan. He had little idea of the size of the gang, guessing there were somewhere between fifteen and twenty members. Nor did he know all the principals or their relations. But the underlying assumptions to his approach got Dugan's attention. Homicide detectives rarely worked with their counterparts in Narcotics, partly for bureaucratic reasons, but also because Homicide looked down on Narcotics. The Department had recently begun making drug investigators detectives after eighteen months' service, as a way of inducing officers into dangerous undercover work. Veteran detectives who'd waited ten and fifteen years for their gold shield felt that their new colleagues were underqualified, and shunned them. More unprecedented in Dugan's eyes, however, was the idea of lumping Manhattan and Bronx cases together in the same indictment. Cops from different boroughs occasionally shared information, but there was no mechanism, no formal protocol—except under extraordinary circumstances—for co-authoring investigations within the Police Department. Yet Rather seemed confident that HIU could assemble the necessary task force and that Manhattan would take the lead position.

When Dugan left HIU with Dimuro, his head was spinning. Rather had turned his skepticism into optimism and given his investigation a new sense of direction. He felt the pressure to make arrests lifted; now he could take a step back and encompass a "broader view of the situation." What's more, he liked Rather personally. He seemed very sharp and attentive. Perhaps most important, he shared Dugan's enthusiasm for the case.

THE CARGILLS also liked Rather. He had called them to brief them on their son's case, and they drove down to HIU with their eldest daughter one afternoon in early February. Innes had been in Boston the night before on business, had downed a bottle of scotch before getting a few hours of fitful sleep, then risen at 4 A.M. so he could put in a morning's work at his office in Tarrytown. Now tired and hungover, he listened to Rather as he described the gang he thought was responsible for David's murder and recited the names of the men who may have taken part in the shooting—Sepulveda, Polanco, Platano. Cargill couldn't grasp what Rather was telling him; it just seemed surreal. What possible connection could men like these have with their lives, with their son's life?

Later Arsenault and Quinn joined them and explained HIU to the family and how they intended to proceed. Anne, still abusing pills and alcohol, seemed in a state of shock; at one point she told Arsenault that she had to stop herself sometimes in the morning from walking upstairs to wake David up. "It was one of the most emotionally draining nights," Arsenault recalled. "We're used to family members who won't even come in, or when they do, they want to know: When am I going to get my car back? When am I going to get the gold out of his teeth? When we have legit people in, it's easy to get crushed by the weight of the tragedy. I told Terry: Thank God not all the victims' families are like this, it's just too heart-wrenching."

A WEEK LATER, Dugan and Dimuro, at the insistence of their captain, set out to interview Lenny Sepulveda, the head of the Cowboys, at Ogdensburg State Prison in northern New York, where he was serving out a year's sentence for gun possession. Dugan was not happy about the interview. The division captain had wanted them to rattle Lenny's cage, perhaps hoping for a quick resolution of the case. But from the little Dugan knew of Lenny—he still recalled the terrified expression in Platano's eyes as he informed on his boss—he didn't expect to get much. Against Platano they'd had leverage. They had nothing on Lenny, other than Platano's exculpatory statement and some sketchy, conflicting FBI reports. Besides, Platano was an enforcer. Lenny was the boss of a big, complex organization: he wasn't likely to break under questioning. It would be an eight-hour drive for nothing.

Dugan and Dimuro's real concern, however, was that talking to

Lenny was premature, a strategic mistake. They could tip off Lenny to the leads they were pursuing, and unwittingly expose weaknesses in their case. But despite Dugan's agreement to share information with Rather, Cargill was still a police case, and Dugan had little choice other than to obey his senior officer.

AT THE PRISON, the guard showed them to an eight-by-eight-foot cubicle off the main area. The room had gray cinder-block walls, a metal table, and three metal armchairs with vinyl cushions. A small window cut into the outer wall gave a view over the roof of one of the cellblocks, a wedge of pale, bright sky. Dugan and Dimuro arranged themselves at either end of the table and set up a chair between them facing away from the window for Lenny.

Dugan's first impression of Lenny as the gang leader entered the room was physical. A rock-hard heavyweight with a square head and heavy eyebrows that knitted together over penetrating eyes and rugged features, he looked huge. In fact, he seemed bigger than he was. According to arrest records, he was five-eleven, an inch or two smaller than Dugan himself. But Dugan's impression was not uncommon. Lenny had an aura of intensity and threat that shrank the space around him. People routinely added three and four inches to his height.

Dimuro motioned him to his seat, and made the introductions, identifying Dugan as a detective with Manhattan North Homicide.

"One of the big guys, huh," Lenny said.

Dugan suppressed a smile. Lenny might not tell the detectives anything, but he wasn't going to jerk them around either. "What's this about?" he asked.

"We believe you might be able to help us in some cases we're working on," Dugan said.

Lenny paused a moment before responding. "I don't think I can help you with anything," he said. "What kind of cases?"

"Homicides."

"Yeah, I can see that." Lenny sat back in his chair, his arms folded in front of him. Nonetheless, he seemed interested in what the detectives had to say, a deal maker considering his options.

"We know that you have knowledge about people who have been killed," Dimuro said.

"What makes you think that I know anything?"

"Some people we've already interviewed."

"Like who?"

"We can't tell you that," Dimuro said.

The conversation circled around several times before Dugan, sensing Lenny's frustration, decided to change tack. He began asking him questions about his background—where he was born, grew up, went to school. Lenny answered minimally without volunteering any extraneous information. He'd been born in the United States; his parents had separated when he was two. He'd lived at several addresses in Washington Heights, finally settling at 640 West 171st Street. He'd attended George Washington High School. He was vague about his friends from the block, and Dugan didn't press him. By rights, Lenny could have ended the interview anytime he wanted.

"Do you have any children?" Dugan asked him then.

"Yeah, a daughter."

"Look, Lenny," he said. "We have evidence against you in a number of cases—we're not going to divulge which ones. If we develop something big, you may never see your daughter again. You may never see your child again. We know that you have knowledge of certain homicides. And there's going to come a point in time when it's too late for you to help yourself."

A look of unease flickered across Lenny's face. "What if I do know something?" he asked.

"If you have any knowledge, now is the time to give it to us," Dugan said. "As we continue with this investigation, we're going to be speaking with a lot of people. These people may have direct involvement with those cases—and naturally, to exonerate themselves, they're going to point the finger at you and say that you did it or ordered it. We know that this may not be true. So don't allow them to get the upper hand."

Lenny nodded, gazing intently from Dugan to Dimuro. He began to jiggle his leg. "What kind of guarantee could you give me," he asked, "if I told you something?"

"There are no guarantees," Dugan said.

Lenny was sitting forward in his chair, his head cupped in his hands, his eyes fixed on Dugan. Then he drew back. "I want to talk to my lawyer first," he said.

I T W A S nearly dark by the time Dugan and Dimuro emerged from the visitors building. They had spent two hours with Lenny. Neither detective was fooled into thinking Lenny was going to confess to killing Cargill. But Dugan was hopeful Lenny would target his adversaries or the weaker, expendable members of his gang. In fact, they would have to be careful not to become Lenny's tool, helping him to eliminate his competition. But Dugan was confident any information Lenny gave them would advance their investigation. Each name would lead to several others, and those would lead to still more, each one a potential informant.

As they passed through Ogdensburg and turned in from the river, heading south toward the city, Dugan realized a door had opened and everything had changed. For the last six months he'd been working a homicide, a senseless, tragic one: now, within the last week, his role had expanded dramatically, and he was part of an investigation into a vast conspiracy of crime. He knew he had an enormous drug gang by the tail—he just didn't know how big it was. The knowledge left him feeling an odd mixture of exhilaration and fatigue. Although he couldn't know it at the time, these heightened, contrary impulses would in some combination rule his emotions in the years ahead.

6

WAR

DUGAN RETURNED to the Three-Four from Ogdensburg that evening only to find himself smack in the middle of a new Cowboy-linked murder investigation. The victim, Danny Montilla, was a typical Washington Heights gangster—a big, heavyset 22-year-old Dominican street-hustler. People in the neighborhood called him Madonna because as a kid he had had trouble pronouncing the name of his favorite restaurant, McDonald's. In the early morning hours of February 2, as Dugan and Dimuro drove upstate to question Lenny, Montilla's body was found on the side of the West Side Highway near 178th Street, two miles north of where David Cargill had been killed. Montilla had been shot in the head and run over.

Dugan was assigned to assist the precinct detective who caught the case. In the first hours of the investigation, Marlene Sanchez, (a pseudonym), a former girlfriend of Montilla's, dropped a bombshell on Dugan. She said that Montilla had been with Frankie Cuevas in the Veinte de Mayo, a restaurant in the Heights, just before he was killed.

Could Frankie Cuevas, Dugan wondered, be the dealer Platano claimed was in the car with Lenny the night of the Cargill shooting? "Was Frankie also known as Fat Frankie?" Dugan asked Sanchez. He was, she told him. Frankie not only knew Lenny but had been in business with him for years. Now, however, they were enemies. In fact, Sanchez was convinced Frankie had ordered Montilla killed because although he worked for Frankie, he had also stayed friendly with Lenny and Nelson.

Marlene didn't know what had caused the rift between Frankie and Lenny, but she was able to fill Dugan in on Frankie's role in the gang. It turned out that Frankie was not simply an associate of Lenny's but a major dealer in his own right with an active spot in the Bronx. In fact, she claimed he *owned* the Veinte de Mayo restaurant in Washington Heights, (in actuality, his brother was the owner). Frankie had his own crew of hired killers, she told Dugan, and ambitious plans to expand—plans clearly in conflict with Lenny's.

BEFORE Madonna's murder, Dugan had seen Frankie simply as a witness in the Cargill case. Given what he knew now, he put Frankie near the top of his wanted list. Clearly, Frankie was a prime mover in a simmering gang war.

Drug gangs were constantly fighting, and with no organizing body like the Mafia's Commission to settle disputes, violence became the final arbiter. The quarrel between the Cowboys and Yellow-Top that led to the Quad murders in the Bronx was but one example of that violence. Earlier that fall, two months before the Quad, George Calderon, a self-styled drug czar who exacted a toll from street dealers throughout the South Bronx, sent a squad of hit men to Beekman Avenue to intimidate the Cowboys, resulting in an extended, Beirut-style firefight embroiling dozens of gunmen from both gangs. Miraculously, no one was seriously hurt. But cars all along the block were pockmarked with small-arms fire, and police later recovered hundreds of shell casings in the street.

Unlike other gang wars, however, the rift between Lenny and Frankie involved the breakup of partners. The war that unfolded promised to be vicious and protracted.

Going over Cuevas' rap sheet, Dugan discovered that Frankie had been convicted on assault charges when he was 19 and sent to state prison for nine years. And he learned from Sanchez that Cuevas' drug business was centered at the Bronx intersection of Watson and Manor avenues, the heavily trafficked corner that Dugan had observed just days before when he scoped out the block where Platano's girlfriend's family lived.

Using the Cargill investigation as a lever, Dugan next began a preliminary investigation of Raymond Polanco, reputedly the third man in the Cargill murder car. What he discovered was a killer no less violent than Platano or Frankie. Crazy Ray, as he was known on the street, was not only a citywide firearms trafficker—supplying guns and grenades to numerous gangs—but the owner of several crack and heroin spots in Brooklyn. Cops in the 84th Precinct, where Polanco lived, told Dugan that Polanco ran the Gowanus projects, a public housing development in southeastern Brooklyn, and was officially a suspect in several murders. Unofficially, they claimed, he had engineered dozens of homicides, and had been shot numerous times himself. In fact, he now walked around with a colostomy bag.

Dugan had no idea where all this information was leading, but his instincts told him to keep digging. He decided to stake out the Veinte de Mayo and the corner of Watson and Manor. In the following week, he spent several long nights tailing Polanco in Brooklyn as he made his rounds of bars, bodegas, and sales spots. It was the kind of surveillance work that is tedious and uneventful, but it yielded important insights into the different groups and their relationships. With the license plate numbers he'd noted, Dugan was able to compile a fuller list of the Cowboy players and associates. By pulling up their parking tickets, summonses, rap sheets, and photos he discovered their hangouts, their criminal activities, whom they were arrested with, as well as whom they called when they were arrested.

Slowly, a picture began to emerge of three interlocking gangs: Polanco's gang in Brooklyn, Frankie's on the corner of Watson and Manor, and the Cowboys, or Red-Top, on Beekman Avenue. Frankie's and Lenny's crews seemed to intermix in the 170s in Washington Heights. Polanco had family that lived next door to Cuevas on 174th Street, and a few years back he had been arrested on a rape charge with Daniel "Shorty" Gonzalez, a manager for the Cowboys and an alleged shooter in the Quad. He was also said to be selling guns through Reuben Perez, the Cowboy-connected dealer who operated on the corner of 174th and Audubon. And Platano, Lenny's top enforcer, was linked to Cuevas' spot on Watson and Manor through his girlfriend, who hailed from the block.

FEARING THINGS were about to explode, Dugan tried to keep close tabs on Platano, who was back on the street. Dugan had learned from FBI reports that he was planning a trip to Florida in mid-February to sell his white BMW, which he apparently felt was too hot. But Platano seemed to have lost the fear he showed while he was under arrest in New Jersey. He told friends that the police had no hard evidence connecting him to any crimes. He made it clear he intended to keep his court dates in Bergen County on the drug charge. It was his first offense, and he felt that if convicted, he would get a light sentence.

Unfortunately, Lenny turned out to be a dead end in the investigation for the time being. His lawyer contacted Dugan several days after his interview with Lenny and instructed him to steer clear of his client. Dugan had arranged with prison officials at Ogdensburg to record Lenny's telephone calls, but they provided no fresh leads.

Dugan had better luck tracking down Felipe Capellan, the registered owner of Platano's BMW convertible. Capellan, a 26-year-old car thief, had been holed up in Massachusetts since the summer, but he had recently moved back to his family's Washington Heights apartment in anticipation of a court appearance on March 25. He had cases pending against him in New York and New Jersey—one of them for assault and reckless endangerment—and seemed cooperative when Dugan contacted him.

Dugan learned Capellan had met Platano two years before through Lenny and his brother Nelson, whom he had known growing up in the neighborhood. Lenny had wanted to buy Capellan's BMW for Platano, but then went to prison before paying him. Nonetheless, Capellan "lent" the car to Platano out of fear, and Platano had kept it indefinitely. Recently Platano visited Capellan at the garage where he worked and tried to exchange it for an M-3—another, sportier BMW that Capellan owned. "I told him that his convertible was a better car, that he didn't want the M-3," Capellan said. "He took out a gun and shot three times into the driver-side door of the M-3. Then he said, 'Now you don't want it either.' "

Capellan got the door replaced and gave the car to Platano.

Despite the information Capellan had given him, however, Dugan felt like he had reached a wall in the investigation. Lenny's lawyer had barred him from speaking further with his client, and neither of the men who had been with Cargill the night of his murder could identify the photos that Dugan had assembled of Lenny, Platano, Frankie, and Polanco. There was little the detective could do but wait for something to break.

As it turned out, he didn't have to wait long. On March 16, a black Ford Taurus pulled alongside Frankie Cuevas as he sat in his car talking to friends on Audubon Avenue and 185th Street. It was almost spring, a brisk, sunny afternoon, and Cuevas had his guard down. His most trusted soldier, Manny Garcia, a man almost as burly and menacing as Cuevas himself, was sitting in the driver's seat beside him. A second bodyguard, Gilbert Compusano, was parked behind them, protecting their rear. Suddenly, the passenger-side window of the Taurus slid down and a gunman opened fire. Cuevas was only winged, but Garcia was hit in the back as he turned from the bullets, and he pitched forward, unable to move. For a moment confusion reigned. Then Compusano took off after the shooter, while Cuevas ran six blocks to the 34th Precinct, where he flagged a ride to nearby Columbia-Presbyterian Hospital.

Dugan stopped in to see Manny at the hospital two days later. The 20-year-old Dominican was lying on his back, his head propped at an angle. He was said to be permanently paralyzed from the chest down. But Garcia still refused to cooperate, even when Dugan offered him official help with disability payments. "Frankie will take care of me," he said.

"No one's going to support you anymore," Dugan said. "You'll be a burden to your family."

"Don't worry about me. I'll get by."

"Do you have a girlfriend?" Dugan asked.

Manny glared at him.

"Don't you realize you're never going to have sex again?" Dugan said. "You're never going to have children? Why don't you help me get the guy who did this to you."

"Fuck that," Manny said. "That's the risk I took. I gambled and I lost."

Dugan went to see Cuevas next, but it was clear Cuevas intended to take care of "the motherfuckers" himself.

CUEVAS checked himself out of Columbia-Presbyterian the next day, against his doctor's advice. A day later, Dugan responded to a call at Cuevas' address on West 174th Street. He found a trail of blood leading from the snow-covered sidewalk to Cuevas' apartment on the fifth floor. Police broke down the door: there was a gun lying on the floor immediately inside the doorway, and a trail of blood that led past a series of bedrooms to the living room. Blood was splattered everywhere, and the furniture was in shambles.

Dugan found two more guns in the apartment and a single set of fresh footprints in the snow on the roof leading to and from the edge.

Dugan quickly pieced together what had happened. Cuevas and at least three others, given the number of guns, had been beating the hell out of someone, trying to extract a confession, or information. That explained the mess in the living room. He figured one gang member—probably Frankie—held a gun on their hostage and at some point, out of anger or carelessness, shot him. Surprised by the violent turn of events, the assailants then tossed their guns and ran, leaving the victim for dead; Frankie, or whoever the shooter was, went up to the roof to ditch his gun over the side. (Police recovered the gun in a lot directly below the roof.) Sometime later, the victim regained consciousness and escaped. Of course, it was possible the victim was dead and Cuevas' henchmen had carried him out of the apartment. But the even distribution of blood on the stairs seemed to indicate that whoever had been shot was ambulatory.

When Dugan called Columbia-Presbyterian to inquire if they'd had any trauma patients the night before, the duty nurse told him that Gilbert Compusano—the second bodyguard at Frankie's shooting— had been treated for a gunshot wound to his head. He was in critical, but stable, condition.

Clearly Cuevas decided Compusano had betrayed him.

After the uniforms had left, Dugan lingered outside the building, surveying the neighborhood. He jotted down plate numbers of the parked cars, a habit of his at crime scenes, and questioned the people at the bodega around the corner. *Yo no se*, they knew nothing. As he returned to the building, he intercepted a slouch-limbed young man in dungarees and an expensive leather jacket as he was about to enter. "May I ask what apartment you're going to?"

The man said he was going to 5A, Cuevas' apartment.

"Who are you going to visit there?" Dugan asked, producing his shield.

The man blanched. He identified himself as Victor Nazar, an off-duty cop from the Four-Oh, Tebbens' precinct. Nazar said he was a friend of Cuevas—that he knew him from the Veinte de Mayo and occasionally dropped by to say hello.

"When was the last time you came by?" Dugan asked.

"Two, three weeks ago. Why?" Nazar asked.

"We're investigating an accident inside the building."

"What apartment?"

"A different apartment," Dugan lied. "But we're limiting traffic going in and out of the building." Encountering a cop who was friendly with Cuevas set all of Dugan's inner alarms off. He didn't want him to see the blood trail inside. But Nazar was already backing away.

AT COLUMBIA-PRESBYTERIAN, Dugan found Compusano sitting on his bed. Dugan realized that Cuevas shot Compusano either because he felt that his bodyguard had set him up or because he failed to take proper actions to protect him. Dugan was hopeful that Compusano could tell him who shot Cuevas, as well as who had assaulted and attempted to kill him. But the neurosurgeon who had operated on Compusano was less optimistic. "He's conscious," he told Dugan. "But you won't get much out of him. I had to remove the part of his brain that has to do with short-term memory."

Compusano's speech, as he responded to Dugan's queries, was slow and slurred. "Who shot you?" Dugan asked him after a few preliminary questions.

"I was shot?"

"Don't you remember? Feel your head." Compusano rubbed

the top of his large round head. It was shaved and stitched together like a baseball.

"Oh, shit," he said.

FRANKIE CUEVAS' EYES slid across the glass toward Dugan, darting left and right, the eyes of a fish in unfamiliar waters. Standing in a darkened corridor on the other side of the one-way mirror, Dugan couldn't help but draw back at the intensity of the gang leader's glare. Cuevas had shown up at the precinct several hours after Dugan had left word with his brother Miguel at the Veinte de Mayo that he was asking for him. Dugan had escorted him to one of the squad's two interview rooms, a cinder-block cubicle with a table, chairs, and a one-way mirror built into its rear wall. He had left Frankie to stew there, and had circled around back to study him through the glass. Thicker through the middle than Lenny, Cuevas had the same powerful build and swarthy skin as his rival; his mouth was turned down at the corners, halfway between a pout and a sneer; and his bushy black eyebrows and mustache concentrated his expression. He was dressed neatly in casual clothes and new sneakers (no chance of matching the treads with the footprints on the roof) and was holding a newspaper from upstate in his big soft hands. Dugan waited until he could see that Cuevas was becoming impatient. He wanted him nervous, not mad.

But Dugan's calculations were for naught. From the start, Cuevas made it clear he wasn't going to cooperate. When Dugan asked him how Manny was doing, Cuevas barely looked up from his paper. "These things happen," he said. "He'll get over it." And later, when Dugan suggested he ought to contribute to his former worker's support, Cuevas claimed he was a worker himself, employed as a manager by his brother's restaurant.

"What kind of work do you do at the restaurant?"

"I order the food and beverages."

"How much do you make there?"

"Two hundred dollars a week."

"What about the cars that you drive?"

"They aren't mine. They belong to my brother." Cuevas' eyes broke off from Dugan and drifted to the newspaper lying on the table. He began to turn the pages as he spoke.

Dugan didn't like Cuevas. He thought he was a bully and a coward. At 19, Cuevas had badly beaten an old woman, who surprised him while he was burglarizing her apartment. (The woman died shortly after, though police were unable to prove her death was caused by the assault.) And after he was shot on March 16, Cuevas had run to the precinct house, abandoning his more seriously wounded bodyguard, Manny Garcia. Cuevas later told Dugan he thought his friend had been killed, and Garcia remained intensely loyal to the gang leader; but Dugan felt that Cuevas had panicked and fled.

Cuevas was a gangster of the old school. He hated the police and, even more than Lenny, ruled by intimidation. There seemed to be no give in the man, no room for negotiation; and Dugan's sources confirmed his intuition. They were not only reluctant to speak to the detective; they didn't want to be seen anywhere near him. With Frankie, they told him, if he suspected you, he killed you.

As Cuevas turned another page, Dugan reached across the table and grabbed the newspaper with a sweeping motion, crumpled it, and tossed it on the floor behind him. The move startled Cuevas; he clearly was unused to being challenged. His shock quickly turned to anger, but Dugan had made his point. "I wanted you at this office because I wanted to talk to you," he said. "Not watch you read the newspaper."

Cuevas just glared.

After a few more questions, Dugan had had enough. Cuevas clearly wouldn't give them anything.

THE ATTEMPT on Frankie's life sparked an explosion of violence in the Heights and the Bronx. A day later, members from Lenny's and

Frankie's crews exchanged gunfire on St. Nicholas Avenue and 173rd Street, wounding Frankie Gonzalez, a dealer with links to both groups. Later the same day, Platano was collared by the police a block from where Gonzalez had been wounded, carrying a 10 mm pistol. Platano told the police he was Paul Santiago and was released on minimal bail. Later that night, Juan Carlos Pena, a Reuben Perez associate, was bounced from a local nightclub for refusing to remove his hat and coat for a security check, and allegedly returned to the club with a gun, fired wildly into a crowd of people at the entrance, and hit a bystander in the head. The next day, the word on the street was that Platano had shot three workers for Orange-Top, a crew thought to be associated with the Cowboys in the Bronx. Three weeks later, 17-year-old Levington Rojas, a rising star in the Cowboy organization known as Mask—the same Mask whom Tebbens had spotted with Platano delivering crack to Beekman Avenue—was shot and killed.

Each new shooting raised questions about the genesis of the war and the quicksilver loyalties of the gang members. Then, on April 14, Platano himself was gunned down while sitting in his double-parked car on St. Nicholas Avenue and 187th Street. The shooter emerged from behind a van that was parked next to him, and fired twice into the car at point-blank range. One bullet entered Platano's side and creased his liver. The other punctured his lung. Critically wounded, he managed to drive as far as 173rd Street, where a friend came to his aid and drove him the rest of the way to Columbia-Presbyterian. Dugan understood he was not expected to live.

But Platano proved to be luckier than many of his victims. Two days after the shooting, Dugan found him alert and on the mend. Although he was weak from his surgery, hooked up to tubes and barely able to speak, his doctors were optimistic. Dugan pulled up a chair. "It looks like you're not going to make it," the detective lied to him. "It doesn't seem right that the person who did this to you should walk away."

Platano nodded, his eyes fixed on Dugan's. "No one had the right to do this to you. Let me do my job and I'll bring the guy in."

Platano continued looking at Dugan, shaking his head in agreement. "Who did this to you?" Dugan asked.

"Frankie," Platano whispered.

O N   A   W A R M   D A Y in early spring, Arsenault went for his daily lunch-hour jog. He'd run the New York marathon the previous November and was already training for the next race. There was a group of dedicated runners from the office who jogged the six or more miles with him, and he enjoyed their camaraderie; but he also used the time to draw back from the myopia of investigative work and to try to gain some perspective on the unit's cases.

He took his usual route behind the Criminal Courts building, through the paved-over Five Points intersection, once home to the city's most notorious gangs; past the Greek Revival Mariners' Temple, its Ionic pillars fronting Henry Street; and down Chinatown's twisty streets to the Lower East Side. The Gheri Curls had occupied his thoughts through the winter, but increasingly the Cowboys claimed his attention. The first one in the office, Arsenault fielded the precinct reports of the preceding night's mayhem. Invariably, he noted, the Cowboys were involved—as shooters or targets, or as friends or relations of the participants. Arsenault remembered the morning that Dugan informed him Levington "Mask" Rojas had been killed in the Three-Four. "Guess who got shot now?" Dugan had begun his report: it became the question Arsenault heard repeated, almost every day it seemed, through the next few weeks.

Arsenault and the others with him turned down Madison Street, past two Italian social clubs, remnants from Little Italy when it spread south below Canal and east to the river. Middle-age wise guys with potbellies and portable radios sat outside on folding chairs, listening to Sinatra or Jimmy Roselli. Sweating lightly, striding easily, Arsenault fell into the unconscious rhythms of the run. His thoughts quickened as he passed through the Rutgers projects on the Lower East Side, then headed north at the river, barely noticing the crack dealers doing a brisk business in the park along the drive. The Cowboys had forced themselves on Arsenault's attention—the sheer amount and audacity of their violence. Quinn had taken to briefing him every afternoon, and lately they'd been having a running argument over which gang was deadliest. Quinn insisted the Cowboys were the most lethal; Arsenault countered that the Spanglers had been equally violent. In fact, the Spangler posse had been larger—some three hundred strong—and with factions all over the world, they'd killed as many as fifty people, Arsenault estimated. But now, despite pride of authorship—every prosecutor thinks the gang he tried is the bloodiest—Arsenault had begun to agree with Quinn.

It was cool and breezy by the shore, and the traffic on the river was light. Arsenault spied a police patrol boat among several yachts, and farther out one of the city's two orange, green, and white sewage ships, trailing seagulls. He realized he couldn't wait any longer on the Cowboys. Despite the unit's already overburdened agenda, he knew he had to get started.

Arsenault picked up his pace. The ball fields where the Fire Department team practiced and cooked out flashed by on his left. He watched them for a moment fielding grounders and shagging flies, and inhaled the aroma of grilling meat. On his right, a group of old Spanish guys fished for striped bass. And looming ahead at the three-mile mark, the 14th Street fire-boat station—an enclosed pier jutting out into the water—came into view. Arsenault turned around and headed back to the office.

Later, he stopped on the eighth floor, as he did most days, to see Nancy Ryan and update her on the unit. As always, he was impressed by her grasp of their investigations, given the number of cases,

many of them already in trial, she had to keep track of. Then he confided his thoughts about the Cowboys. "This is going to be a huge
case," he told her. "The biggest one we've done yet."

Her response was simple and unhesitating. "What do you
need?" she asked him.

M E A N W H I L E, in the Bronx, Mark Tebbens was having problems. His
informants had been more cooperative than Dugan's, and several
months before, on the basis of their statements, Tebbens had been able
to lock up two of the Quad shooters, Stanley Tukes and Daniel Gonzalez.
But since then Tebbens had been losing witnesses as fast as he found
them, the first of whom was Chico Puentes, the small-time felon from
Beekman Avenue who was the first informant to identify Platano as one
of the shooters in the Quad. Having heard that Puentes was wanted for
assault, Tebbens had picked him up and made a deal for his testimony
in exchange for leniency. But somehow the Cowboys had gotten wind of
the deal. In late January, shortly before his arrest in New Jersey, Platano,
along with two other gang members, took Puentes for a ride, suppos-
edly to have dinner at a restaurant outside the neighborhood. Instead,
they stopped by the side of a quiet road, and Platano shoved the barrel
of a gun in Puentes' mouth. "This is what happens to snitches," Platano
told him, and pulled the trigger. The chambers clicked once, twice, then
a third time. They were empty. But Puentes got the message, and disappeared.

Benjamin Green, the young man who had accompanied
Tebbens in the surveillance van on Beekman Avenue, had also had a
change of heart. Threatened by the Cowboys, he'd signed a letter in the
office of one defendant's lawyer recanting his statements to Tebbens.
Then, on February 12, two Cowboy enforcers cornered James Singleton, a third witness in the Quad case, in a yard behind his home. Saying "Snitches get stitches," one of the gang members pinned Singleton's

arms, while the other slashed his face. Tebbens was able to arrest and lock up the offenders a week later and to get the resources to relocate Singleton to a new address. But increasingly the detective felt like a juggler who tries to keep too many plates spinning, as one after another they wobble and fall.

Moreover, Tebbens' bosses in the Bronx were pressuring him to wrap up the Quad case. As a rule, the Department allots precinct detectives four days to work on homicides before they begin catching cases again. Because of the exceptional nature of the Quad, Tebbens had been allowed to pursue the case exclusively, and had been assigned a small task force of three investigators to assist him. But by March, with the precinct under siege, Tebbens was fielding new cases once more. What little time Tebbens was able to give to the Quad that spring was frequently his own.

The Cowboys were under no such constraints. Despite an increased police presence in the wake of the Quad shootings, the gang seemed to be operating at full force. In early January, Anthony Villerbe, a former Corrections officer, was shot dead in his car while apparently trying to buy crack from Red-Top. And almost every day through the winter, Four-Oh cops received complaints and reports of violence from Beekman Avenue.

Tebbens and his colleagues were able to lock up a number of lower-level gang members, but the Cowboys could easily replace them from the pool of neighborhood youngsters. What concerned Tebbens far more, however, was Dugan's revelation, during one of their periodic meetings to go over their separate investigations, of a possible link between the gang and Victor Nazar, the off-duty Four-Oh cop Dugan encountered in front of Cuevas' building. Tebbens recalled that Nazar had spent an inordinate amount of time hanging around the detectives' squad room at the Four-Oh. Internal Affairs was investigating Nazar, and had placed him on limited duty. (Nazar resigned from the force and later was arrested with Frankie Cuevas on a gun charge but was never prosecuted.) But Tebbens couldn't discount the possibility that Nazar had learned details of the Cowboys investigation—the names of informants and potential witnesses—and had sold or given the information to the gang.

But whether or not Nazar had compromised his witnesses' anonymity, Tebbens was aware that their identities would become public soon enough—through either court proceedings or their own loose tongues. Moreover, he knew that he would not get the time and resources he needed to protect them.

Then, on March 20, a seemingly routine murder on Beekman Avenue changed the course of the investigation. Though it would take him another month to realize the implications of what had happened, Tebbens was about to encounter a family who could help him take down not only the killers in the Quad case but the entire Cowboy organization.

7

CATCHING A BREAK

SPRING 1992

IN THE END, it was mere chance that brought the Morales family to the attention of Mark Tebbens. Elizabeth Morales had agreed to testify against Cowboy enforcers Pasqualito and Frankie Robles in an assault case. The police arranged to put Morales and her son Tito—the target of the attack—up at a hotel outside the precinct for protection. The next morning, however, the hotel complained that she had boarded her entire family—more than twelve children and relatives— in the room. "I can't leave my family behind," Morales told them. "[The gang] would kill them." Forced to move to a shelter, they found conditions intolerable. Families were segregated into male and female living areas, and Elizabeth and her husband were forced to quit their jobs and withdraw their children from school.

Morales called the precinct daily, pleading for help. She realized that convicting Pasqualito and Robles wouldn't protect her family against reprisals by the rest of the gang. In desperation, Morales hinted to the detective in charge of her case that she could supply him with information on other cases, including the quadruple murder on Beekman Avenue. The detective inexplicably made no attempt to draw Morales out or to hook her up with Mark Tebbens, whose search for potential informants from Beekman Avenue was well known to the squad. It was weeks later that another Four-Oh detective, fielding one of Morales' calls by chance, advised her to contact Tebbens.

For the next two weeks, Tebbens visited the shelter almost every day to interview Elizabeth and her children, and to help them out in whatever small ways that he could. But even before he left their apartment that first day, he realized his investigation had taken a giant leap forward.

ELIZABETH MORALES had lived in the Beekman Avenue area all her life. Her parents had come from Puerto Rico in the 1950s, part of the postwar flood of migrants who'd colonized East Harlem, then spilled across the river to the South Bronx. As the city's newest arrivals, Puerto Ricans were low men on the economic totem pole. They competed for a dwindling number of manufacturing and union jobs with white ethnic and African-American workers, and they bumped up against blacks in their search for decent housing. Segregation was the rule then, and the South Bronx had become a ghetto, a uniformly poor community without Harlem's institutions, bourgeois neighborhoods, or political clout.

Elizabeth's father found work as a super at several buildings in the neighborhood, and spent four nights a week at their kitchen table drinking himself into oblivion. When she was 16, she married Angel Luis Cruz and began having children of her own. Her mother had married at 12.

But for all the hardship, life in her South Bronx neighborhood was good. In the warm months, the men cooked out and the women pulled picnic tables together and closed off the block. Neighbors were like family then; they watched over each other's children and came to each other's aid in hard times. There was crime—Mr. Philip, an elderly Italian gent said to be "connected," lived on the corner and ran the numbers and other sundry rackets—and there were gangs: the Bachelors, the Suicides, and the Ching-A-Lings. But they didn't carry guns and there was relatively little violence.

Drug sales first spilled onto the street in the 1970s. When Elizabeth moved with her mother and burgeoning family onto Beekman Avenue, there were "cheese lines"—queues of drug customers—in front of the abandoned buildings on Beech Terrace at the north end of the block. But the operations were small and self-contained, and rarely impacted on the neighborhood. It wasn't until the late 1980s, after a fire destroyed their stronghold on Beech Terrace, that the Cowboys moved into the Hole, the alley adjacent to Morales' building at No. 348, and life changed forever.

The gang announced their arrival on the block with a flurry of murders and assaults. Almost every day, Pasqualito and Victor Mercedes, one of the original Cowboys, seemed to be beating someone up. It was common knowledge in the neighborhood that Pasqualito had shot and killed a dealer on Beech Terrace, and Morales witnessed him slashing the throat of another potential competitor who sold crack in a vacant lot across from No. 348. Another local dealer lived downstairs from Morales. She remembers looking out her window one day, after hearing a commotion, and seeing Pasqualito firing into his second-floor apartment from the street.

The gang solidified their hold over the neighborhood in 1989, when they publicly executed two dealers from another part of the Bronx whom they suspected of murdering one of their friends, in the killing that became known as the Double.

Bribing and bullying the residents of No. 348, the gang quickly gained control of the building. They picked up tenants' rent, used their apartments to stash drugs and guns, and hired tenants as low-level workers. Nearly all were grateful at first for the infusion of cash and jobs. But the relationship soured once the Cowboys moved in—and then it was impossible to move them out.

When Loretta Baker tried to sever her "sublet" plan with the Cowboys—they had slapped her niece and treated the place as their own—Lenny, Nelson, Platano, and Ulysses Mena, a Cowboy enforcer known as Dominican Chino, paid her a visit. Platano had tossed a bag of crack onto the living-room table, aimed a gun at her, and mouthed "pow-pow-pow." He placed the gun on the table, and Mena picked it up and shot her in the head. They dumped Baker's unconscious body in the hallway—a message to other uncooperative tenants. (Baker later recovered.)

Baker was not the only tenant bullied by the Cowboys. Elizabeth Morales' downstairs neighbor fled the building, leaving her belongings behind, after her brother was beaten by the gang for stealing their drugs. When another neighbor ran afoul of the gang, they broke into her apartment and hanged her dog, and shot at her through her peephole.

Elizabeth also made a deal with the Cowboys, to her subsequent regret. Her husband had left her five years before with four children to support. She had begun living with Chino Morales, a laborer in the Hunts Point grocery market, and she had found work in a nursing home. But with her mother, various relatives, and the addition of another child and four grandchildren, she had nineteen mouths to feed. So when the gang offered to pay her to cook for them, she accepted, only too glad to have the extra money coming in to help feed and clothe her family. In exchange, her living room became a kind of clubhouse for the Cowboy hierarchy.

Before long, Lenny, Nelson, and Platano became regular visitors. They'd slip her fifty dollars to fry up *chorizos* with rice and beans, and hang out on her couch, discussing the day's business or watching TV. The arrangement worked well enough. They called her Ma, and her husband Pa, and Lenny briefly dated her oldest daughter, Ita. But good relations only went so far with the Cowboys. Platano used to tip Joey, her youngest, fifty dollars to carry a book bag full of drugs from his car to the Cowboys' stash apartments. Michael and Tito, now 16 and 18, started as lookouts at 14, and became part-time managers. When they began cutting school, Elizabeth complained to Lenny and Platano.

"They're in a man's world now, and they got to learn to live by a man's rules," Lenny had told her.

M E A N W H I L E, sales at the Hole skyrocketed, with clients pouring in from bedroom communities in New Jersey, the North Bronx, and Westchester. The Hole became a cash machine operating twenty-four hours a day, seven days a week. During its peak, between 1988 and 1991, the organization grossed $30,000 per day.

As the money flowed in, Cowboy justice became not only vicious but capricious—a kind of impulsive mayhem that couldn't be explained by any street code. In May 1991, Oscar Alvarez, a Cowboy seller, was shot dead after his best friend absconded with company crack and cash, even though Alvarez had offered to work off his debt. Six months later, the Cowboys caught another worker, a local youngster named Eddie Maldonado, stealing from them. Platano, Tukes, and others surrounded him in St. Mary's Park one afternoon. Amidst a crowd of children, they pulled out machetes and a serrated Rambo-style knife and gutted Maldonado.

As frightening as these eruptions of violence were, they were still connected, however tenuously, to the operation of the gang's drug business. But there were gratuitous acts of violence as well, the sudden, casual use of force to solve even small, everyday problems: Lenny punching out his girlfriend during an argument, leaving her unconscious in the street; Stanley Tukes throwing a thirty-pound weight from the roof of 348 Beekman at a young deaf girl because he felt she was making a disturbance. (The weight hit her in the head, causing permanent brain damage.)

Worse, the gang's culture had begun to seep into the life of the block, poisoning relations among neighbors and corrupting the youngsters who grew up in their shadow—Morales' sons among them.

But Elizabeth felt trapped. It was dangerous to complain to the Cowboys, and the city landlord did nothing. A few tenants organized patrols, but they were powerless against the heavily armed dealers. The police had done virtually nothing in three years to curtail the gang's activities. And with her sons all working for the organization, what would she say to them? Besides, everyone on Beekman Avenue knew that the gang had a cop in their pocket. Complaints to the precinct seemed to be channeled back to the Cowboys. Nor could Elizabeth afford to give up her rent subsidy. Where else would she find a four-bedroom apartment for $93 a month?

In the wake of the 1991 Quad murders, things seemed to calm down in the neighborhood for a while. Lenny was in jail, Nelson was rumored to have absconded to the Dominican Republic after killing a customer—the former Corrections officer, Anthony Villerbe—in early January, Platano rarely visited the block after narrowly escaping the police, and Stanley Tukes had been arrested. The Hole still did business, but much of the sales seemed to have migrated a block east to Cypress Avenue, where the gang had another spot.

Then, on March 20, all hell broke loose in the lobby of 348 Beekman. Marion Frazier, the 18-year-old son of Louise McBride, Elizabeth's upstairs neighbor, held up Esteban Clemente, a Cowboy manager, who lived across the hall from Elizabeth with her friend Fat Iris. Frazier had been acting strangely. Just a few days earlier he had shot and killed a local dealer for insulting his mother. When Clemente refused to hand over the cache of drugs and cash he was carrying, Frazier shot him in the stomach and fled. Fatally wounded, Clemente made it back to his apartment, and begged Fat Iris to get the bag of drugs and cash he was still holding out of the apartment before the police arrived. Fat Iris gave the bag to Ita, Elizabeth's oldest daughter, who in turn gave it to her brother Michael.

To Michael and his brothers, a bagful of crack and cash was a windfall, and they set off on a shopping spree, oblivious to the ramifications. By noon the next day, Pasqualito had traced the pilfered drugs to the Cruz-Morales family and had cornered Elizabeth's oldest son, Tito, in front of their building. While Elizabeth and her youngest daughter, Iris, watched in horror from their window, Pasqualito, accompanied by Frankie Robles, pistol-whipped Tito into unconsciousness.

Elizabeth raced Tito to the hospital. But when the police questioned him in the recovery room, Elizabeth ordered him not to say anything. She was still unaware of the extent of her children's folly or the magnitude of Pasqualito's rage. Hours after bringing her son back from the hospital, Pasqualito and Frankie showed up at her apartment demanding their drugs.

"I don't know nothing about your drugs," Elizabeth had said. "I was at work all yesterday. I don't know what went on here."

"Ask your kids," Pasqualito said, waving his gun between her mother and her granddaughter. Elizabeth had never seen him so angry. He was pointing a gun as big as a hair dryer at the back of her mother's head. "I'll kill her right now if I don't get my drugs back."

Frankie Robles stood in the narrow hallway to her apartment, his short, fat frame blocking the front door, a cocked gun at his side.

"He's going to kill us," her granddaughter Daisy said. "The man is going to kill us, Mama." Only three years old, she knew about death the way children in war zones knew about death.

Fear, like nausea, roiled Elizabeth's stomach. She knew if Pasqualito harmed her mother, he would have to shoot them all. Suddenly, everyone was talking. Fat Iris, who'd come from next door; Elizabeth's husband, Chino, who emerged from the living room at the rear of the apartment and was pleading with Pasqualito to spare his family. Loudest of all was her mother's defiant incantations. *"Reprendre el Dominica,"* she keened repeatedly. "Take back the devil."

"Take the old lady inside," Pasqualito snapped. Elizabeth's daughter Iris hustled her off to her bedroom, but they could hear her prayers through the paper-thin walls.

"Please, let's talk," Chino begged Pasqualito. "Don't do anything to my family. We were working. We didn't know nothing about this."

"I'll get you your money," Elizabeth promised. "If I have to give you my whole paycheck."

"Talk to your kids," Pasqualito said. "Get all the drugs and money." He started for the door. "You have until midnight," he said.

ELIZABETH and Fat Iris searched the apartment, turning up crack bottles from under the washing machine, from the back of closets. The kids themselves couldn't remember where they'd hidden all the drugs. Then the two women went to Ita's apartment to recover her share. But her husband, Edgar, told them he had nothing to give back, and Elizabeth could see why. All around them was the evidence of their day-long shopping jag: a new baby crib, Nintendo, expensive stereo equipment.

An hour later, Elizabeth handed Pasqualito a bag with the drugs and cash she'd been able to retrieve. He began counting the bundles.

"If there's something missing, please let me pay you back," Elizabeth offered again. "Don't hurt my family."

"I'll think about it," Pasqualito said.

"Are we all right?" Elizabeth asked. "Is my family all right?"

Pasqualito's sidekick, Frankie, laughed at the question.

THE NEXT DAY, Chumpy, a young man from the neighborhood who worked for the Cowboys, advised Elizabeth to take her family and leave. A Cowboy enforcer known as Tezo had permission from the "big boss" to kill them if she didn't return all the drugs and money that day.

Morales didn't know whom to appeal to. Ramon Madrigal, one of the local managers, told her to speak to Platano, and offered to get a message through to him for her. Platano, after all, had been a regular at her apartment, and everyone knew he had a crush on her youngest daughter, Iris. But by the end of the day, she hadn't heard from him. Finally Chumpy returned, advising her to leave immediately. "Don't take anything with you or they'll know you're leaving. They've already decided that even if you return the drugs, they're going to make an example out of you."

TEBBENS FOUND that the Cruz-Morales family were hardly ideal witnesses. Elizabeth was sly, cantankerous, at times profane; and her children were street kids—wild, defensive, barely articulate, and full of attitude. But they had been living on Beekman Avenue since before Lenny and Nelson opened their first location, and they knew all the Cowboys and the inside workings of their operation. Elizabeth had stashed the gun that Lenny used in the Double. Michael had closed down the Hole on orders from Platano a half hour before the Quad, and he'd seen Pasqualito's partner, Daniel Rincon, handing out weapons to the shooters in the hallway of 348 Beekman. More important, his younger brother Joey, who'd witnessed eight murders by the time he was 14, had seen the entire incident from the street and was ready to testify that Platano was one of the shooters.

With the Cruz-Morales family as witnesses, Tebbens was finally ready to go to the Bronx DA with his case.

8

BUMPS IN THE ROAD

SPRING 1992

WHEN TEBBENS took the Quad case to the Bronx DA back in January, it was treated as a multiple homicide and assigned to an assistant named Cindy Elan-Mangano. Elan-Mangano, 32 years old, was a solid prosecutor whose record of convictions had earned her a promotion to deputy bureau chief. But she was also pregnant, and didn't feel she could undertake a long, arduous and dangerous investigation. After meeting with the Cruz-Morales family and indicting Platano, she begged off the case, and it was transferred to Ed Freedenthal, the chief of narcotics investigations. Freedenthal assigned the case in mid-May to Don Hill, whose steady, low-key competence made him the best choice to head up the investigation. With a long, boxy face, heavy-

framed glasses, and receding hairline, Hill, in his mid-thirties, projected an aura of solemnity and order. But although he was fair-
minded and unpretentious, beneath his placid surface he could in fact
be something of a hothead. Colleagues were used to his slow burns, his
stiff-necked resistance when pushed too far. It was the kind of fire and
grit that would serve him well in handling a difficult and complex assignment like the Quad murder case.

When Hill first read through the case file, he realized just how
weak his position was. There was no physical evidence linking any of
the defendants to the crime. The witnesses against two of the defendants, Stanley Tukes and Daniel Gonzalez, were criminals themselves.
And the witnesses against Platano—namely, several members of the
Cruz-Morales family—were no more presentable. Nearly everyone in
the family had worked for the gang, and despite their mother's efforts,
the boys had dropped out of school. With their street accents, they
would be difficult to understand, and even when understood, barely
credible. He knew they were also extremely wary about testifying. Elizabeth Morales had approached Tebbens with trepidation, desperate to
protect her family; and though the detective had managed to gain the
family's trust, it was a limited trust that did not extend to the DA's office.

What's more, Elan-Mangano had compounded these flaws in
her deposition taking. Trial attorneys usually debrief difficult witnesses
extensively, making sure their statements are consistent and free of errors and embellishment before committing them to paper. Even the
most reliable and cooperative witnesses usually require some preparation to sort out the vagaries of memory. But Elan-Mangano was concerned about the Cruz-Morales family. At one time heavily involved in
the drug trade, they seemed jittery and unreliable, likely to disappear
or recant their statements if the Cowboys got to them with threats or
inducements; and Elan-Mangano was eager to memorialize their testimony as quickly as possible, even at the risk of creating an inconsistent
record later on. As a result, she had a stenographer take down the Cruz-
Morales family's statements without much preparation, then allowed

them to testify in a like manner before a grand jury in order to indict Stanley Tukes, Daniel Gonzalez, and Platano. Reviewing the minutes of their testimony, Hill shuddered. They read like a mixture of street myth and rap stories, told more for effect than accuracy. The witnesses contradicted themselves and each other, as well as earlier statements they had given to Tebbens. A good defense lawyer would have a field day with them on cross-examination, using them not only to impeach the witnesses' testimony but to undermine the prosecution's credibility.

Hill did what he could to stanch the damage, spending hours with Elizabeth Morales and her children, gently probing their stories and putting them at ease. But the family's earlier testimony was irreversible; and in his haste to indict a fourth suspect, Daniel Rincon, a top-ranking Cowboy known as Fat Danny, he put two of the Cruz-Morales children before the grand jury, adding still more inconsistencies to the record.

Fourteen-year-old Joey Morales, for example, tended to be melodramatic. He claimed one of the shooters used a "street sweeper," a type of shotgun, which put him at variance with his sister Iris' testimony and with the ballistics recovered at the scene. He also named as suspects Cowboy gang members who Hill was fairly certain were not involved. And at times he placed himself on top of the action; at other times crouching behind a car on the opposite side of the street. None of these errors were fatal to Joey's credibility, and once Hill convinced him to stop trying to make the case and just tell the truth, he returned to the story that he'd originally told Tebbens and that matched the particulars by and large of the other witnesses. But Hill knew that Joey was going to get hammered on cross-examination, and there was little he could do about it.

Hill almost overlooked a note in the case file requesting that he call Dan Rather at the Manhattan DA's office. When Hill phoned him several days later, he learned from Rather that his investigation of the Quad murders and HIU's investigation of the Cowboy gang overlapped. Rather encouraged Hill to consider working together. But Hill had all he could do to prepare for the upcoming trial of the Quad case, and he wasn't much interested in Manhattan's fledgling conspiracy case.

HIU WAS HAVING its own troubles developing its case against the Cowboys. The heart of their case was the gang's drug conspiracy, the multimillion-dollar crack-selling business that had already sparked dozens of murders, shootings, and assaults. As a result of his investigation into the Cargill murder, Dugan had created files on some of the Cowboys' main players: Lenny, Nelson, and Platano; explored their tangled relations to the Cuevas crew, to whom he'd linked the Madonna, Compusano, and Platano shootings; and looked into Raymond Polanco, who Dugan knew had supplied guns to both Cuevas and Lenny. And Tebbens, in locking up three of the shooters in the Quad murders, had identified a number of the Cowboys' top managers, and illuminated some aspects of their drug-selling activities in and around Beekman Avenue.

But so far, neither Dugan nor Tebbens had been able to prove a connection between those activities and, Platano excepted, any of the Cowboy leaders; and HIU, busy with the Gheri Curls investigation, had not contributed much to the case. Rather had collated information gleaned from Dugan's and Tebbens' investigations, and along with Quinn had undertaken some preliminary intelligence gathering— reading through unsolved homicide files, looking for links to the Cowboys; ordering up rap sheets on known gang members; and putting together a photo book for use when questioning informants.

But both Rather and Arsenault knew that penetrating the upper levels of the gang would entail a long, resource-intensive narcotics investigation—including video surveillance, undercover buys, and the execution of warrants on stash apartments and crack kitchens. Moreover, Arsenault knew that HIU didn't have the manpower to undertake that kind of investigation on its own. With only six full-time detectives, and at least three open cases in addition to the Gheri Curls, the unit simply had no one to spare. In the past, they'd recruited partners from other agencies to carry out these operations. Arsenault had teamed up with federal ATF agents when he targeted the Jamaicans. More recently in the Gheri Curls and several other cases, HIU had successfully joined forces with a team of NYPD detectives from the federally sponsored HIDTA (High-Intensity Drug-Trafficking Area) program. Arsenault wanted to reenlist HIDTA in the Cowboy case, and the HIDTA detectives were eager to continue working with HIU. But the NYPD wanted their elite teams such as HIDTA making cases that produced either large amounts of cocaine powder or numerous arrests—the kind of arrests that got the police on the local news as a result of a raid that confiscated ten or twenty or more kilos, or a "street sweep" that netted fifty or a hundred collars in a weekend. The sight of mountains of intercepted cocaine or dozens of drug dealers being hauled off in paddy wagons made community leaders feel like something was being done, even if the cocaine represented a fraction of current supplies, and even if the dealers were fungible, low-level workers, many of whom would be back on the street within days.

Retail crack gangs that sold to the public, such as the Cowboys, rarely kept much cocaine on hand. Though they might sell hundreds of kilos over the course of a year, they bought and marketed their product in small amounts and rarely had more than a kilo in their possession at any one time. What's more, locking up gang leaders like Lenny or Nelson, who insulated themselves from their organization's street operations, entailed extraordinary risks and could easily tie up the unit for six months or a year. Over a year's time, other narcotics units often generated hundreds of arrests. The fact that these gang leaders were responsible for numerous murders and shootings was beside the point for a narcotics division; credit for arrests in those cases were given, in accordance with police procedure, to the precinct detectives who had originally worked on the investigations.

Finally, there was the never-ending issue of turf. HIU cases were run out of the DA's office, not the NYPD's 1 Police Plaza. Even though HIDTA operated autonomously in the field, and HIU was careful to credit them as full partners in press releases and at press conferences, there was no doubt among the media or law enforcement that when they worked with HIU, Manhattan DA Robert Morgenthau was calling the shots. After working four investigations under the auspices of the DA's office, Charles Rorke, the NYPD lieutenant in charge of HIDTA team No. 3, was under pressure to initiate cases of his own.

Arsenault was in a bind. He could, of course, reach out to other agencies or to other units within the police. But developing a good working relationship with detectives as talented as Rorke's HIDTA team would not be easy. Moreover, the Cowboys—as a result of their escalating war with Frankie Cuevas—demanded attention. Throughout the spring the two factions had clashed with increasingly violent results. In the weeks after Platano's April 14 shooting, Cowboy enforcers repeatedly drove by Cuevas' spot at the corner of Watson and Manor, spraying the area with gunfire. Once, Cuevas' men were waiting for them. They piled into two cars and chased the Cowboy gunmen through the Bronx and back to Washington Heights, where the two crews squared off at 181st Street and Fort Washington Park. Remarkably only one person was wounded in the ensuing firefight, though police later recovered more than sixty shell casings.

Three days later, a group of gun-wielding Cowboy associates barged into Cuevas' restaurant, the Veinte de Mayo, after midnight looking for the gang leader. The gunmen forced ten people down to the basement, then set the place on fire, locking the doors behind them. The hostages managed to escape by throwing chairs through the plate-glass storefront, narrowly averting a catastrophe. Called to the scene, police exchanged gunfire with the fleeing Cowboys at 181st Street and Amsterdam. But they broke off their pursuit after one cop took a bullet in the foot.

Meanwhile, the gang continued to raid Cuevas' drug spot. One day in May, they shot six people, one of them, a bystander, fatally. A month later they shot eight people, killing another.

Faced with the spiraling violence and fed up with HIDTA's vacillations, Rather decided to reach out to a joint DEA-NYPD narcotics task force called Redrum ("murder" spelled backward). Part of a federally funded program that targeted violent drug gangs in key cities, Redrum seemed like the perfect unit to partner with HIU. But when Rather talked to Arsenault about them, Arsenault expressed reservations. Although Redrum's New York unit had just been set up, the program had been operating for some time in Washington, D.C., and Arsenault's sources told him they were more flash than substance—a lot of high-profile arrests and low-profile acquittals. Moreover, Arsenault was still hoping HIDTA would sign on. He told Rather to set up a meeting with Redrum, but not to make them any promises.

The meeting Rather arranged with Redrum took place at HIU in early summer. In addition to Rather, Arsenault and Terry Quinn sat in. From the start it was clear that the units held widely different philosophies. Redrum's agents wouldn't do inside buys, meaning the Hole was out of bounds. Instead they wanted to develop the conspiracy case using wiretaps. It was a clean, safe approach, with no messy surveillance or undercover work. And by letting gang leaders incriminate themselves with their own words, it obviated the need for skittish, suspect witnesses. But Arsenault felt that, besides being extremely labor-intensive, wiretaps were a lot less effective in dealing with retail organizations like the Cowboys. While they were fine for investigating the Mafia or big drug importers and wholesalers, "street gangs, almost by definition, do most of their business standing around on the corner."

Arsenault's approach to gang investigations at HIU was to get as close to the action as possible. Typically, that meant doing video surveillance and using undercover detectives to make recorded buys, then arresting lower-level workers and managers and getting them to tie the leaders and top enforcers into the conspiracy. Nothing, in Arsenault's opinion, persuaded a gang member to cooperate faster than seeing himself selling drugs on TV. And no evidence was more convincing to a juror than a tape that showed defendants actually committing the crimes they were charged with. "Our approach was down and dirty," Arsenault would say later. "The more violent the people are, the closer to the street they are. We feel that to get those people, we have to stay close to the street, to do buys instead of wiretaps, to get out from behind the desk, not sit in an office following paper trails, listening to phone calls."

One of the Redrum agents claimed that you couldn't do video surveillance in Washington Heights. "Bullshit," Quinn responded. Arsenault later explained: "There was an old canard among some detectives in the Three-Oh and Three-Four that the neighborhoods were too close-knit to bring in men and equipment without being detected. But I knew it could be done. Hell, we'd done it in our last four cases. Of course, you couldn't just drive onto the block in a shiny new air-conditioned van, which was how the Feds liked to do surveillance. It took a little imagination. In the Super-King Bodega investigation—another Dominican crack case we were working on—our undercovers rented an apartment across the street from the target location. Quinn used to get to and from the observation post dressed up as an old woman, complete with wig and cane."

More irksome to Arsenault and Quinn was Redrum's hubris. Somehow they'd got the impression that the case was already theirs, and with a typical federal attitude they were telling HIU what they were going to do. "The way it usually worked with HIDTA was when they were using their undercover, they called the shots; and when it was our undercover on the line, we were in charge," according to Arsenault. "But even when they had the final say, we liked to think we had some influence on who they targeted and how and when they took them down. Basically Redrum was saying to us: 'We'll take the case and see you in a year.' " It was clear to Arsenault the two agencies could never work together.

Unfortunately, Dan Rather came away from the meeting with a different impression. He thought the negotiations had gone well enough, and told the Redrum agents that he would be in touch with them shortly. Clearly, Rather, who was heading the investigation, and Arsenault, who ran the unit, were not on the same page. A few days later Charles Rorke called Arsenault; HIDTA was ready to go forward with the investigation. The two men agreed on the spot to work together. Rather was taken aback when he heard the news. He was embarrassed at having to go back to Redrum without an offer, but more to the point, he felt he'd been left out of the decision-making process in a matter critical to his case.

Arsenault had never concealed his preference for using HIDTA, and Rather would also have favored the HIDTA team, had he known they were available. But the misunderstanding pointed to the uneasy relations between Rather and Arsenault, which continued to fester under the surface. Since his arrival at HIU in January, Rather had felt unwelcome. Shunted off to a desk in the squad room, he had to wait months for an office. He was assigned to help Fernando Camacho prepare for the Gheri Curls trial, and told not to work on any new cases of his own— even though he'd come to HIU specifically to expand an auto-theft-ring investigation he'd been working on. At one point he felt that he was the target of a bizarre hazing ritual. Rather felt that when Arsenault dismissed Redrum, by extension he had dismissed Rather himself.

Whether Rather's grievances were real or imagined, they went unnoticed by the rest of the unit. Not only were they unaware of any tension between Rather and Arsenault, they thought the two men had hit it off well together. Arsenault's injunction against opening new cases applied to all the unit's prosecutors—HIU's investigators were simply jammed up at the time. Moreover, Arsenault had assigned one of HIU's biggest cases to Rather within weeks of his arrival.

Nonetheless, Rather was stung by Arsenault's decision to go with HIDTA. The fact that his chief seemed oblivious or, worse, indifferent to his mounting dissatisfaction only sharpened his sense of estrangement. His frustration would come back to haunt the Cowboy case in the months ahead.

D U G A N, prompted by Rather, had broadened the scope of his investigation. Since February bodies had been dropping at the rate of one per week, not including the three Orange-Top workers shot by Platano on Cypress Avenue or the fifteen people wounded and killed as the result of Cowboy drive-bys on Cuevas' crack location. Dugan used each case as a spade to dig deeper into the vast subterranean network of the Cowboy gang. Every few days, Dugan, armed with new lists of victims, suspects, and their associates, would trek downtown to the Bureau of Police records, pull their rap sheets and arrest folders, and painstakingly copy out their pedigrees. Then he transferred the information to file cards and cross-referenced them, looking for connections. Madonna, the Cuevas soldier murdered on February 2, turned up in the photograph of a car that belonged to Lenny's brother, Nelson. Levington Rojas, the Cowboy soldier known as Mask, was shot and killed in a red Plymouth, the same car he'd used to drive Cuevas worker Frankie Gonzalez to the hospital just three weeks before, after Gonzalez was shot and wounded by an unknown assailant—thought to be Platano—in the Three-Four.

Each new piece of evidence spawned new questions. Did Lenny and Cuevas represent warring factions within the same gang? Or were they separate gangs battling over turf? What was the origin of their rift? Even as he scrambled to identify the names and affiliations of new players, Dugan revisited the starting point and center of his investigation, the West 171st Street block that Lenny called home. Working with local beat cops, Dugan spoke to several neighbors willing to give information about the Cowboys. One of them, known as Blue Eyes (a pseudonym), described a core group of boys who had grown up together:

Lenny, Nelson, Victor Mercedes and his half brother Daniel Rincon, and a fifth crew member named Jose, who he felt was running things while Lenny was in jail. Jose was playing the "big man" on the block, setting up a basketball court and showering the youngsters with toys and sneakers—a way of recruiting future workers for the gang. Some weeks later, after exchanging information on the case with Tebbens, Dugan realized that Jose was Jose Llaca—Pasqualito—the Cowboy enforcer who had been a defendant, along with Mercedes, in the Double murder case, and who had beaten Tito Cruz and threatened his family.

Dugan began meeting regularly with Mark Tebbens at this point. Tebbens' sources informed him mainly about the gang's activities on Beekman Avenue. Dugan's informants were knowledgeable about the Cowboys' Dominican hierarchy and their Manhattan-based rivals and allies. Tebbens had also told Dugan about the Cruz-Morales family. Tebbens thought they could help link the two investigations. Already, they had supplied Tebbens with enough probable cause to collar Platano, who was still recovering at Columbia-Presbyterian. The two detectives agreed to meet at the hospital and interrogate Platano one last time before Tebbens formally arrested him.

Platano was still not out of the woods when Dugan and Tebbens visited him on the morning of May 11. His wounds had become infected, and he was scheduled for another operation that day. Dugan decided to play on Platano's vulnerability, as he had once before, and on whatever religious impulses Platano had retained since his service as an altar boy. Tebbens used a different tack: He told Platano that he had massive evidence against him in the Quad and other cases, and that even if Platano survived his operation, he would likely spend the rest of his life in prison unless he began cooperating.

"I know you did the Quad," Tebbens told him. "But I also know that there were others involved. You don't want to go down the tubes on this when there were others who did worse things than you."

"You're still a Catholic?" Dugan asked him. "You still believe in God and your immortal soul?"

Platano nodded his head affirmatively.

"What happens if you die today?" Dugan went on. "What happens to your soul? I know you've killed a lot of people. I know that you've shot and wounded a lot of people. I know about the thirteen-year-old girl. You don't want to die with this on your shoulders."

At one point, Platano opened his mouth to speak, and Dugan bent close to hear him. But though his lips moved, no sound came out. Finally Tebbens' sergeant told him to wrap it up and make the arrest. Even then, Dugan stayed another forty-five minutes, cajoling Platano until the hospital technicians came to prepare him for surgery. But either Platano was confident he'd pull through or his fear of eternal damnation wasn't as powerful as his fear of Lenny's retribution. No confession was forthcoming—nor would Platano ever confess.

9

LENNY

C O W B O Y   L E A D E R Lenny Sepulveda was released from the Tombs at 6 A.M. on June 8, having served an eight-month sentence for gun possession. He walked up Centre Street to Canal in the fresh early morning air, the sun poking through the side streets, throwing long shadows across the intersections, and bought a beer at a twenty-four-hour deli. Then he hitched a cab ride with another inmate, stopping first at his mother-in-law's apartment on West 171st Street and then at the Queens high-rise where his wife and daughter lived. By afternoon, word had spread that Lenny was "out."

That evening, Lenny drove with his two brothers-in-law to Cypress Avenue in the Bronx to check on the business. A light rain was misting as they saw Fat Danny, his girth enormous in the arc light, standing in front of Miraya's, the ground-floor apartment at 354 Cypress that the Cowboys used as their clubhouse. He looked uneasy when they pulled up in an unfamiliar car, but relaxed when he saw Lenny get out. "I was expecting you," he said, hugging his former boss.

"You looked at the car kind of nervous," Lenny told him.

"There's a war going on," Danny said.

Inside Miraya's the mood was festive. Pasqualito was showing off his new gun—a .454 Magnum with bullets "big enough to stop an elephant," in Lenny's words. The neighborhood girls kept coming into the room on one pretext or another.

"Yo, Len, they're coming to see you," Pasqualito said.

"Don't play me," Lenny said. But he was pleased. He hadn't been certain what kind of reception he'd get. Before starting his sentence, he'd made sure the organization was running smoothly, and he'd called the block every day from prison. But a lot had happened since he'd left—the blowups with Frankie Cuevas and Yellow-Top, Nelson's departure to the Dominican Republic, Platano's shooting and arrest. Lenny knew plenty of gang leaders who'd lost control after spending time in the joint, and Lenny's relations with Pasqualito and Fat Danny had been rocky in the past. But they seemed genuinely glad to see him now.

"Let's go where we can talk private," Pasqualito said.

The two men repaired to Rob Lopez' apartment in the next building. Pasqualito had transformed the manager's living room into the gang's new headquarters, adding a weight machine and video games, as well as a safe and counting table. Fat Danny joined them, and he and Pasqualito filled Lenny in on the hostilities with Frankie. After Cuevas had shot Platano, they told him, they'd organized several drive-bys at Frankie's spot on Watson and Manor, and firebombed his restaurant, hoping to draw him into retaliating at the Hole. They'd posted gunmen on the rooftops at Beekman, and ordered their workers to shoot Cuevas and his men on sight.

Lenny listened quietly, and then the three locked themselves in the bathroom to insulate themselves from the stream of Cowboy workers passing through the apartment, to hammer out an arrangement among themselves.

"Business is slow," Pasqualito told him, which made it clear to Lenny why the others seemed so happy to see him.

With Fat Danny seated on top of the toilet to the right, and Pasqualito propped against the opposite wall, they formed a ragged triangle, the geometry of friendships and rivalries dating back to early childhood. Growing up on the same block, they had changed over time, spurred by drugs, guns, and more money than they'd ever imagined. Danny had been a big, soft kid, glad just to hang around the older Lenny and Nelson. Pasqualito had grown up with religion, thanks to his mother, a Jehovah's Witness; the other kids used to tease him, calling him "church boy." Lenny himself had changed too, he realized. How much? In what ways?

From what he was being told by Pasqualito, the business was in trouble. The Quad had burnt Beekman Avenue; the Hole, when it was open, generated a fraction of what it once earned. Moreover, Pasqualito and Fat Danny proved to be even less adept at management than Nelson. They were sloppy about details, spent more than they brought in, and owed money to their supplier, who withheld "work" from them. As a result, the gang's sales spots were often without product—*the* cardinal sin, Lenny had often told them, in running a crack operation.

But Lenny wasn't put off by Pasqualito's bleak assessment. He knew what was wrong with the business, and he knew he could fix it. The problem was, he wasn't eager to go back to the old arrangement. He didn't want to be a street boss anymore; he didn't want anything to do with Beekman Avenue. In fact, he'd been thinking of getting out of the business altogether—joining his brother in the Dominican Republic, or taking up Detective Dugan on his offer to wipe the slate clean.

But what else could he do? he wondered privately. What else

would bring him a fraction of the cash or respect he got from dealing? Besides, he liked the nuts and bolts of the business, the details involved in running a complex operation. The socializing he could do without— the nightclubbing and the joyrides, the drinking and the shooting. Eight months in the joint had sobered him up, and he'd never loved that part anyway. What he'd missed was the day-to-day stuff, making sure of the supplies and the receipts, making it all work. It was the first thing, perhaps the only thing besides sports, that he'd been able to make sense of, that he'd been good at. He liked that feeling, without being able to articulate it. It made him feel powerful, just as it made him powerful now to know that he could take Pasqualito's and Danny's mess and make it work again, make it efficient, make it profitable.

Lenny looked at Pasqualito and Danny. Their faces looked worried. Good.

"Don't worry," he told them. "I'm here now."

NAMED AFTER the Russian revolutionary and party leader— Lenny's parents belonged to a generation of Dominicans that believed in sweeping social reform—Lenin Sepulveda was born in New York shortly after his parents emigrated from the Dominican Republic. His father, Roberto, the son of a Santiago blacksmith, repaired radios and televisions; their mother found factory work. But neither parent assimilated well. Roberto developed a drinking problem, bickered strenuously with his wife, and separated from her when Lenny was three.

After a series of moves through the Heights, the family settled at 640 West 171st Street, not far from Roberto Sepulveda's tiny repair shop. But Lenny hated his father for the way he left his mother—homeless and penniless—and for his heavy drinking, which had taken on a public aspect. Once, walking home from school with a group of friends, he ran into his father, unkempt and smelling of alcohol. Asked who the older man was, Lenny replied, "Just some bum I know."

Lenny was headstrong from the start. His mother, a quiet,

religious woman, tried to curb his impulsiveness. But with four other children to care for, she was often overwhelmed, and Lenny had a willfulness that couldn't be tamed. "We lived in the same room and fought all the time," recalled his older brother Nelson. "I used to beat him up, but he just kept coming."

Lenny's first love was sports, especially baseball. At seven, he used to wander over to nearby Inwood Park to watch the other kids play. Later he organized pickup games in the neighborhood. But his school didn't have an athletic program, and there was never money to join a league.

School was also a disappointment. Bright but undisciplined, Lenny was bored by classwork, too young to understand its purpose or importance, like so many fatherless children growing up in the slums without role models to provide guidance. He showed an aptitude for drawing in grade school, and a teacher fostered his talent and offered to help shepherd his application to one of the city's magnet design schools. But the teacher was transferred unexpectedly, and his replacement was indifferent to Lenny's interests.

As Lenny entered his teens, gangs ruled the Heights. The Ballbusters held sway from 135th to 145th streets, the Playboys from 160th to 171st streets. Uptown was the province of the Bad, Bad Boys, whose leader was a tough banger named Frankie Cuevas. These gangs were social in the tradition of *West Side Story*'s Jets and Sharks, mostly concerned with turf—who owned what streets, what schools, what playgrounds. They stole cars and snatched gold chains, mostly to buy beer and weed; but their association wasn't about money. It was about status; neighborhood boys like Lenny looked up to the gang leaders as celebrities, and dreamed of being tapped to join them.

A big, scrappy kid, Lenny was a natural for membership. Even before high school, he was constantly in trouble—cutting classes, jumping turnstiles, getting into fights. When he was 15, he joined the Playboys and gained a reputation for toughness, once shooting at and fending off some twenty members of the rival Ballbusters. But the gangs were already in eclipse. "At one point, gangs died because when we grew a little, we finally realized we were fighting for nothing," Lenny remembered. "Then all of a sudden the Heights became a snowstorm of cocaine. To have coke meant status. Everybody wanted to be a part of that."

By the early 1980s, the Dominicans had replaced the Cubans as the Colombian cartels' wholesale suppliers in New York, but they hadn't yet begun to exploit its vast retail potential. Then, in 1982, two former members of the Bad, Bad Boys, Santiago "Yayo" Polanco and Eduardo "Capo" Mejias, both 21, started Coke Is It, an outfit selling grams and half grams of cocaine along Audubon Avenue, east of the George Washington Bridge—a prime drug location because of its suburban traffic from New Jersey. The operation was small, but profitable enough to enable Polanco to walk into an Englewood Cliffs car dealership in 1984 and plunk down $43,000 in cash for a Mercedes-Benz.

At first Coke Is It operated along Audubon from 173rd to 175th streets, just around the corner from where Lenny and Nelson lived, and employed local teenagers, many of them former gang members, to sell their product. But when crack hit the streets and profits soared, Yayo and Capo imported a team of hit men from their families' village in the Dominican Republic to protect their organization's turf and ease its expansion. By 1985, they had wrested control of the intersection of Edgecombe Avenue and 145th Street—a prime spot, with easy access to the Bronx across the 145th Street Bridge—from a group of Jamaican dealers and opened a string of new spots in Harlem and the South Bronx.

Polanco became the first dealer in the Heights to use marketing techniques to sell crack. He changed the name of his brand to Basedballs, packaged it in distinctively colored vials, and offered free samples and specials to local addicts whenever he opened a new spot. As Basedballs' business expanded, so did its organization. Polanco secured a major supplier, a Dominican who dealt directly with the cartels in Colombia. Polanco also centralized Basedballs' operations in a head-quarters at 2400 Webb Avenue in the Bronx. There, his workers cooked, packaged, and stockpiled crack in separate apartments. And he arranged with one of the many money-changing companies along up-per Broadway in Manhattan to launder Basedballs' revenues through an investment company he set up in the Dominican Republic.

Meanwhile, Polanco began distancing himself from Based-balls' day-to-day operations, adding layers of bureaucracy and spend-ing more and more time in the Dominican Republic. By the summer of 1986, Basedballs employed as many as nine mid-level managers to deal with street-level managers at a score of locations around the city. Each location manager, in turn, supervised teams of dealers, none of whom were supposed to know the people more than one level above them.

Lenny was a sophomore at George Washington High School and a member of the Playboys when he first heard about Yayo and Basedballs. Two of the toughest Playboys stuck up one of Basedballs' spots. That same afternoon Yayo and Capo, and a carload of their en-forcers, drove over to George Washington in Yayo's signature yellow Mercedes, descended on a group of gang members hanging out in front of the school, pummeled one terrified teenager, and sent the oth-ers running in all directions. Lenny, who barely escaped, realized he'd just seen the A-team, and he became determined to work for them.

He didn't have to wait long.

Lenny had already begun to distance himself from the Play-boys. Along with some of the gang's newer recruits—Miguel Castillo, Ramon Tijada, and Jose Reyes, a former schoolmate of Lenny's known as El Feo (The Ugly)—he formed his own group, the Young Playboys, as they sometimes called themselves. In part, the reason for breaking away was a matter of style. The older Playboys were part of the Hip-Hop generation—break-dancing, graffiti-writing, going to parties, dressing sharp. Lenny and his pals were into a different kind of cool,

Gangsta Cool—rap music and baggy pants. But they also had another aim: to break into the drug business that was then turning enterprising young hoods into millionaires. Lenny apprenticed with a dealer from 125th Street; El Feo interned with an old-time drug lord from his block known as Chocolate.

Smart and ruthless, El Feo moved up the ranks of Chocolate's organization, becoming Chocolate's right-hand man, taking over the reins when his mentor went to jail. Lenny, however, was having a hard time just getting paid. His boss had neither Chocolate's clout nor his savvy. Then, in early 1985, Mike "the Dom," a top manager for Yayo who'd grown up on Lenny's block, began recruiting youngsters from the neighborhood to work in Basedballs' expanding operation. Lenny volunteered.

Lenny was not the only one from the neighborhood to join Yayo's organization. Nelson signed up too, as well as friends Miguel Castillo and Ramon Tijada. But they just wanted to make some extra cash to attend sports camp. Lenny saw his job as an opportunity to rise in the organization. In a business notorious for unreliable workers, Lenny was industrious and dependable, as well as tough, and after trying him out at spots in the Bronx and the top of the Heights, Yayo installed Lenny at 166th Street and Amsterdam Avenue and promoted him to manager.

Lenny went to school on his bosses. He learned how to set up a secure location, how to supply his spot from stash houses, how to run the business and keep his workers in line. Yayo himself taught him the most important lesson: always stay open, never run out of "work." Crack customers are, almost by definition, creatures of habit. If you provide them with a quality product at a reasonable price, they will keep coming back. But if you allow them to go elsewhere—even once—you might lose them forever.

For all his success, Yayo was a difficult boss to work for: greedy, demanding, bullying. When the revenue from the spots Lenny and Nelson were managing failed to meet his expectations, he fired them.

In the fall of 1985, Nelson opened his own spot in an apartment at 603–605 Beech Terrace in the Bronx, a tenement at the north end of Beekman Avenue. But he had a hard time making a go of it. Crack was still a relatively new drug in the South Bronx, good local workers were scarce, and rival crews kept undercutting Nelson's sales. Nelson had never been a careful manager like his brother; he didn't have the same patience for details or single-minded focus. In fact, Nelson was still in school, playing football and hoping to graduate; he had to delegate authority, and his workers exploited his absence, slacking off and stealing from him. Finally, around Christmas, Nelson came down with pneumonia, and asked Lenny to run the spot.

The change was immediate and dramatic. Nelson had been buying his crack already cooked and packaged, kicking back 70–75 percent of his revenues to his suppliers. After paying his workers and taking care of expenses, he was barely breaking even. Lenny sought out wholesalers who'd front him raw cocaine in bulk (El Feo was his first supplier), then set up a crack kitchen, got Ramon Tijada to teach him how to cook, and began producing and packaging the signature Red-Top brand—not only improving quality control but more than doubling his profit margins. Meanwhile, he fortified the apartment in which he sold against stickups and police raids, hired new workers, brought in Miguel Castillo as a transporter to make sure they were always well stocked, and initiated a marketing campaign, distributing free samples to neighborhood users.

Business boomed. The line of Red-Top customers stretched through the building's first-floor hallway, out onto Beech Terrace, where the chill December wind gusted in from St. Mary's Park. As news of Lenny's success spread back to the Heights, Lenny's childhood pals started showing up, looking for work: Pasqualito, then Victor Mercedes and Fat Danny, who brought Platano, who in turn brought Freddie Sendra, a former running mate from the neighborhood. Lenny employed them all as managers and enforcers, insulating his brother and himself from the street, much the way Yayo and Capo had.

That strategy was only partly successful. While Lenny and Nelson never touched the drugs they sold, their workers expected them to "pull the trigger" when necessary. In early 1987, for instance, Lenny shot a disgruntled customer who attacked him with a machete in a lot outside 603–605 Beech Terrace. Nelson, who had rushed to his brother's side, was arrested and took the blame for the shooting. He eventually pled to gun possession, and was sentenced to five years' probation. Lenny, meanwhile, took a monthlong "vacation" in the Dominican Republic, where he hooked up with Yayo, who was also fleeing U.S. law enforcement.

When Lenny returned to Beech Terrace, the spot was humming along more profitably than ever; crack was then selling at $10 per vial and the brothers were clearing about $15,000 per week. As crack revenues climbed, competition for prized locations increased, and turned ever more vicious. Guns proliferated, as did the circumstances under which the younger, hungrier dealers were prepared to use them. And each new increase of violence attracted more attention from the police.

Lenny came back to Beech Terrace colder and more ruthless. He beefed up security and initiated a shoot-first, ask-questions-later policy. "One year everybody had guns," Lenny recalled. "It seemed like the whole world was going crazy, that every week, everywhere you looked someone you knew was getting killed. I wasn't going to let no little kid make his name off me."

Lenny had grasped, sooner than most rivals, that they were operating in a new paradigm, and adjusted quickly. Unlike Yayo, who didn't like mixing guns and drugs at his sales spots, Lenny made sure his managers were armed with automatic weapons, and expected them to use them, to counter threats and slights with calculated, preemptive violence. More than most, if not all other gangs, the Cowboys gained a reputation for knee-jerk brutality.

Initially, Lenny's tactics served as an effective deterrent, but the genie of violence, once out of the bottle, became impossible to contain. It not only spurred competitors to new heights of aggression. It also had an unpredictable, at times destabilizing effect on members of Lenny's own gang. Platano had been an auto mechanic and wheel-man when Lenny hired him in 1987 to transport his crack. Small and frail, he changed once he learned to use firearms. With a gun in his hand, he became a fierce, unpredictable killer, the gang's most feared enforcer. Pasqualito underwent a similar transformation. Growing up, Pasqualito had struck Lenny as a mama's boy. No one was more sur-prised than Lenny when Pasqualito, in 1988, gunned down Guy Gaines, a former Corrections officer and stickup artist who had been preying on Red-Top's customers and workers.

But while Platano was content to remain a loyal soldier of the gang, Pasqualito's forays into violence emboldened him to the point where he began to challenge Lenny's leadership. Arrested for Gaines's murder, Pasqualito spent five months in jail before he was acquitted at trial in December. Back on the streets, Pasqualito was a changed man—cockier, more assertive, and tougher than before. When Red-Top moved to Beekman Avenue after their spot on Beech Terrace burned down, Pasqualito led the way, shooting and slashing local dealers who failed to make way for the gang. By spring, he, along with Fat Danny and Victor, was lobbying Lenny for his own spot in the neighborhood.

Power in New York's drug world was a constant negotiation. There were no deeds or titles to crack spots, no legal contracts or stocks or bonds that defined ownership. There weren't even rigid hierarchies or reinforcing rites or traditions as there were among Mafia-type or-ganized crime groups. The city's drug gangs were loose-knit associa-tions of mostly violent young men with guns and authority problems. A leader's signal virtue—more important than his connections, his or-ganizational skills, or even his toughness and charisma—was a kind of brutal pragmatism, an ability and willingness to accurately size up his strengths in relation to his competitors, to know when to quash a rival, when to pay out line.

In the summer of 1989, Lenny agreed to set up Pasqualito and Danny on 138th and 141st streets, each location a few blocks from the Hole. But he attached a stringent set of conditions to the deal. Pasqualito and Danny would have to buy their product packaged from Lenny, and return up to 80 percent of their revenues to him. They would have to sell orange-capped vials, to distinguish them from Red-Top's better-established brand. Most important, they would have to stay off Beekman Avenue.

Pasqualito balked at the conditions. He felt he'd been doing the lion's share of the work—he, Victor, Danny, and the other managers—supervising the workers, providing muscle, and policing the block. They were entitled to at least an equal cut of the profits. Hell, they didn't need Lenny anymore. Pasqualito and Danny got "Caballon," a major dealer from the Heights, to front them cocaine, and began selling on Beekman Avenue.

Lenny confronted his former workers in a tense meeting on Beekman Avenue. Outgunned and outmaneuvered, Pasqualito and Danny retreated to the terms of their original agreement, narrowly averting a war. But ill feelings among the onetime childhood friends continued to simmer.

Meanwhile, Lenny had forged an alliance with Frankie Cuevas, back on the streets after serving eight years in prison for burglary and aggravated assault. While Cuevas had been a celebrity in the Heights as the leader of the Bad, Bad Boys, by the time of his release in November 1989 he was an anachronism. The cocaine revolution, then two generations old, had passed him by. His former running mates had already made their fortunes, and most young men Lenny's age, just kids when Cuevas was arrested, viewed him as a relic. But Lenny remembered Frankie and respected him. Lenny was looking to expand his business, and Cuevas, who had secured a crack spot at the profitable intersection of Watson and Manor, was desperately seeking someone to set him up in the business. Lenny agreed to front Cuevas in exchange for a cut of his profits—$2,000 for each kilo Cuevas sold.

The spot flourished, and Lenny and Cuevas became fast friends, hanging out at each other's home and clubbing together.

Though their friendship contained elements of gratitude and respect, it was also grounded in violence, a shared readiness to use force—even lethal force—to achieve their ends. When one of Cuevas' local workers absconded with a stash of drugs in early 1990, Lenny helped orchestrate Frankie's response, "renting" two hot cars and driving with Platano, Cuevas, and Cuevas' chief enforcer, Smiley, to the building where the worker lived, blasting the apartment with "heavy artillery," shattering windows and serving notice on the neighborhood. Similarly, whenever Lenny needed assistance, Frankie was there for him. At the height of Lenny's quarrel with Orange-Top, Lenny wanted to put out a "contract" on Fat Danny, but didn't want to use anyone from his own gang. So Frankie "lent" him Smiley, who shot Danny seven times on the pretext of some minor argument. (Danny eventually recovered.)

But the seeds of Frankie's and Lenny's own rivalry had been sown earlier that spring, when El Feo had opened a spot on Watson and Manor right next to Cuevas'. Lenny promised to handle El Feo, but Frankie decided to take matters into his own hands. That afternoon, he loaded two cars with armed workers and drove over to El Feo's Manhattan stronghold at 167th Street and Amsterdam Avenue. Nelson and Lenny were already there, sitting with El Feo on the stoop of his building, trying to negotiate a way out of their dilemma. When Nelson saw Frankie's armada rolling up the block, he intercepted them and managed to defuse the situation before any shots were fired. But the damage had been done. Frankie had invaded El Feo's turf, earning El Feo's implacable enmity; and Cuevas, discovering that Lenny was a friend of his competitor, began to question his partner's loyalty.

THE VIOLENCE continued unabated. Two days before the new year, Lenny ordered the executions of a dealer and his pregnant girlfriend at the request of Supra, Lenny's hot-car connection. There were rumors Lenny was also behind the murders of two dealers in the Beekman Avenue area, and he was known to have shot another, Miguel Guzman, over a business dispute. Stanley Tukes got 1991 off with a bang, shooting Quentin Lee five times at a New Year's Eve party. A couple of weeks later he shot Nathan Wilder, a potential witness to the Lee shooting, seven times, blinding him. A month after that he allegedly tossed Renee Brown off a balcony at 370 Cypress, critically injuring her. Platano, in one drive-by in the Bronx, shot and accidentally killed a 13-year-old girl. Freddy Krueger, El Feo's chief enforcer, carried out several hits for El Feo in the Heights, then teamed up with Platano on June 4 to gun down Cuevas' onetime enforcer, Smiley, and a friend of Smiley's.

Some of these acts were gratuitous or just careless, like David Cargill's shooting. Other assaults were so savage that they shocked even Lenny. In January, Red-Top workers hauled a stickup artist named Quincy Norwood into St. Mary's Park and set him on fire, burning him to death. It was later in the year that Platano, Tukes, and others disemboweled Eddie Maldonado.

In September, George Calderon, one of the Bronx's biggest drug lords, sent a squad of armed "rent collectors" to the Hole, sparking the Beirut-style firefight that riddled cars with bullet holes the length of Beekman Avenue. Sensing the violence closing in around him, Lenny decided to take a plea on a gun charge that was coming up for trial. He was sentenced to a year in jail (eight months with good behavior). Before leaving, he made peace with Pasqualito and Victor, agreeing to pick up disputed fees owed to the gang's lawyers for the Double murder case they had been charged with. He placed his brother in charge of the Hole, and made Platano second-in-command.

Given his careful preparations, Lenny's subsequent falling-out with Frankie Cuevas mystified everyone. Some members of his gang thought Cuevas was trying to move in on Beekman Avenue, that he felt slighted because Lenny hadn't asked him to take over the Hole during his prison term. Lenny, however, thought that Freddy Krueger, on orders from El Feo, hit Frankie in retaliation for his aborted drive-by on 167th and Amsterdam, as well as to take over his spot on Watson and Manor. Krueger had brought Platano along for the ride, and since Platano was Lenny's man, Frankie would have reasoned that Lenny was behind the shooting. But as they all knew, logic was hardly necessary. In their tinderbox world of threat and counterthreat, the smallest spark of suspicion was enough to ignite a conflagration. And once started, the fire was nearly impossible to contain, much less extinguish.

LENNY SLOWED as he turned onto Manor, timing the light so he'd hit the intersection when it was green. He knew if he had to stop, he risked getting made. Frankie's crew were likely to spot him anyway, given the unfamiliar car and tinted windows. Tezo huddled in the passenger seat, adjusting his bandanna; Freddy Krueger, behind Tezo in the backseat of the Taurus, tinkered with the Uzi in his lap. A fourth Cowboy soldier, seated next to Freddy, had a Glock .45. Halfway down the block, Lenny began checking for snipers, straining to see over the low rooftops. Nothing moved. No one stirred.

Lenny and Pasqualito had hammered out a deal that first night of his release from prison. Fat Danny would take 138th Street, Pasqualito would take 141st and the Hole. They'd manage the spots, take care of the workers; Lenny would handle the supplies, and they'd split the money three ways.

Freddy had prodded him since he got out of jail to hit Frankie's. Lenny didn't much see the point. He knew he'd never catch Cuevas exposed at his own spot. All through the spring, Pasqualito and Fat Danny had been shooting Frankie's workers, without much effect on Frankie's operation. Still, Lenny knew that some gesture was expected of him, if only a symbolic one.

The jagged rows of tenements narrowed ahead, converged onto a corridor of light where Watson crossed Manor. The signal turned green, and Lenny feathered the accelerator. They swept past the corner, crowded despite the late hour.

"There's Cubita," Lenny said. Frankie's short, stocky enforcer was standing thirty yards from the corner, shirtless in the warm weather.

Lenny continued down Manor, then circled back to Watson, heading once more for Frankie's spot. He was completely concentrated now, looking for police, ticking off escape routes to the nearest highways—the Bruckner, the Cross Bronx—maintaining a steady interval between him and the car in front of him. His chief concern was not getting boxed in. Hit a highway and be out, he thought. He could lose any cop on a clear road. Even in a Taurus. The first turn, a cop will be thinking about his wife and kids. Lenny'd be having fun. Getting away was his rush.

The spot loomed up, a hundred yards on his right. He saw Cubita standing in front of the corner store, and his workers talking to some guys parked in a brown sedan, a Grand National or Buick Regal, he wasn't sure. He'd pull alongside the sedan, he told the others. They'd get them too. He shifted into low gear. Around him he heard the action of guns cocking, the whir of electric windows sliding down. He felt a chill in his stomach, an animal sense of trespass.

Lenny didn't enjoy killing the way Freddy or Platano did. He had to psych himself up for it, screw up his mind like a tightly wound propeller, then let it go, pull the trigger while it was still a red blur of anger. Not that he felt a lot of sympathy or guilt for his victims. The truth was, he tried not to feel much of anything at all, outside of the anger and adrenaline. The rules were very clear: Do it to them before they did it to you.

And then you got the hell out of there. You didn't look back at the damage, you never saw the damage. When the anger was gone, you didn't feel anything, and you tried not to think about it anymore. You just moved on.

"Get ready," he said. Then he lurched forward, braking beside the brown sedan.

The next few seconds were filled with the sound of gunfire and explosions. Lenny barely noticed the shattering glass, scrambling bodies, punctured flesh. Once he saw that Frankie's crew weren't firing back, he checked the mirrors for police, the street ahead for traffic, waited about five seconds for a lull in the firing, then gunned the engine.

"Damn, we should have got out of the car," Freddy said, moments later. They were sharking down Bruckner Boulevard in the shadowy lee of the expressway. Lenny started to laugh. The last thing you wanted to do on a drive-by was show your face.

"We should have got out and made sure we done Cubita," Freddy said. Lenny accelerated up the ramp to the expressway. Ahead, the lights of upper Manhattan sparkled against the starless night. Lenny didn't want to make sure. He didn't even want to know. Later he'd hear that Cubita had taken a bullet in his buttocks. He would never find out that they'd shot six people that night, or that one of them, a 19-year-old local kid named Kevin Nazario, would not live to see the morning.

10

POINT, COUNTERPOINT

SUMMER 1992

THE SUMMER of 1992 would prove to be among the most violent in the history of upper Manhattan. Despite HIU's success against the Jamaicans, the murder rate was inching back up to record levels; drug dealers ruled the streets; and there were riots in the Heights. Yet even against this background, the Cowboys stood out. "Once we started doing the intelligence, the case just kept getting bigger and bigger," Arsenault recalls. "It seemed like every time we turned over a rock, there would be the Cowboys."

Law enforcement seemed powerless against them. Operating out of the Three-Four in Manhattan, Dugan had yet to put together enough evidence to arrest any major players; and the precinct detectives who caught Cowboy-related cases were faring even worse. Tebbens in the Bronx was also frustrated. He'd transferred out of the Four-Oh to the Bronx DA's detective squad in order to devote more time to the Cowboys. But with evidentiary hearings scheduled to begin in September, Don Hill was focused exclusively on the upcoming Quad trial; and Tebbens' new bosses—busy with their own cases—weren't interested in helping him expand his investigation.

Of the several Cowboy inquiries, HIU's nascent conspiracy case was the most ambitious, targeting the entire gang and their full range of activities. But it was also the least evolved—a patchwork of evidence and intelligence culled mainly from outside sources—and it showed few signs of stirring itself. Throughout the summer, Rather continued to connect the dots between Dugan's and Tebbens' findings; and by August, Terry Quinn, heading up the investigative side of the case, had begun plotting strategy in earnest—reaching out to his police contacts, combing the jails for disaffected gang members, and peppering Arsenault with reports and recommendations. But Arsenault was busy helping Camacho prepare for the Gheri Curls trial in September, as were most of HIU's investigators. That left HIDTA to advance HIU's case against the Cowboys, and they were running into problems of their own.

TOWARD THE END of June, HIDTA's Charles Rorke sent a 32-year-old detective named Eddie Benitez to the Four-Oh to talk to Mark Tebbens and check out the case that Quinn and Arsenault had been trying to sell HIDTA since April. Benitez already knew about the Cowboys. He'd worked on the Gheri Curls investigation with HIU and had been hearing scuttlebutt for months about Lenny, Platano, and company. Tebbens had been trying to get Narcotics to investigate the gang's crack operation on Beekman Avenue even before the Quad, and he presented Benitez with a chilling picture of the gang, backed by flow charts, maps, rap sheets, crime scene photos, and old case files. But it wasn't until Benitez and his partner, Al Nieves, drove out for a tour of the gang's turf that Benitez realized just how ruthless the Cowboys were.

Using an undercover vehicle disguised to look like a gang-banger's car, the two detectives trolled the long square block bordered on opposite sides by Beekman and Cypress avenues. Benitez got a couple of good looks at the alley adjacent to 348 Beekman, the daunting concrete corridor that the Cowboys called the Hole, and at the ground-floor apartment of 354 Cypress, the gang's informal headquarters. It was a warm summer afternoon, and a group of Cowboys were sitting out on the stoop in front of the building. Driving past them, Benitez saw five or six pairs of hard eyes follow him down the block, then several crew members charge inside, almost certainly to arm themselves. The second time the detectives rode past, the gang rose as one, and a barrel-chested young man, whom Benitez recognized as Pasqualito, strode out into the street, gun drawn, and challenged them. Benitez had never seen anything like it. He felt a thrill of fear, a sense that if Nieves, who was driving, idled a moment longer, shots would come raining down on them. Nieves felt it too and peeled off. Later, back at the precinct, barely able to contain himself, Benitez called his sergeant at HIDTA. "We have got to get these guys," he said.

Getting the Cowboys, however, was not going to be easy. Benitez, the primary on the case, and his eight-man team were all experienced narcotics investigators, but the Cowboys' drug operation was as cleverly designed as any Benitez had seen, the Hole practically invincible. A frontal assault was out of the question. His men would be detected long before they got to the entrance of the alley, much less the walkway where the sales were actually conducted. He could try "buy and busts"—have a plainclothes officer make a routine purchase, then arrest the seller after he exited the Hole—but that would only net him low-level workers on minor charges.

He could also send in undercovers to "buy up the ladder"—incrementally increase the amount of their purchases, thus triggering the participation of high-ranking managers. In the Gheri Curls case, HIDTA agents had made "hand-to-hand" buys from most of the leaders, locking them into the gang's drug conspiracy. But this approach would be tricky with an outfit like Red-Top that specialized in small retail sales. What's more, the Cowboys' record for violence and rip-offs militated against extensive undercover work.

To confiscate drugs in any quantity, Benitez realized, he'd have to raid one of the gang's stash apartments; but first he'd have to locate it. The Cowboys moved their stores around, and he couldn't get a warrant for the entire building. He'd need an informant to direct his efforts, and no one seemed eager to play that role.

One thing Benitez decided to do was to compile an exhaustive video surveillance of the sales spots, then use it in combination with at least some tape-recorded undercover buys to show a jury how the Cowboys operated. But as soon as he began searching for a discreet site with a clear view of the Hole, he ran into difficulties. Nearby rooftops and vans were out of the question; the Cowboys had their own rooftop lookouts, and neighbors were not to be trusted. He thought of setting up cameras on lampposts, disguised as air pollution meters, but his tech people nixed the idea; they were too easily detected, and in any case wouldn't deliver clear pictures of what was going on inside the alleyway. Benitez did manage to secure an apartment overlooking the gang's Cypress Avenue clubhouse, but he couldn't find a venue from which to film the Hole.

Benitez also had larger, strategic issues to deal with. For starters, there was confusion over what HIDTA should include in their surveillance. Tebbens and Don Hill felt that the Hole, and to a lesser extent the neighboring Orange-Top locations at 138th and 141st streets, were the key to the Cowboys' drug operation. But Manhattan, casting a wider net, also wanted HIDTA to set up observation posts overlooking Cuevas' spot on Watson and Manor, as well as suspected Cowboy outlets in Washington Heights. Benitez followed HIU's surveillance recommendations, but balked at their requests to increase the number and volume of buys his team made from Red-Top workers. Benitez had a bad feeling about the Hole. When he and Nieves, pretending to be building inspectors, toured the place, they noted that the alley walls were pocked with bullet holes. What's more, without an observation post, Benitez couldn't provide appropriate backup for his undercovers. Finally, and perhaps most important, Benitez and Rorke were under mounting pressure from their bosses in the Department not to stick their necks out.

Tensions between the police and the city's minority neighborhoods were running high that summer, and nowhere more than in Washington Heights, which was becoming a war zone. The year before, the Three-Four had led all other precincts in homicides, and was on track to repeat. But those numbers, as troubling as they were, didn't begin to convey the daily, potentially deadly, skirmishing between the police and the gangs for control of the streets. Dealers double- and triple-parked on narrow streets, effectively barricading their sales spots against radio cars, and dropped bricks on beat cops who ventured onto their turf. The police, for their part, rousted gang workers, beat up resisters, and extorted money and drugs from traffickers.

On the night of July 3, long-simmering tensions ignited into a full-scale conflagration. Shortly after midnight, Michael O'Keefe, a Three-Four street crimes officer, had attempted to stop and frisk a local drug dealer named "Kiko" Garcia. Garcia resisted, and O'Keefe ended up shooting and killing him. Though O'Keefe was later exonerated by an exhaustive, DA-led investigation—Garcia had been trying to wrestle away O'Keefe's gun when he was fatally wounded—the incident quickly turned into a referendum over police policy in the Heights. Blithely ignoring the facts of the case, community activists depicted Garcia as a hardworking father of two, the victim of excessive police force.

The debate touched off a firestorm of publicity and sparked

three days of rioting, much, if not most of which was orchestrated by area drug dealers. As always in these situations, the police looked to City Hall for leadership, a signal by which to measure their own response. They didn't have to wait long to get it. Within twenty-four hours of the shooting, Mayor David Dinkins, who was heavily beholden to the Latino community for his 1989 election, visited Garcia's family to offer condolences and promise justice—a gesture he'd failed to make to the family of a Three-Four officer killed on the job during Dinkins' tenure as Manhattan borough president, just several years before.

Dinkins, who ordered the city to pick up the tab for Garcia's funeral in the Dominican Republic, was not the only notable to sympathize with the drug dealer. A host of local officials and TV and newspaper reporters had also prejudged O'Keefe's actions; to his credit, Dinkins *did* try to make amends to the officer and his colleagues when the facts of the DA's investigation emerged. But it was too late. The Department, ever sensitive to the prevailing political winds, had learned that aggressive policing in the Heights, even when wholly justified, was not to be encouraged.

THE COWBOYS knew they were under investigation. Dugan's interviews with Platano and Lenny, Tebbens' Quad arrests, the surveillance cameras and increased police presence on Beekman Avenue had made them wary—but little more. All their lives the gang had literally gotten away with murder. Pasqualito beat two homicides, one of them in front of dozens of eyewitnesses; Platano killed more than a dozen people before he was even arrested; and virtually all the gang's hierarchy had been committing crimes on a daily basis for years without legal consequences. What little time any of them had spent in jail they considered to be the cost of doing business, and so far it had been a small cost to pay. Most recently, Fat Danny, charged with four counts of homicide in connection with the Quad, had been released on bail and was back on the street doing drive-bys. His trial was months away—a lifetime to a dealer—and neither Danny nor his associates thought that he, or any of the other Cowboys arrested for the Quad, would ever be convicted.

In fact, many gang members, far from retrenching, regarded the increased police attention as an occasion for sport. When Benitez and his men tried to follow the Cowboys from Beekman Avenue to Manhattan, the Cowboys picked up on the tails and toyed with their pursuers, eluding them at will. Most transporters for the gang used motorbikes, which they routinely drove onto the sidewalk or the wrong way down one-way streets. "They were playing with us," Benitez said. He began looking for other ways to keep tabs on his quarry.

In other respects, too, the gang seemed to be acting bolder. In June, after taking a few precautionary measures—switching the trademark color of their crack vials from red to black, diverting some customers to their other outlets—the Cowboys resumed selling full-time at the Hole. In July, they opened a new spot in the Brighton Beach section of Brooklyn, sending two scouts—Rafael Perez, the high-ranking manager known as Tezo, and his sidekick Ramon Madrigal—to recruit local workers and sell discounted samples to prospective customers. And throughout the summer the gang stepped up their "enforcement" activities, unleashing a spate of violence in support of operations new and old.

On July 14, the Cowboys announced their arrival in Brooklyn with the murder of a local competitor, known on the street as Papito. Four days earlier, Papito, unaware of the gang's ruthless reputation, had assaulted Tezo with a tire iron and ratted out Madrigal to the cops. Tezo returned to Brighton Beach in a car with Lenny, Pasqualito, and Rennie Harris, a Cowboy enforcer. Tezo and Pasqualito, wearing ski masks, got out of the car and walked up to Papito in the middle of the street. "Remember me?" Tezo asked him, lifting his mask. Before he could answer, Pasqualito drew a gun and shot him three times in the chest.

A week later, Gilbert Compusano, Cuevas' battered ex-body-guard, back in Manhattan after six months of rehabilitation in Florida, was attacked on a Harlem street corner in the middle of the afternoon, probably by the same people who had shot him in Cuevas' apartment four months before. A black sedan pulled alongside Compusano as he was walking along, and one of the passengers offered him a lift. Compusano gladly accepted, and the sedan drove him to a neighboring precinct. But when Compusano exited the car, the passenger called him back and shot him six times in the chest and stomach. Compusano kept walking several blocks before a passing bus driver stopped at the sight of Compusano's bloody shirt, and asked him what happened.

"I think my friends shot me," he answered, a bewildered look on his face. Then he collapsed and died.

Two weeks later Dugan was in the Three-Four squad room when a call for backup came over the radio. A street-crime unit was in pursuit of a black Ford Taurus with tinted windows, the subject of an attempted car stop. It sounded to Dugan like the Cowboys. He hopped in a squad car with another detective and joined the chase—a wild ten-minute ride through the streets of Washington Heights—arriving at the West Side Highway moments after Anti-Crime had forced the suspects over on the roadside. The cops already had the car's occupants hand-cuffed against the car. Dugan counted three young Hispanic men. One of them, he realized with a start, was Lenny.

Back at the precinct, police booked the trio for reckless endangerment, resisting arrest, and criminal possession of a weapon—the cops had seen them tossing guns out the passenger-side window during the chase. Dugan gave Lenny a wide berth—the gang leader's lawyer had enjoined Dugan from talking to his client after his Ogdensburg interview. And the detective was only mildly interested in the second suspect, a typical street tough named Manny Crespo, who claimed he had been hitchhiking and had no idea who his companions were. But Dugan was eager to talk to the third subject, who turned out to be Jose Llaca, a.k.a. Pasqualito.

The burly enforcer was built like a torpedo—five feet seven or eight, 200 pounds, with a round shaved head, narrow setback eyes, and thick sensual lips. Sitting calmly across from Dugan in one of the Three-Four interview rooms, he seemed serene, almost Buddha-like, until he began talking. Then his expression became animated, and he turned cocky, loquacious, even jovial, but he made it clear that he had no intention of cooperating. He said he hadn't been aware that the police were chasing them. He didn't see anyone throwing guns out of the window. He couldn't remember who was driving. At one point he asked Dugan how much money he made in a month.

"Enough to get by," Dugan replied amiably.

"Five thousand dollars?" Pasqualito asked. "I make that much in a week. So don't waste your time asking me all these questions."

Still, as Pasqualito rambled on, he couldn't help divulging information. He'd just bought a new Pontiac for his girlfriend and had been on his way to show it to her in a lot on Broadway and 177th Street. (Dugan later located the car and traced the plates to an address in nearby Riverdale, a luxury apartment building where Pasqualito holed up with his girlfriend.) And Pasqualito admitted that the black Taurus belonged to Nicholas Bohan, "a guy from my block who loaned it to me."

Dugan decided to pay Bohan a visit.

One of the few Irish-Italian families still residing in the Heights, the Bohans—Nicholas, his parents, grandmother, and four brothers and sisters—lived in a dilapidated three-bedroom apartment at 620 West 171st Street, directly across from Pasqualito's home. They seemed to have no visible means of support. Nicholas' father, Steven, was a recovering addict; his mother, Jude Anne, was unemployed. Nicholas himself turned out to be 14.

When Dugan arrived the morning after the arrests, Jude Anne answered the door. A large, harried, unkempt woman in her forties, she was dressed in dungarees and a loose-fitting blouse. Behind her lay the wreckage of an overcrowded, undertended apartment—walls caked with dirt, piles of unwashed dishes, a clutter of toys, ashtrays, newspapers, and knickknacks on every surface. A pungent dog odor wafted out into the hallway.

After Dugan identified himself, Jude Anne became nervous. Nicholas, she told him, was out. When he told her that her son's car was the subject of a criminal investigation, her anxiety deepened. Her son didn't own a car, she insisted; the car belonged to Pasqualito. He'd registered it in Nicholas' name against her express orders, though she couldn't explain why Pasqualito had chosen her son. Dugan suspected that her relationship to the gang leader was more complicated than she was letting on, and resolved to find out what other services she was providing Pasqualito. In her eagerness to exculpate her son, Jude Anne told Dugan that Pasqualito and Lenny had been calling the block since their arrest, bragging that the police had failed to find several guns hidden in the Taurus' clavo—a secret compartment built into the car's dashboard.

Later that day, after checking with Rather, Dugan had another go at Pasqualito's Taurus. Prying open the clavo, he found the guns. What's more, Ballistics was able to match fingerprints found on bullets in an ammunition case to Pasqualito's. The evidence, the investigators felt, should have compounded the case and kept the defendants in jail—at least Lenny, who was on parole from a previous gun conviction. But that gun case was never indicted. According to Dugan, Rather had failed to obtain a warrant before Dugan searched Pasqualito's car, making the search potentially improper under New York's strict laws. Rather states that "there was no mistake on my part or Detective Dugan's regarding the warrantless search." However, Dugan says that Rather had beeped him to advise him he needed a warrant shortly after conferring with him the day of the search, though by the time Dugan received the message, he'd already uncovered the guns. In any case, after their arraignment the following day, the gang members easily made bail.

With Lenny and Pasqualito back on the street, Dugan had a more pressing concern, however. Why had the two gang leaders been driving around the Heights with a mini-arsenal in their car?

He was about to find out.

MARK TEBBENS had repeatedly warned Michael Cruz, the 16-year-old son of Elizabeth Morales, not to venture back to Beekman Avenue. The price the Cowboys had put on his head made it risky to confide his whereabouts to even his closest friends. But the cocky teenager had ignored Tebbens' admonitions, slipping in and out of the neighborhood all summer to visit his girlfriend. On August 14 someone tipped off Pasqualito and Lenny that Cruz was on the block, and intended to drive to Queens later that evening with his brother-in-law, Edgar Agosto, to call on Agosto's mother. The two gang leaders got hold of the address in Queens and headed over with Manny Crespo to wait for them.

Fortunately for Cruz, Agosto spotted the Cowboys just before he and Cruz reached their destination, and they doubled back to Brooklyn at high speed. When they got to the shelter on Chauncy Street, Michael was shaking. He was pretty sure they'd eluded their pursuers, but it had been a close call. Agosto parked the car in front of the tenement where they lived, while Michael searched under his seat for a tape; he wanted to listen to music and calm down before he went upstairs. Suddenly he heard Agosto's voice nudging him: "Look who's here." Michael straightened up in time to see Pasqualito and Lenny getting out of a car beside them, guns drawn. He ducked as five or six shots rang out. He heard the thwack of bullets—glass shattering, plastic splitting—then it was over. Michael looked up and saw Pasqualito's and Lenny's retreating figures and, closer in, blood splattered on the windshield and dashboard. He asked Agosto if he was hit.

"It's not my blood," Agosto said to him. Cruz saw Agosto

looking at him strangely, and reached up to the spot on his cheek that Agosto was staring at. There was a hole there—wet, tender. A wave of fear and nausea passed through him, and the numbness began to subside, and pain flooded in its place. He took his hand away. It was covered with blood. Then he sank back in his seat and waited to die.

11

LOSING GROUND

AUGUST 1992

MIRACULOUSLY, the bullet that hit Michael Cruz, tearing through his head and exiting behind his right ear, was not fatal. But the incident had a lasting impact on the course of the Cowboy case.

At the time of the shooting, the investigation was just a jumble of loosely related initiatives, each with its own objectives, timetable, and tactical approach. Investigators from the Three-Oh, Three-Four, Four-Oh, Four-Six, Manhattan North Homicide, HIU, HIDTA, and the Bronx DA's Narcotics Investigations Division were all looking at pieces of the Cowboys operation, many of which overlapped, but no one as yet had taken charge of the various inquiries or developed a rational battle plan. As recently as August 12, just two days before Michael

Cruz's shooting, HIDTA had tried to do something about it. Caught between the Manhattan and Bronx DAs' competing agendas, they invited
principals from the two offices to sit down with them and work out a
common strategy.

The main obstacles dividing the two camps were institutional,
the very questions that always seem to crop up whenever law enforcement agencies try to work together: Who's going to have control? Who's
going to contribute what? Who's going to get the credit? But there were
also differences over strategy. HIU, in line with their basic philosophy,
wanted to take out the gang as a unit, and they felt that they alone had
the resources and expertise to do it. All they lacked were the cases. Except for the Cargill shooting, virtually all the Cowboy-linked homicides
had taken place in the Bronx. The Bronx DA's office, however, was not
prepared to undertake a broad, long-term investigation.

Quinn and Rather both felt that the Bronx DA's conventional,
case-by-case approach was misguided. Focusing just on the Quad
murders would not effectively shut down the gang. Quinn's concerns
were mainly tactical—protecting witnesses and not scaring off the
leaders. Rather, on the other hand, thought that Hill's upcoming Quad
trial was unwinnable. He wanted the Bronx DA to abandon the case
and throw in his lot with Manhattan and HIU in bringing down the entire Cowboy gang.

Hill, however, had no intention of letting go of the Quad. Although he didn't particularly look forward to trying it, it was a Bronx
case and he felt duty-bound to see it through. He wanted to make sure
that those responsible for the four Bronx deaths got the maximum
punishment. Although Hill welcomed HIU's support, he wasn't at all
sure that their aims coincided with his. He felt that Manhattan's priority was the Cargill homicide—a big press case with headlines written all
over it—and that HIU wouldn't hesitate to compromise the Quad prosecution if it helped them gain convictions against Cargill's killers.

Hill had particular reason to be chary of HIU's overtures. His
colleagues had been burned a number of times in joint investigations

with outside agencies who used their influence and superior resources to gain control over the cases, then relegated the Bronx assistants to bit roles in the courtroom and the press. Morgenthau's office bestrode its neighboring DA's offices in the other New York City boroughs like a colossus. Morgenthau himself was an outsized figure, easily the most powerful official in New York law enforcement. Endorsed by all the state's major parties, with acolytes in the press and virtually every county prosecutor's office, he had a reputation as a shrewd horse trader with a habit of muscling his way into plum cases outside Manhattan's bailiwick. Hill, on the other hand, was the least political of prosecutors. He made it a point to leave the turf building and credit grabbing to others. Yet even he understood that working *with* Manhattan meant working *for* Manhattan.

So far none of these concerns had developed into a problem. In fact, Hill and Rather maintained cordial relations. They exchanged information on a timely basis, mainly through Detectives Tebbens and Dugan, and Rather had even trekked up to the Bronx to interview the Cruz-Morales family himself. But the lack of closer ties had begun to impede both their inquiries. Tebbens, who had transferred to the Bronx DA's squad so he could work full-time on the Cowboys, had been frustrated by Hill's narrow focus on the Quad case. Now, sensing an opportunity to rally additional troops to Beekman Avenue, the detective had begun to press HIDTA to begin making "buy-and-bust" arrests of Red-Top's workers so he could flip them against the gang's hierarchy.

But HIDTA, taking HIU's lead, was looking at other operations besides Red-Top's—Cuevas' spot on Watson and Manor avenues and suspected Cowboy outlets in Washington Heights. More important, Benitez was reluctant to do "buy-and-busts" on Beekman Avenue. Even before the meeting, Hill had told him that he couldn't guarantee that the dealers Benitez' men arrested would get jail time. Bronx judges were extremely liberal, and its jury pool, tainted by police prejudice, was unpredictable. Benitez, already troubled by safety conditions in the Hole, refused to send in undercovers unless he was sure of a payoff.

There was a solution, however. Manhattan's Special Narcotics Court, created in the mid-1980s to hear the city's increasingly complex, volatile drug cases, operated under the purview of Leslie Crocker Snyder, a no-nonsense jurist who understood the dynamics of violent street gangs and did not hesitate to remand their workers. Manhattan's administrative judge had assigned all of HIU's cases to Snyder, and Benitez, who knew her from the Gheri Curls case, wanted HIU to arrange to have his arrest subjects transferred from the Bronx to her court. Unfortunately, neither Arsenault nor Rather wanted to alienate the Bronx by poaching minor drug cases in its backyard. They planned to incorporate the Quad and other Bronx homicides into their conspiracy indictment—regardless of whether or not Hill tried them separately—and they knew that they would need Hill's cooperation down the road.

All these different agendas were at play when investigators crowded into a cubicle at HIDTA's downtown Manhattan headquarters on August 12. Among those at the meeting were Dan Rather and Terry Quinn from HIU; Mark Tebbens, assistant DA Don Hill, and Hill's supervisor, Ed Freedenthal, from the Bronx; and Eddie Benitez and his CO, Charles Rorke, from HIDTA. The meeting ran smoothly, at least at first. Hill and Freedenthal had come prepared to cooperate with Manhattan, and they agreed to cede jurisdiction over HIDTA's drug busts as long as Rather was willing to share information and include them in any cases that developed later on. When Rather assured them he was, the parties quickly hammered out a three-pronged strategy: HIU would carry on investigating Cargill and other homicides linked to the Cowboys; HIDTA would step up their probe into the gang's drug operations; and Hill would prosecute the Quad with support from HIU and HIDTA.

It was a viable plan, a good first step toward a more formal arrangement later on, and the meeting might well have ended then. But Quinn, who had taken charge of the discussion, was already racing ahead to the endgame, proposing investigative lines that would topple the Cowboys and net the gang's elusive leaders. "Terry was trying out different strategies, and he decided to float a trial balloon," Hill recalls. "But Terry doesn't float balloons, he lobs grenades—and this one blew up in his face."

As the self-appointed moderator, Quinn went around the room, querying each party about their specific plans, probing the limits of their cooperation. Tebbens, seeing Quinn in action for the first time, was impressed. He wanted nothing more than to expand and accelerate the investigation, and he recognized in Quinn a kindred spirit, someone who would step up and get everyone working together.

But Hill's impression was less benign. Troubled by Quinn's dismissive attitude toward the Quad, Hill saw him as a stereotypical Irish cop: hard-charging, hardheaded, blunt, and supremely sure of himself. He understood that Quinn's agenda was different from his, that his agenda was a Manhattan agenda—solve Cargill; get Lenny, Cargill's presumptive killer. And he'd worked with enough men like Quinn as both a cop and a prosecutor to know that on some level he was being tested, that Quinn would not stop pushing him until Hill made it clear where he stood.

For a while, the two men sparred—Quinn nudging the investigators to focus on the conspiracy aspects of the case, and Hill reiterating that the Bronx was all for rooting out the Cowboys and locking up Lenny but that their priority was the Quad, the Quad must be tried first. Then Quinn decided to force the issue: "We should flip Platano against Lenny," he told the group. "Or if that doesn't work, we should indict him and then flip him."

Although Hill was in many ways the opposite of Quinn, deliberate, taciturn, at times aloof, he also had a nasty temper; as a prosecutor, he had learned that it could be an effective tool, especially in contrast to his normally placid demeanor. But Quinn's statement genuinely shocked Hill. Platano was the linchpin of the Quad, Hill's No. 1 defendant. Making a deal with Platano in order to get to Lenny was tantamount to scuttling the case. "Are you implying that one white kid in Manhattan is worth more than four lives in the Bronx?" Hill asked Quinn.

"No, and you know I don't mean that," Quinn replied. "But sometimes you've got to make choices. Not all homicides are equal, you know what I mean? Those victims in the Quad were either dealing or using. I'm not saying they deserved to die, but Cargill was just a nice kid who got popped for being in the wrong place at the wrong time. That could have been my kid. Hell, it could have been yours. How would you have felt then?"

"That's bullshit," Hill said. "Platano's a stone-cold killer. For all you know he's murdered twelve, maybe more than twelve, and that's not including the Quad. You're asking me to make a deal with someone like that?"

"Hey, I've had Jamaicans testify for me who've killed more than a hundred people."

"Well, good," Hill said. "But they didn't murder a hundred people on my turf."

The meeting broke up moments later. Rather, as a peace offering, invited Hill for drinks at a nearby bar. It turned out to be an odd, pleasant interlude in the case. Hill had already formed a good opinion of Rather as a prosecutor; he seemed serious and competent. But Hill had not been prepared to like him personally. Hill knew he was being courted for his cases, that however tactfully Rather smoothed over Quinn's blunder, he still harbored the same agenda as his outspoken investigator. Nor did Rather's celebrity aura add any appeal for Hill—if anything, it put him on guard against any sense of entitlement Rather might have. But as the two men traded biographies over beers, Hill found himself disarmed by Rather. They discovered they'd both attended universities in D.C., Hill as a congressional worker for conservative causes while at American University, Rather at Georgetown. Rather talked about his fishbowl existence at Georgetown in a folksy, self-effacing manner that both surprised and beguiled Hill. The prosecutors reaffirmed their commitment to the case, their shared concerns over the witnesses and cleaning up the battered Bronx neighborhood still controlled by the Cowboys. An hour later Hill exited into the late afternoon sunshine much reassured. Nonetheless, he understood that he and his Manhattan counterpart were traveling along separate, perhaps even divergent tracks.

Those divergent paths, however, began to converge with the shooting of Michael Cruz. The attempted assassination not only injected a new sense of urgency into HIU's investigation—within weeks of the failed execution Quinn's detectives were staking out Cowboy hangouts in the Heights—but broadened the scope of the Quad case. In the aftermath of the shooting, Hill realized that he could no longer focus exclusively on his case and his defendants and ignore the rest of the Cowboy gang, without jeopardizing the safety of his witnesses. Now everyone—Rather, Quinn, Hill, Tebbens, Benitez—agreed that their first priority must be getting Lenny and Pasqualito off the street.

ON AUGUST 18, four days after Michael Cruz's shooting, Mark Tebbens and HIDTA detectives John Scaccia and Cesar Ortiz were searching the Four-Oh for Lenny and Pasqualito when their radio crackled. Eddie Benitez was calling from HIDTA's Cypress Avenue observation post. He'd spotted Lenny and Pasqualito across the street, hanging out with two young male Hispanics in front of the gang's headquarters at No. 354. Moments later, the detectives parked around the corner from Cypress and proceeded on foot.

As soon as Benitez saw Tebbens with his men, Benitez freaked. Tebbens' size made him stand out at a distance, and both Lenny and Pasqualito knew him from past encounters. But it was too late to change plans. Pasqualito had just ducked into a playground between Cypress and Beekman. Benitez radioed the information to the detectives, but they let him go. Tebbens had spotted Lenny not more than thirty feet ahead of him. The gang leader was standing in front of the stoop of No. 354, flanked by two kids from the neighborhood. He was dressed casually—jeans, sneakers, a white T-shirt, and a black wind-breaker—and his hair was cropped close to his head, shorter than Tebbens remembered. But there was no mistaking Lenny—the coiled posture, the muscular air of command. For a second or two their eyes locked, then Lenny turned abruptly and jogged up the steps to No. 354, followed by his two young acolytes.

Tebbens charged after him, unholstering his gun as he ran; he bounded up the stairs three at a time. At the rear of the entrance hall he came to a corridor that traversed the building and led on his left to a walkway overlooking a vacant lot. Lenny's companions were standing near the door to the bridge. Tebbens lined them up against the wall as Scaccia arrived, panting from the run. Behind Scaccia, he spied Lenny.

Tebbens realized Lenny must have darted into an apartment, reemerging after the detective passed him in the hallway. He trained his gun on the gang leader, and motioned him against the wall next to the others. Then he holstered the gun out of Lenny's sight and, pulling Lenny's right arm behind his back, started to cuff his wrist. In the same instant, Lenny pushed off the wall with his left arm, momentarily freeing himself and sending the cuffs flying. Tebbens recovered and tackled Lenny from behind as he tried to escape, driving his face into the floor. But when Tebbens reached behind him for the cuffs, Lenny broke free again, and made for the door to the bridge.

Tebbens was taken aback by Lenny's strength. He knew from experience that a subject who didn't fight, who focused his energy on getting away, had an advantage over his pursuer, no matter how small or frail he was, and Lenny was neither. Tebbens also knew it was extremely difficult to cuff someone who was actively resisting. Still, given his size and conditioning, Tebbens was used to overpowering his prey.

As Lenny lurched toward the exit, Tebbens managed to trip him up and grab on to his jacket collar. But as they wrestled for a second time, Lenny slipped out of his windbreaker and away from Tebbens. Scaccia, a former football player, broke away from the two teenagers he'd been guarding and grabbed at Lenny. But Lenny bulled past him and out onto the walkway.

Tebbens knew where Lenny was heading. The ground underneath the bridge sloped away from the street at a sharp angle. It was a twelve-to-fifteen-foot drop from the walkway to the lot below, a rutted, rocky patch of ground between buildings. If Lenny jumped, there was no way Tebbens could follow him down. He lunged at Lenny as Lenny hoisted himself up the metal retaining wall, and grabbed at the tail of his T-shirt. But the shirt just ripped, and Lenny dove headfirst over railing. Tebbens helplessly watched him fall. The Cowboy gang leader landed on his right side and rolled over; clutching at his knee, he limped behind the building and out of sight.

Tebbens, joined by a dozen cops now, canvassed the neighborhood and staked out the area, but Lenny, having ducked into one of the connecting buildings, was holed up somewhere, probably in a friend's apartment. At nightfall, Tebbens' supervisors, concerned about safety and overtime, had to call off the operation.

Lenny's escape was a devastating blow to the investigation. Not only had Tebbens let him literally slip through his fingers, but he'd scared him into hiding, making it unlikely the detectives would get a second chance to apprehend him soon. For weeks afterward, Tebbens replayed the chase and capture in his mind. He realized he'd acted precipitously, that he should have called in backup and surrounded the building before going after Lenny. In fact, he probably shouldn't have gone after him at all. But the prospect of personally putting the cuffs on the man he'd been pursuing for nearly three years had dulled his judgment. He swore to himself he wouldn't let that happen again.

THE COWBOYS continued their intimidation tactics in the wake of Michael Cruz's shooting. A day after the incident, Elizabeth Morales, having moved with her family to a new shelter in Queens, returned with Tebbens to her Brooklyn apartment to pick up her belongings, and found it had been broken into and ransacked. Photographs of her family had been ripped from their frames and taken. A few days later, when Elizabeth was driving back to Queens after visiting her son in the hospital, she noticed a Cowboy enforcer following her, at one point writing down her license plate number. When Tebbens learned about it, he realized it was no longer safe for Elizabeth Morales or her family to remain in the city. He made arrangements through the Bronx DA's office to move them to an apartment motel upstate.

Around that time, the gang attacked another Quad witness, 24-year-old Raymond Jimenez. A longtime resident of Beekman Avenue, Jimenez, like many of his neighbors, made his living as a small-time scam artist—hustling, burglarizing, selling drugs. He had worked from time to time as a spot manager for the Cowboys. But he drew the line at wanton murder. Jimenez had been repulsed by the Quad, and he was one of the few witnesses who'd come freely to Tebbens and offered to testify against the shooters. Somehow the gang had found out about it, and Lamar Taylor, a local arm-breaker, confronted Jimenez with a six-inch hunting knife. Mouthing the enforcer's mantra— "Snitches get stitches"—Taylor attempted to slash his face. Jimenez warded off the blow, but nearly lost two fingers from his right hand in the process.

Tebbens was able to track Taylor down and arrest him on an assault charge. But as long as Lenny and Pasqualito remained at large, he knew his witness problems would continue.

Just before Labor Day weekend, with the Quad trial about to begin, a series of events occurred that baffled even the most cynical investigators in the case. On Thursday afternoon, September 3, Benitez, along with three HIDTA detectives, apprehended Pasqualito while he was picking up receipts at a Cowboys crack spot on 141st Street, around the corner from the Hole. The arrest had been difficult. Pasqualito had resisted when the detectives tried to cuff him, wrestling with them in the street, drawing a crowd of about fifty. As the mob closed in, Pasqualito began moaning about brutality, inciting them to intervene, and some onlookers began tossing bottles and stones at the detectives, forcing Benitez to call in emergency backup.

"What the hell's wrong with you?" Benitez asked Pasqualito, once he got him back to the Four-Oh.

"I've always got to fight," he replied. "I don't just give up."

"You're lucky you didn't get shot."

"I can handle myself," Pasqualito said, smiling, at ease now. He seemed eager to talk. "Why the hell are you locking me up anyway?" he asked.

"On account of the kid you shot."

"I don't know what you're talking about," Pasqualito said.

"Really?"

"Yeah. I'm just a cabdriver."

"Yeah? What are you doing with twelve hundred dollars in your pocket?" Benitez asked, referring to the wad of bills the police had taken off the burly enforcer.

"I had a good day."

As it turned out, Pasqualito also had a good night. Benitez processed his arrest in the Four-Oh, then transported him to Brooklyn, where Benitez swore out a complaint for Pasqualito's role in Michael Cruz's shooting. Benitez was careful to inform the young recording prosecutor about the circumstances of the case: the difficulty the police had apprehending Pasqualito, the fact that Cruz was a witness in numerous murder cases, and Cruz's importance to ongoing investigations in the Bronx and Manhattan. Benitez also notified Don Hill, who drove to the Brooklyn courthouse that night to make sure the arraignments judge understood the gravity of the arrest. Now that the Cowboy investigators had Pasqualito, they were determined not to lose him.

But then the inexplicable happened. Not only did the judge deny the prosecution's request for remand, but he granted Pasqualito a relatively low bail of $25,000—even though Pasqualito had just shot a government witness in the head, was a suspect in at least four other homicides, including the month-old Brooklyn murder of Papito, and belonged to a violent drug organization whose members were known to skip to the Dominican Republic.

The Brooklyn DA's office used an assembly-line system, breaking down cases into their constituent parts—complaint, indictment, arraignment, trial—with the youngest, least experienced assistants responsible for the early stages. The ADA who handled arraignments that night was not the ADA who took Benitez's statement. Moreover, Hill had gone home moments before Pasqualito's appearance, having been told by Pasqualito's lawyer that his client was in lockup for the night and wouldn't be produced until the following morning. But none of that altered the facts of the case that were communicated to the judge, however inexpertly, by the arraignments assistant. Eddie Benitez was shocked to discover, when he arrived at work the next day, that Pasqualito was back on the street.

12

THE INFORMER

FALL 1992

THROUGHOUT the fall of 1992, Walter Arsenault arrived at work with a heady, pulse-quickening sense of anticipation. In October his last two Jamaican murder cases pled out, winding down what had been, by any measure, an enormously successful three-and-a-half-year campaign against Manhattan's posses; and the Gheri Curls trial—the unit's first big conspiracy prosecution—was slated to begin in November. With nearly twenty gang members agreeing to testify against the six top leaders and enforcers, the prospects for conviction were good. But having so many witnesses multiplied the burdens of preparation, and the stakes for HIU—in the press, in the office, and on the street—were immense.

What's more, the unit was suffering growing pains. Having already doubled in size since Arsenault's arrival in 1988, HIU had begun another round of expansion in the wake of the Gheri Curls takedown. The added administrative duties were crowding Arsenault out of the courtroom, and HIU's rising profile had triggered distractions in and out of the unit. Arsenault let Nancy Ryan handle the larger office politics—the inevitable squabbles over resources, perks, and publicity—but it was difficult to ignore the grousing in his own ranks. Some of the old-time investigators, who had worked with Hoyt, resented Arsenault's ascendancy, and Terry Quinn, who worked closely with Arsenault, was unhappy reporting to James McVeety, the former Jade Squad sergeant whom Ryan had installed as the unit's chief investigator.

Adding to the ferment at the office, Arsenault was about to become a father again. His wife, Beth, a 35-year-old telephone company executive, was due to deliver a girl in February, and at inappropriate moments—while viewing crime scene photos or teasing out the details of a horrific murder for a grand jury or sitting through an arid administrative confab—Arsenault would feel an unreasonable happiness welling inside him.

With all this going on, the Cowboys, nonetheless, were a constant presence in his thoughts. At the end of each day, Terry Quinn would stroll into Arsenault's unkempt office and hold forth on the latest developments in the investigation. Since the end of August, Quinn had been interviewing potential cooperators, many of them gang members who'd been locked up and were looking for a deal. Much of the information he extracted was fragmented, inconsistent, exculpatory, slanted, or just plain made up. Still, Quinn, working closely with HIDTA, was gradually able to piece together a picture of the gang, its size and structure, its allies and rivals, its method of operation, its history, and many of the past crimes that contributed to its myth.

As always, Arsenault was stunned by the sheer wealth of information Quinn had been able to gather on a group that, until recently, had been largely nameless and faceless. But two themes that troubled him emerged from the welter of detail. First, unlike the Gheri Curl leaders, none of the Cowboy bosses participated in their organization's drug sales. Although it was exactly what he'd predicted about a gang involved in retail sales, it meant that prosecutors would have to rely on witnesses—most of them gang members themselves—to tie higher-ups like Lenny and Nelson into the conspiracy. Second, it was becoming increasingly clear to Arsenault that the Cowboys really were a Bronx case, as Hill and Tebbens had been insisting all along. Based on his conversations with Hill and his supervisor, Ed Freedenthal, Arsenault was confident that their office would continue to cooperate with HIU. But Arsenault also understood that he would have very little leverage should their two agencies clash over policy later on. In short, HIU needed the Bronx far more than the Bronx needed them.

Those caveats aside, the Cowboys were already becoming HIU's biggest case ever. Quinn estimated that even without the Frankie Cuevas and Reuben Perez pieces, the gang numbered forty to sixty members, more than double the size of the Gheri Curls. And even those numbers underestimated the magnitude of the case. Retail drug gangs are violent by nature. Since their product is fairly standardized, their capital is their location, and their workers must be prepared to use force to repel would-be competitors from their turf, as well as to defend themselves against stickup artists and rowdy customers. Most gangs employ specialists to handle the bulk of their enforcement tasks—the contract hits and drive-bys. Like Platano, they strive to build cultlike reputations in the street that shield their organizations from vagrant attacks. Usually gangs employ one or two such enforcers, rarely more than a handful. But as far as the Cowboys were concerned, Quinn observed, "they were all shooters."

EVEN AGAINST that backdrop, the Cowboys' Victor Mercedes stood out as a loose cannon. Fat Danny's older half brother, Mercedes, 23, had grown up next door to Lenny and was one of the gang's original members, serving as a manager-enforcer. As far back as 1987, he was rumored to have killed a rival drug dealer in the Melrose section of the Bronx and to have blown off a chunk of his own thumb while running from the scene. Then, in 1988, he gunned down another competitor in St. Mary's Park, wounding him in the arm. More recently, he'd fired the shot that set off the Double, the blatant, public executions in 1989 that solidified the Cowboys' hold over Beekman Avenue and led a month later to Mercedes' arrest and jailing by Mark Tebbens. Although he spent nearly two years in prison until his release in 1991, after the witnesses in his case disappeared or recanted their testimony, the experience had done little to curb his appetite for gunplay. Just two months after his release on October 18, he fired a bullet into the leg of Michael Turner, a reputed drug dealer visiting Cypress Avenue. Neither Turner nor his cousin, who witnessed the shooting, would file complaints against Mercedes, but three weeks later, Mercedes copped a plea in his still-pending 1988 case and returned to jail, where Quinn found him in August 1992.

Short and stocky, with a pumped-up prison physique and sullen, shifty demeanor, Mercedes was not a promising interview subject. But as Quinn quickly discovered, Mercedes was nursing grudges against several of the Cowboys and could not resist taking shots at them. He blamed the Quad on Platano, Stanley Tukes, Nelson, who he told Quinn had fled to the Dominican Republic, and a fourth individual Quinn had not heard of before named Tezo.

Mercedes talked about several other murders as well, including the Compusano and Mask homicides, which he claimed was the work of Frankie Cuevas. But he seemed to reserve a special animus for Tezo. According to Mercedes, Tezo had shot and killed a small-time weed dealer known as El Gordo in Washington Heights the previous fall on Halloween night. Quinn had been tracking the homicide, which he suspected was linked to the Cowboys through Reuben Perez, El Gordo's competitor in the marijuana business. Until now, however, Quinn had been unable to identify the shooter, who had worn a Halloween mask. Of course, Mercedes might be lying, implicating Tezo in crimes that actually he or one of the other gang members had committed. But Mercedes' description of Tezo matched the one in police reports: a tall, slim, dark-skinned Dominican, 23 or 24 years old, with a "fade" hairstyle.

Quinn began a search for the new suspect. Mercedes thought that Tezo's real first name was Rafael, and he recalled that he'd recently been arrested with Lenny's brother-in-law, Rafael Fernandez, in a car stop near the 207th Street Bridge in the Heights. But Quinn's initial efforts to find him were unsuccessful.

As it turned out, Quinn was not the only one looking for Tezo. Richard Gwillym, a Brooklyn detective investigating the July 14 murder of Papito, was also searching for the lanky young man, who, according to witnesses, had pointed out Papito to Pasqualito, just before the Cowboy enforcer fired six shots into his chest. Gwillym didn't even know Tezo's street name—his informants referred to him as Flaco—but he learned that earlier that summer Tezo, or Flaco, had opened up a spot in the area with a partner named Ramon Madrigal, whom Papito had caused to be arrested. In a nifty piece of police work, Gwillym got hold of Madrigal's arrest folder and discovered that his bail had been posted by Rafael Perez. Was this Flaco? Then Gwillym ran Perez' name through the Bureau of Criminal Investigation records, and found that on July 21—just a week after Papito's murder—Perez had been arrested for possession of nearly 400 vials of crack and an AK-47 in the Three-Four, not far from the 207th Street Bridge. Gwillym figured this must be his man. Perez' record indicated that he had a court date on September 11 in Manhattan. Gwillym decided to arrest him when he arrived.

In one of those odd coincidences that often befall law enforcement, Gwillym bumped into Terry Quinn in the lobby of the Criminal Courts building on the morning he went to arrest Tezo. Gwillym had worked for Quinn on a Manhattan task force in the mid-1980s. The two men exchanged pleasantries, and Gwillym mentioned his current mission to collar Perez. At the time, Gwillym didn't know Perez was called Tezo, and Quinn had no idea that Tezo was Perez.

Back in Brooklyn, however, after arresting Perez, Gwillym called the Three-Four to get some background on Tezo prior to questioning him. Gwillym was referred to Garry Dugan, who just that afternoon had discovered Tezo's identity. (Dugan had run Rafael Fernandez' rap sheet and found he'd been arrested with Tezo, just as Victor Mercedes had told Quinn that he would.) Dugan told Gwillym to contact Quinn. When Quinn heard the news, he gathered up Rather and Mark Tebbens and headed over to the Six-Oh in the Coney Island section of Brooklyn, where Tezo was being held.

The Brooklyn prosecutors were hardly thrilled to see the Manhattan contingent, and kept them at bay for four and a half hours, while they conducted their own interviews with Tezo. Finally, around 3 A.M., Gwillym made Tezo available to Rather and Quinn. But it was worth the wait. While the investigators didn't feel they had enough solid evidence against Tezo to confront him with the Quad or the Halloween murder, Tezo was voluble on a broad range of subjects, including the Papito homicide, which he ascribed to Pasqualito.

Tezo had known Lenny from the Heights for ten years and had started working for him about a year ago as his driver and aide. With an insider's knowledge of the gang, he was able to provide the investigators with much more detail about its operation. Lenny, he confirmed, was the gang's boss, and Nelson, his brother, his second-in-command. Platano was the gang's chief enforcer, but Pasqualito had taken his place since Platano's arrest. Jimmy Montalvo, a 300-pound Dominican known as Heavy D because of his uncanny resemblance to the eponymous rap singer, was the general manager of Lenny's spots. Other high-ranking managers included Rennie Harris, who ran their Red-Top spot, and Frankie Robles, who managed Orange-Top.

The gang cooked up their crack 100 grams at a time in coffeepots in an apartment on Sedgwick Avenue and 183rd Street in the Bronx. Three to four workers did the packaging, and then a transporter named Mikie brought the "bundles" to Heavy D, who distributed them as needed to several sales spots in the Beekman Avenue area. Confirming the estimates of other informants, Tezo calculated that the business, which operated continuously, grossed $30,000 per day.

Tezo was also able to provide background on Lenny's war with Frankie Cuevas. He told them that the two men had been associates until Cuevas tried to take over Lenny's spots while Lenny was in jail and that Lenny retaliated by ordering Platano to kill Cuevas. This was familiar ground to the investigators. But Tezo added a new wrinkle. Platano had indeed set up Cuevas' execution by paying off Gilbert Compusano to give him the address of Cuevas' cocaine supplier and the time of his next pickup. Then he'd hired out the contract to a hit man known as Freddy Krueger.

Neither Quinn nor the other detectives had heard of Krueger. Tezo told them he was notorious within the Washington Heights community, feared even more than Platano. Krueger, Tezo said, worked for a big weight dealer in the West 160s who was closely allied with Lenny. But there was another reason why Krueger did the hit, Tezo explained. Cuevas had given Krueger's boss a "bad package" a couple of years ago and didn't make up for it. Krueger's boss—whom Quinn later discovered was Jose Reyes, or El Feo—had wanted to kill Cuevas then, but Lenny had intervened. Now all bets were off.

Quinn was taken aback. As if their investigation wasn't complicated enough with Cuevas' and Lenny's gangs, now a third drug organization had entered the picture, along with someone purportedly more lethal than Platano. How many bodies would they find this time? And who was Freddy Krueger?

Quinn reasoned that if Krueger was even half as infamous as Tezo claimed, other informants would know about him as well, and he'd almost certainly have had some contact with the law. Mark

Tebbens recalled a Red-Top manager named Freddie Sendra who fit Tezo's description of Krueger. He'd been arrested on Beekman Avenue a few years back for shooting at police. But when Tebbens pulled Sendra's record, he saw that Sendra was still in prison serving out a seven-year sentence: he couldn't have been the shooter in the March attempt on Cuevas.

Nevertheless, Rather wanted Sendra brought in. His highest priority was to talk to former gang members and top-ranking managers who could give him some perspective on the Cowboys. "We were looking at each individual event: How did it relate?" Rather recalls. "We'd start to see patterns, like a jigsaw puzzle. The first pieces were Cargill, the Quad. Sometimes we'd get pieces from another puzzle, like the ballplayer shooting, or the Chicken Store murder, where Platano was supposed to have killed a 13-year-old girl. Then there were the drive-bys and the shootings around Frankie Cuevas and Gilbert Compusano.

"We were working forward and backward, asking ourselves: Who are these guys? What was their relationship to each other? What was their past? It was incredibly fertile ground. We kept uncovering old crimes, and new crimes were happening all the time. We were working on all levels.

"The worst investigation is a dead one, one where you're not getting any information. But this was very different. Almost everywhere you looked there were significant things. Someone would get shot and we would be trying to figure out why. Who was the victim? Who was he aligned with? Why was he shot? Who's going to replace him?"

Rather hoped that Sendra would help provide some of the answers.

Framed in the doorway of Rather's office, Freddie Sendra was tall and big-chested with a gruff, handsome face, hulking shoulders, and a fighter's big, soft hands. Rather had figured him for a hard case. Sendra had drawn down on police during a drug bust, taken a stiff plea, and kept his mouth shut. Rather was prepared to negotiate with him for his cooperation, but Sendra's first words preempted him: "I've thought about what you want," he said, "and I've decided to tell you everything."

Thus began one of the more remarkable episodes of the investigation for Rather. Freddie Sendra had been stewing in prison for nearly three years—his former mates had visited him just once during that time, and then only to ask him to whack another inmate, Victor Mercedes—and he was eager to talk. He told Rather he didn't even want a deal, just a letter to his parole board saying he'd cooperated.

Rather could scarcely believe his good fortune. Until his arrest, Sendra had spent nearly every day with the gang from the time he was a student at George Washington High School, where the gang coalesced, until well after they'd formed Red-Top and moved their operation to the Hole. The story Sendra told Rather during the late fall months of 1992 was the story of the gang's origins, and it provided Rather with the foundation for what had been, until then, an utterly confusing and fragmented investigation.

"At first there was Lenny, Nelson, Platano, Maximo, Victor Mercedes, Pasqualito, Frankie V.," Sendra began. "We'd meet at the handball court behind school. We started stealing cars in Manhattan—then Riverdale, Whitestone, La Guardia, Kennedy, and over to New Jersey: Englewood, Englewood Cliffs, Tenafly and Teaneck. Three or four cars a day. Everybody learned to drive on stolen cars.

"My first car was a Toyota Celica with MD [doctor's] plates. Crashed it. I got caught with Max in New Jersey, two times with Frank in New Jersey and New York. Got ROR [released on own recognizance] and never went back [to court]. The third time, they sentenced me to seven years. Charged me with thirty-two cars. They had surveillance up [at the lot]. I did two years four months. I was sixteen or seventeen."

Sendra was candid, detailed, and articulate. His father owned his own store; his mother was straitlaced, religious. But they couldn't shield him from the street, any more than he could protect himself. At times, he'd tried to straighten out—to study or get a job—but the excitement, the camaraderie, the swagger and notoriety of gang life always lured him back. Every day was a day off—pickup football games that were an excuse for mayhem; midnight motorcycle races down the West Side Highway; scams to make money. After stealing cars, Sendra and his crew turned to marijuana sales.

"Joe schooled us in marijuana," he said. "He had a game arcade over on Audubon. We'd hang out, buy weed from him. When we started selling, he called us all in, told us, 'This is how you do it.'

"We were finished with cars by then. Everybody had his own little spot. Hector had a connection down in Texas. What cost a thousand dollars in Washington Heights cost two-fifty to three hundred in Texas. They needed someone to go down, they picked me. Paid for eighty pounds, they gave me ninety-eight pounds. I skimmed the extra off the top.

"They'd pack it in Saran Wrap and fabric softener in a duffel bag. Went once every two weeks with Elvis. He got arrested. We used to stop in Midland-Odessa—real small airport—drive back to Dallas or Love. Immigration pulled him off a bus with two big bags full. They thought he was Mexican, an illegal alien. Hector put up his bail. He's still running."

By then, Sendra said, crack was making its appearance in the Heights, and their friends were offering them coke on consignment. Sendra had been out of the business, working as a doorman at 163rd between Broadway and Amsterdam, when Platano took him out to a spot he'd said he'd found on Beech Terrace, a curved drive at the north end of Beekman Avenue in the Bronx. Sendra quit his job the next day.

"Lenny was running the show," Sendra recalls. "He was the strong-arm. Nelson was the bookkeeper. Everybody had their own personalities. Pasqualito and Platano were always bragging. Victor Mercedes also. Platano was the clown. He liked big cars, Caddies. He liked cracking them up. A guy we called Capone was the *GQ* of the group, the ladies' man, the dresser.

"During the week, we'd be hooking up a car, then racing Saturday night at Hunts Point. We'd go to clubs too—Roseland, Palladium, Tunnel, Gotham. And Highbridge Pool. We fought there with the 145th Street guys over turf. We'd get high, race cars. Cops? We used to slow down for cops, sit on their tails. They wouldn't do nothing."

Within a year or two, the money was rolling in faster than they could spend it. Lenny, Sendra said, was the nominal leader, the one who was always there, who understood the business, who told you what to do. But the Cowboys were a conspiracy of equals, according to Sendra. Any one of the top-ranking members, Sendra claimed, could go to the company safe and take as much as he wanted. (Rather doubted this.) If one Cowboy bought a cycle, they all bought the same cycle; and every week they set up their cars for the Saturday night races, spending eight or nine thousand dollars to install a nitro bottle and reseal the engine. Then they would crash them and start all over again.

"We never thought it would end," he said. "Figured we'll think of something. We can always make more money."

By the time he'd finished, Sendra had described a freewheeling, beeper-quick, totally self-indulgent existence—a group of violent young men who ran roughshod through the streets, careening from one lucrative racket to another, and literally thumbing their noses at the police. Nothing was denied them. Nobody said no. The schools they barely attended promoted them without prejudice. Parents turned a blind eye to their exploits, as did the law. They turned the roof of 352 Beekman into a firing range and took target practice, shooting at or near the legs of strollers in St. Mary's Park. (Tebbens had investigated more than twenty incidents traced to sniper fire from the gang's headquarters.) Anyone who got in their way—or merely brushed against them, as Cargill did—was beaten or killed, and because they rarely suffered any consequences for their actions, they felt invincible.

"When I saw the cops coming, there was no fear or hesitation," Sendra told Rather, trying to explain the shoot-out with police that landed him in prison. "I thought, 'All right, let's do it.' All I can say is it's Washington Heights, the way we were brought up."

WHILE QUINN and Rather were debriefing potential witnesses, HIDTA was figuring out the gangs' drug operations, making buy-and-bust arrests, and providing HIU with new cooperators. But the process started slowly. Benitez focused first on Cuevas' spot on Watson and Manor, identifying his workers and on September 10 raiding one of his stash pads. But the raid was disappointing—Cuevas had moved his drugs to another apartment a few days before—and it soon became evident that there was no overlap between Cuevas' crew and the Cowboys on Beekman Avenue.

HIDTA had even less luck in Washington Heights. Working with HIU investigators, Benitez set up an observation post on West 171st Street, the block where Lenny, Nelson, Pasqualito, Fat Danny, and Victor Mercedes grew up and their families still lived. But the detectives were unable to connect the Cowboys with any local drug activity, and stakeouts of Reuben Perez' spot on 174th Street and Audubon Avenue were equally unproductive. Not only was Perez' operation limited to marijuana sales, but his main customers seemed to be the Cowboys themselves, many of whom rolled up two and three times daily to buy the pot-stuffed cigars they called blunts. (Though none of the high-ranking Cowboys used their own product, virtually all of them got high on weed all of the time.)

But when Benitez turned his attention to Beekman Avenue, his efforts started to pay off. On September 21 he was finally able to secure an apartment—a small flat in the rear of 353 Cypress Avenue—with a clear view into the Hole. The next day he installed a twenty-four-hour time-lapse camera, and shortly after that his team began making buys from Red-Top's workers. But HIDTA's biggest coup came as the result of a windfall. On September 23 a disgruntled Cowboy worker turned up at the Four-Oh saying that the gang had cheated him and offering detectives information on the whereabouts of Red-Top's stash apartment. By luck, Benitez was in the precinct at the time and overheard the informant mention Beekman Avenue. Benitez debriefed him on the spot, got a search warrant from Judge Snyder overnight, and on September 24 HIDTA detectives and Bronx police converged on Louise McBride's fourth-floor apartment at 348 Beekman Avenue.

THIRTY-SEVEN-YEAR-OLD Louise McBride's door seemed to explode off its hinges, as the police battering ram crashed through the doorway and the eight-man police team positioned outside charged in. Suddenly she found herself facedown on the floor, something sharp—Benitez' knee, it turned out—pressing into her back, and there was the feel of metal around her wrists. Then she was right side up, a long, bony face an inch away, and yelling, "You-gotta-fucking-problem-lady-you're-going-to-jail-for-life." It didn't help she was high as a kite.

Nor did it help that McBride had a record dating back to 1975, or that earlier that fall, Benitez, masquerading as a building inspector, had observed her in the Hole selling Red-Top crack. But most devastating for McBride was that Benitez had timed the raid to the start of the 4 P.M.-to-midnight shift, so that there was a full stash of crack on the living-room table. To McBride, her arrest seemed just one more piece of hard luck in what had been a harrowing life. But McBride's misfortune was HIDTA's gain. After sweeping the apartment, police recovered 500 vials of crack cocaine, a .30-.06 rifle with a telescopic sight, an 11 mm Cobrey machine gun, a beeper, and $795 in cash. They also collared two mid-level Red-Top managers, David Polanco and Frank Blair, in the kitchen. With prior convictions for assault, weapon possession, and drug sales, McBride was facing serious jail time; Benitez was confident he'd delivered to Rather and Quinn the inside cooperator they'd been clamoring for.

Meanwhile HIDTA scored a second coup, though it would be some time before they recognized its significance. On October 13, Detectives Cesar Ortiz and John Scaccia were doing auto surveillance on West 171st Street when they observed a van with two unknown Hispanic men and a woman pull up in front of No. 641, where a group of Cowboys, including Pasqualito and Fat Danny, were hanging out. Normally laid-back, the gang members made such a fuss over one of the van's occupants, a stocky young man in a wheelchair, that Ortiz and Scaccia were convinced they'd stumbled onto one of the Heights' Mr. Bigs, perhaps the Cowboys' supplier. After conferring with Pasqualito and Fat Danny for several minutes, the man in the wheelchair and his two associates drove off. The detectives followed them to a motel in nearby Montvale, New Jersey. The next day they got the New Jersey police to do a car stop on the van. Ortiz and Scaccia already knew the name of the van's driver from the motel registry. But it was the second man they were interested in. He told the police that he'd been paralyzed in a shooting the year before, and identified himself as Jose Reyes—the gang leader whom Quinn would later identify as El Feo, Lenny's main ally and Freddy Krueger's boss.

JUST AS HIDTA's investigation began to pick up speed, the Bronx's Quad case hit a bumpy patch. Throughout the fall, in a series of hearings, Don Hill sparred with defense lawyers over what evidence he'd be allowed to introduce at trial. A normal part of criminal procedure, such hearings aim to shield defendants from attacks by the prosecution that are irrelevant, capricious, unduly prejudicial, or based on information illegally obtained. What's more, the Quad being a big, complex case, Hill expected to be strenuously challenged, and having argued several times before Ira Globerman, the presiding judge, he anticipated at least some "defense-friendly" rulings. But by year's end, Hill was chafing under strictures he felt had been unreasonably placed on his prosecution.

Indicative of the way things were headed was Globerman's decision late that fall to bar one of Hill's witnesses, a jailhouse informant named Ramon Rodriguez (a pseudonym). In prison for a 1987 homicide, Rodriguez had advised the Bronx DA's office in early September that he had information about several Cowboy murders and that he wanted to cooperate in exchange for help with his sentence. On October 22 Garry Dugan and Mark Tebbens drove up to Attica State Prison, where they debriefed Rodriguez for nearly five hours. Among other tidbits, Rodriguez informed the detectives that he'd been incarcerated at Rikers Island earlier in the year, and while there had run into Platano, who'd told him about his involvement in the Quad. A few weeks later, HIU arranged for Rodriguez to be brought into their offices for further interviews, and he was transferred once more to Rikers Island, where he was accidently thrown together again with Platano and his associates, generating further statements about their illegal activities.

Hill wanted to call Rodriguez as a witness to testify about these statements, but the defense objected, claiming that once the authorities had made a deal with Rodriguez, he'd become their de facto agent, and under terms of the so-called Massiah law, should not have been speaking to their clients without disclosing his status. Hill argued that no deal had been offered Rodriguez, much less struck, and that Rodriguez had talked to the defendants on his own initiative. Globerman ruled in favor of the defense.

In fact, Rodriguez, a convicted murderer whose interests were clearly served by implicating the Cowboys, was never going to be a strong witness. Far more troubling to Hill were pending defense objections aimed at the heart of his case. Hill wanted to introduce testimony that tied the defendants to the Red-Top drug operation, as a way of explaining why they shot their victims. Their lawyers argued that Hill didn't need to show motive to get a conviction, that the defendants were not being tried for drug or gang-related crimes, and that making them out to be members of a drug gang would unduly prejudice jurors against them. By the end of the year, Globerman still hadn't ruled on the issue, but Hill got the impression that he would disallow any reference at trial to Red-Top's activities.

Nevertheless, Hill was willing to take his chances in court. He wasn't daunted by the legal aspects of the case. If Globerman continued to rule against him, he even had contingency plans to reindict the case on conspiracy charges, a strategy that would allow him to introduce evidence pertaining not only to the Cowboys' drug operation but to other crimes as well. Rather, it was events taking place outside the courtroom that were eating at Hill.

BY NOVEMBER, more than six months had passed since the Cruz-Morales family had vacated their Beekman Avenue home in the dead of night and entered the city's shelter system. A lot had happened since then, not much of it good. The children, uprooted from their schools, had fallen behind in their studies and lost what little sense of structure and discipline they'd known before their exile. And the entire family was cut off from the network of friends and relatives centered in the neighborhood where they'd spent all their lives. Meanwhile, Elizabeth's closest brother suffered a fatal heart attack, brought on, she was convinced, by their travails at the hands of the Cowboys. And then, of course, Michael had been shot and nearly killed.

No less troubling to Elizabeth was the disintegration of family life. Never easy to control, her brood seemed to be spinning off in separate directions. Tebbens recalls an occasion when he brought them take-out for dinner. Each of the children grabbed a portion and skulked to a different part of the apartment to eat. The idea of sharing a meal didn't seem to occur to them.

Tebbens tried to check the family's dissolution. He visited them as often as he could, worked tirelessly to normalize their living conditions, and counseled the children in everything from grooming and etiquette to life skills and safe sex. But the constant moving, the anomie and isolation, and the ever-present fear of reprisal militated against his efforts.

Then, on November 9, while shopping at a supermarket near the Newburgh motel where she was hiding out with her family, Elizabeth Morales was accosted by two Dominican men. Approaching her from the rear, they told her not to look back, and one man put a knife to her throat and walked her out of the store to a patch of woods by the roadside. Morales was convinced she was going to die. Yet she kept her eyes forward and made no effort to struggle against her captors. The whole foolish enterprise—running from the Cowboys, informing on them—had been useless. When they were out of sight of the road, the men told her to stop, and one of them, reaching around her, shoved a series of photographs in front of her. It was nearly dusk, and a thin, wintry light filtered through the bare branches of the trees; still she could make out the worn, familiar images of her family, photographs that had been stolen from her Brooklyn apartment a few months ago. "We know what your children look like," the man was saying. "If you talk to the police, we will kill them all."

The men let Morales go, but the incident left her badly shaken. Coming on top of Michael Cruz's shooting and Raymond Jimenez' slashing, it convinced Hill he didn't have the manpower to guarantee the safety of his witnesses. Even Tebbens, frustrated by the DA's squad's lack of interest in his investigation, had transferred back to the Four-Oh and begun catching other cases.

Hill did what he could. He compiled a list of the incidents of witness intimidation and made ex parte reports to Globerman; and he prevailed on the judge to conduct sealed hearings and issue protective orders. But he realized that sooner or later the Cowboys would deduce the identities of the witnesses they didn't already know, and that one more serious reprisal would send them all fleeing for cover.

13

COLLARED

WINTER 1992–93

D O N   H I L L had always tried to separate his professional and per-sonal lives. He rarely discussed his cases with his wife, Janelle, a 32-year-old software consultant, and never in front of his daughters, Katie, four, and Ellen, two. If he brought home work—cases to read, briefs to prepare—he waited until after the children had gone to bed before get-ting started.

Hill lived on West 110th Street near Columbia University in a turn-of-the-century two-bedroom apartment. Most evenings, he man-aged to get home by 6 P.M., when he would shower, change into sweat pants and a T-shirt, and play with his daughters until his wife returned from late rounds of food shopping. Dinner was a ritual in the Hill household. Hill and his wife rarely ate out; they made a point of sitting down with the girls over a home-cooked meal. "We were trying to impose our own ethos on Manhattan," Hill says. "We were trying to create a slower, more easy life."

Lately, however, that had become impossible to do. The extremes of the Quad case—the attacks on witnesses, the legal morass, the chilling particulars of the crime itself—simply didn't chime with the rest of his life. He couldn't fully decompress when he came home to his children, and he felt raw and emotional when he returned to work the next morning.

The day he prepped Chico Puentes, Tebbens' first eyewitness to the Quad, marked a turning point in Hill's handling of the case. A small-time hustler, Chico had made a deal to cooperate, then disappeared after Platano stuck a gun in his mouth and dry-fired it repeatedly. He resurfaced after Platano's arrest, and Tebbens held him to his promise to testify in the upcoming trial. Hill, however, wasn't thrilled to see Puentes. He made a poor witness. A street kid with a record and an attitude, he was often contrary, and Hill couldn't understand half of what he was saying. It took the prosecutor nearly an hour to get him to listen to his questions.

Still, Hill felt sorry for him. They spent most of the morning going over Puentes' childhood—his alcoholic and abusive mother, the way he'd slip out onto the fire escape to avoid beatings. He hadn't had much of a chance. Slight, no more than five-five or five-six, with sallow skin, pouty lips, and a crew cut, Puentes was hardly twenty, although his face looked forty from the wear of street life.

At lunchtime, Hill ordered Puentes a sandwich, then raced by subway to his elder daughter's school in upper Manhattan, arriving just in time to see her in her Christmas pageant. The contrast between Chico's childhood recollections and the soft-lit, innocent faces in front of him jabbed at Hill.

In the afternoon Hill and Puentes sorted through the Quad. No matter how many times Hill heard the story, it still got to him, and

Puentes had a way of using body language to make the details even more graphic. That day he acted out the narrative, cocking his hand as if it were a pistol, jamming it under Hill's chin in imitation of the fatal shootings. At times like that, Hill had no trouble imagining Chico in Platano's or Stanley Tukes's place.

That night, Hill pursued his usual routine at home. He showered off the Bronx; changed into sweats; boiled water for spaghetti; and read to his daughters. But even as he undertook these simple, prayer-like tasks, images of the day's events kept cycling through his thoughts: Chico's grimacing face as he reenacted the Quad, the victims—Cynthia Casado lying in the street, clutching a vial of crack like a vanished dream; Manuel Vera crumpled in a doorway, shot fourteen times—and Chico again, younger now, huddled in the alley behind his apartment, waiting out the wrath of his mother.

Hill's elder daughter, Katie, was pressed against his back, and Ellie stretched out on the floor, absorbed in the exploits of Pat the Bunny; but Hill was thinking about Chico, peeling back layers of his short rude life, imagining him as a child, a teenager. That made him think about the Cruz-Morales boys, Joey and Michael—were they any different now than Chico had been at their age? And how great a leap was it from Chico to Nelson or Lenny? The lines among them blurred. Where do you reach the point where a troubled kid becomes a danger-ous adult? Who's responsible? More important, how do you fix it?

Hill had no answers to these questions, the same ones he'd been asking in one form or another since becoming a prosecutor. But now they'd invaded the calm and privacy of his home, the world he'd built to cushion his children—and himself, he realized—from the rig-ors of his work. The case was spinning beyond his control. And so he made a decision that night he knew would derail the trial.

Hill filed a motion that asked the court to take extraordinary measures to shield the identities of his witnesses—to allow them to testify anonymously, in some instances with masks on and voices disguised. His papers described a clear pattern of witness intimidation by the Cowboys, implicating some of the defendants' lawyers in the gang's campaign. Benjamin Green, the brother of one of the victims in the case, the motion noted, had recanted his statements to police in the offices of one of Stanley Tukes's lawyers and Hill's papers charged that one of Platano's attorneys was the suspected go-between in a $15,000 bribe offer made to another witness, Janice Bruington.

Hill understood that the motion would effectively disqualify some of the defendants' lawyers from litigating the case—indeed the impugned lawyers immediately resigned—and delay the start of the trial for at least several months. Moreover, he knew that his office barely had the resources to protect his witnesses now, and that any substantial postponement would force him to reach out for help from another agency, HIU or perhaps even the Feds. But he felt a responsibility to make the strongest argument possible on behalf of those witnesses who wished to remain anonymous in order to ensure their safety.

The day after Hill filed the motion, he and Ed Freedenthal journeyed to Manhattan to meet with HIU to discuss joining forces and enfolding the Quad in HIU's conspiracy case.

The meeting between the two boroughs' DAs went smoothly. Arsenault gave Hill and Freedenthal HIU's pitch, but the Bronx prosecutors had already decided to throw in their lot with the unit. Nor did they require written agreements, memos, or detailed discussions of procedure. Having met with Arsenault several times during the investigation, they had been impressed by his candor and expertise. They merely wanted to make sure that the Bronx would be an equal partner in the case and that the Quad would not be given short shrift in favor of Cargill. In particular, they wanted guarantees that Fat Danny and Pasqualito would be locked up at the first opportunity. That they were roaming free in the Bronx was an affront to Hill, as well as a grave risk to his witnesses.

Arsenault, for his part, was happy to agree to the Bronx's conditions—terms that seemed more than reasonable under the circumstances. Despite HIU's attempts to link the Cowboys' illegal activities to Manhattan, it was now clear that the gang operated outside the unit's normal jurisdiction. In fact, with the exception of Cargill and the two Brooklyn shootings, virtually all the violent crimes in the case, as well as the crack sales, had occurred in the Bronx. "If [Hill and Freedenthal] hadn't come to us, I doubt there would have been a Cowboy case," Arsenault says. "If we had tried to do the conspiracy without them, we wouldn't have had any overt acts, and we wouldn't have had the leverage to flip the people we did."

With the Bronx on board, HIU's investigation ballooned. Overnight their case gained six homicides, and they inherited a wealth of new informants and witnesses. But Arsenault, looking ahead, was troubled. In previous cases, he'd learned the importance of locking up main targets—the so-called must-haves—as early as possible. The timing of these arrests was always tricky. Move too soon and you risked tipping your hand to the rest of the gang and scuttling an investigation prematurely. Wait too long, however, and the leaders might get wary and take off. The last thing you wanted to do was try a gang's low- and mid-level workers without their bosses. But of the Cowboys' hierarchy, only Platano was in jail. All the other leaders were at large and in a position to flee. Nelson, according to several CIs, had already absconded to the Dominican Republic and was not expected to return. Fat Danny and Pasqualito were out on bail and, at least for the moment, untouchable. And Lenny, who was in the city *and* wanted on several charges—the Double and Michael Cruz's shooting among them—had so far eluded the authorities.

Cowboy investigators had been tracking Lenny throughout the fall and early winter. They'd set up surveillance on Cypress Avenue in the Bronx, where he'd last been seen fleeing from Tebbens; on the West 171st Street block in Manhattan, where his family lived and the gang occasionally hung out; and at a luxury apartment building near Shea Stadium in Queens, where, according to an informant, Lenny was living with his wife and daughter. But Lenny knew he was being hunted and took evasive measures. He rarely went out, avoided old haunts when he did, and mediated his calls through a trusted lieutenant.

Then, at noon on February 4, Lenny took everyone by surprise.

"THEY JUST CALLED from the courtroom," Dan Rather yelled over to Quinn. "Lenny's there. Let's go, let's go." Rather was poised at the entrance to the squad room, his jacket half on. Quinn didn't ask him for details. He knew that Lenny, along with Pasqualito, had been scheduled to appear in court that day—in a gun case stemming from their August 4 car chase with Anti-Crime cops in the Three-Four. And Quinn was reasonably sure that Lenny's lawyer had told Lenny he could get the charges against him dismissed, if Lenny would just appear. Still, Quinn hadn't expected Lenny to actually show up at the Criminal Courts building. He'd spent the last six months dodging the police, and he'd ignored a series of court dates leading up to now.

But then Quinn hadn't reckoned with Lenny's disdain for the system.

Although Lenny knew that Bronx detective Mark Tebbens was after him, possibly for the Quad or the Brooklyn shooting of Michael Cruz, he had no idea that Manhattan was tracking him as well. In Lenny's experience, the police were parochial and almost blindly bureaucratic. They seemed to have little knowledge of, and even less interest in, what happened in the next precinct over, much less in another borough. For years Lenny and his cohorts had tilted with law enforcement, tendering false identities, as Platano did in New Jersey, and employing lawyers schooled in the vagaries of the system; and the authorities had rarely connected the obvious dots in the gang's records to discover the true nature and extent of their criminal activities. And he had no reason to believe the police were about to now. As far as he knew, the Three-Four cops who'd arrested him on the gun charge were ignorant of his operation on Beekman Avenue, and neither Lenny nor his lawyer suspected that Rather, who was handling the gun case, had any interest in Lenny beyond that charge. Ironically, Lenny felt safer from arrest in Manhattan Criminal Court than he did on the streets of the Bronx. This time, however, he'd miscalculated.

Sitting with Pasqualito, his co-defendant, in the gallery, Lenny noticed several court officers eye them. When Pasqualito stood up to use the bathroom, one of them waved him back down, announcing that the courtroom was temporarily closed. Lenny confided his suspicions to Pasqualito, and as soon as the bailiff turned his back, they scrambled out to the hall. With several officers in pursuit, they headed toward the south stairwell. As Pasqualito hustled down to the lobby, Lenny, surmising that the cops would follow Pasqualito, ascended to the third floor.

Meanwhile Quinn, accompanied by his case officer, Bobby Tarwacki, and another investigator, hurried after Rather, past banks of geriatric elevators, down thirteen flights of stairs to the second-floor courtroom where Lenny had been spotted. He wasn't there. Cursing, Quinn ran over to the mezzanine railing and, looking down, saw a commotion at the south end of the lobby. A phalanx of white-shirted officers were leading a burly young man back into the building. Quinn and Tarwacki met them at the head of the stairs and checked out their prisoner. "That's Pasqualito," Tarwacki told the officers. "You can let *him* go."

"Shit, where's fucking Lenny?" Quinn said, certain they'd lost him again. He began checking the building exits.

"He's up there," Tarwacki shouted. Quinn followed Tarwacki's eyes to the mezzanine and glimpsed Lenny limping along the railing. A blue neoprene cast extended the length of his leg, a souvenir, no doubt, from his scuffle with Tebbens in August. Quinn and his men bolted back up the stairs, mounting the steps two, three at a time.

Lenny was trapped. As soon as he'd exited on the third floor, he'd begun looking for a way out. He knew he only had moments before the officers caught Pasqualito and began looking for him. He'd hobbled past the elevators on his left—too slow—then headed for the stairwell at the opposite end of the hall. He'd planned to double back to the mezzanine, check out the lobby, and if the way was clear, escape through the portals at the north end of the building. He'd got as far as the second-floor landing when an alert officer spotted him and began herding him back toward the courtroom he'd just escaped.

Tarwacki got to Lenny first, pushed him brusquely against the wall, and began cuffing him. A moment later Quinn was at Lenny's other side, and it was all over. When Quinn saw Lenny's lawyer striding toward them from the courtroom, and felt Lenny stiffen, he decided to send the gang leader a message. Crooking his knuckle into the shape of a gun barrel, he slipped it between Lenny's buttocks. "I ain't playing wit' you," Quinn whispered into Lenny's ear. "If you try to run, I'll blow your nuts off."

IN ALL HER YEARS at the Brooklyn DA's, her colleagues had rarely seen Lori Grifa take a step backward. She worked punishing hours, took every case that came her way, and never let herself be intimidated.

Strikingly attractive with raven hair, smooth olive skin, and a lithe, athletic body, she leavened even her harshest attacks with an easy, knowing humor. "Lori takes her cases seriously," Dawn Adelson, Grifa's former trial partner at the DA's office, says. "Not herself."

Still, Grifa's hard-charging style had earned her her share of detractors. They viewed her candor as aggression, her exuberance as ambition; and it didn't help that she had a knack for cultivating mentors among the male-dominated senior staff.

But none of her colleagues doubted her abilities as a prosecutor. She was a shrewd assessor of cases who knew when to cut her losses and take a plea, and for all her feistiness, was cool and precise in front of a jury. "She wasn't a showboat," says Joseph Alexis, who later

worked with her in the Homicide Bureau. "She didn't try to be spontaneous or to turn a fancy phrase. She relied on preparation."

Nobody outworked Grifa. She switched on the office lights at
the start of the day and flicked them off well after dark. But it was her
activities outside the office that distinguished her. Grifa learned early
on in her tenure that police were a scarce resource at the DA's office. In
the Police Department's view, once an officer had made an arrest in a
case, his job was done. What happened after that was the prosecutor's
responsibility. The problem with this kind of assembly-line justice was
that the standard of proof needed for an arrest was often shy of the
standard required for a conviction, and some cops, trained to get violent subjects off the street as quickly as possible, played a forensic version of *Name That Tune*: I can arrest this guy on just two scraps of
evidence. Just getting a cop into court to testify could be a struggle for
an ADA, much less getting him to enhance your case or track down a
reluctant witness. Even when cops wanted to help out—and the good
ones almost always did—their supervisors were not cooperative. Police
don't get credit for convictions, only arrests, and a cop working on a
case that's already been cleared is a cop not out clearing new cases.

Grifa began doing her own legwork. She visited crime scenes,
canvassed witnesses, was a regular at precinct houses that didn't see
many prosecutors. She was gathering new evidence and additional testimony, but she was also breathing life into her cases, getting them off
the page—attaching faces to names in affidavits, giving sounds and
smells to neighborhoods seen only on maps or in photographs, making sense out of the convoluted logic and improbable passions that lay
beneath the surface of many crimes. And when the cops saw her taking
an active interest in their investigations, they found ways of helping
her out.

But Grifa's strongest suit, according to Geoff Kern, a fellow
prosecutor, was her "urban mentality"—her instinctive feel for all
kinds of people and her ability to communicate with them. No one
was better, Kern says, at picking a jury, and she had a way of express-

ing herself—confident, straightforward—that made them respond. Equally important, she knew how to reach the witnesses, victims and cooperators—many of them poor and uneducated, street people who were skittish about any contact with the system.

In early February, Grifa got an urgent phone call from HIU's Dan Rather. Rather told her he'd just arrested the unindicted perpetrator in one of her cases, a gang leader named Lenny Sepulveda. Sepulveda, Rather informed her, had been one of the gunmen who'd fired shots at Michael Cruz, the government witness who had nearly been killed. Then Rather explained why he was calling. The yearlong conspiracy investigation he was working on was still months away from the grand jury, and the other charges against Sepulveda—a four-year-old double homicide in the Bronx and a weak gun case—were not enough to keep him in jail. He needed Grifa to draw up a warrant for the Cruz shooting.

Grifa was backed up with work at the time, and the case had little meaning for her. On paper Cruz's shooting looked like a typical drug-related dispute; Cruz, after all, had been arrested twice for crack dealing. But Grifa told Rather to send over a detective with the paperwork and she would write up a complaint. It was a courtesy among prosecutors, and Rather had conveyed a sense of urgency, the excitement of a big Manhattan homicide investigation that required, in some small way, her services. But Grifa certainly had no idea when she put down the phone that her career was about to change.

THE INVESTIGATION gained momentum through the winter and into spring, each new break leading to other valuable sources of information. Almost every week, prospective witnesses turned up for interviews at HIU. The Cruz-Morales family members were still the hub of the case. They had detailed, firsthand knowledge of the gang's drug operation, had witnessed each phase of the Quad from planning and preparation to execution, and they could link Lenny, as well as

Pasqualito and Victor Mercedes, to the Double. Michael had seen Lenny shooting at one of the victims as he tried to get away in a hijacked car, and the gang leader had ordered Elizabeth Morales to stash the gun he'd used in her apartment.

But the Cruz-Morales family members were not alone on HIU's prospective witness list. With Nelson in the Dominican Republic, and Platano and Lenny in jail, Tebbens had been able to coax several Quad witnesses—including Chico Puentes and Benjamin Green, who had recanted their original statements—into cooperating once more. Meanwhile, HIDTA's detectives produced a handful of low-level workers who had witnessed a spate of Cowboy shootings and stabbings that Rather and Quinn were tracking.

But what continued to surprise the investigators was what they didn't know, the staggering number of shootings, assaults, and rapes that went unreported because of the victims' fear or cynicism. Chico Puentes told Quinn about the skirmish that took place in the fall of 1991 when a rival gang headed by drug kingpin George Calderon invaded Beekman Avenue. As two carloads of gunmen pulled up in front of the Hole, Lenny recruited neighborhood youngsters to defend the block, supplying them with automatic weapons and promising to pay them $150 each for their services.

More often, gang members directed their violence against the community. When the elderly owner of a local bodega refused to extend their credit, three Cowboy thugs, including Quad suspect Daniel Gonzalez, broke into the cash register, then set fire to the store and broke all the windows with pipes.

But the gang reserved its fiercest savagery for its own. Cowboy managers routinely disciplined their workers by crushing their knuckles with a brick. Repeat offenders were gouged, stabbed, shot, or molested. Twenty-two-year-old Martha Molina was typical of a group of women employed by the gang. Crack-addicted and destitute, Molina began pitching for the Cowboys in 1990 as a way of supporting her habit. Molina performed her chores reliably, but in the spring of 1992, her spot manager decided that she had shorted the count—withheld receipts—and smashed her face with a gun butt. Later he discovered he'd made a mistake in his calculations, but by then it was too late. Molina developed a blood clot near her eye, slipped into a monthlong coma, and woke up blind. She recovered her sight, but only bits and pieces of her memory.

She did recall her assault, however, and described it in some detail to Quinn. Molina considered herself lucky; under similar circumstances, she said, Cowboy enforcers dragged another worker into St. Mary's Park, raped her, beat her, and stuffed twigs and dirt into her vagina. Lulu, a pitcher for the gang and the girlfriend of a Cowboy manager known as Rob Base, was a bystander in 1990 when Fat Danny Rincon got into a dispute with a motorist on Cypress Avenue. When Rincon fired wildly at the driver, Lulu was hit in the head. She recovered eventually, but later, while she was pregnant with Rob Base's child, Nelson shot her in the leg for tampering with Red-Top's product.

What was most troubling to the DAs was the way the victims told their stories and their depiction of the brutal character of life at the bottom rungs of the gang's organization. "In any conspiracy case of any scope you deal with crimes you feel you can prove and crimes you can't prove but feel happened," Hill says. "That first set of crimes—those are the bones and tendons and sinew of your case. Those other crimes, the ones you can't prove or that don't rise to the level of a felony, are the case's flesh—the penumbra, what in legal terms we call the surrounding circumstances. That's what we were getting into during that period, and the chilling aspect of that was that these stories came out so matter-of-factly, so routinely, not because they were traumatic or devastating—although they were—but because they weren't isolated or extraordinary. What made the Cowboy case unique was the stuff we left out—the crimes that would have been major crimes in another case, but that had never been reported, and then barely mentioned, because there was no expectation on the part of the victims that anything would be done about them, or that if they did say something, they would just get hurt again."

And Hill felt that their expectations had been justified. What would have changed for the people of Beekman Avenue had he tried the Quad murders in the Bronx? Even if he'd been able to protect his witnesses, even if he'd won convictions in that case, the Cowboys would have continued to operate the Hole, a new generation of enforcers would have replaced Platano, Stanley Tukes, and the other defendants, and the murders and beatings would have gone on unabated. Worse perhaps for the neighborhood's law-abiding families, so too would the muggings and harassment, the petty theft and rampant drug abuse that multiplied in the margins of gang violence. But now working alongside Rather, Arsenault, and Quinn, with ample resources and a plan to lock up the entire gang, Hill felt for the first time as though he was able to make a difference.

14

DISSENSION

IN FEBRUARY, two days after Walter Arsenault's wife delivered their second child, the jury in the Gheri Curl trial handed down its verdict—guilty on all counts. HIU's first big conspiracy case had culminated in a landmark victory and vindicated a long, resource-intensive investigation. Arsenault didn't realize how complete HIU's triumph had been until sentencing six weeks later. Judge Leslie Crocker Snyder, appalled by the gang's wanton murders, parceled out prison terms of more than 100 years to most of the defendants; Rafi Martinez, the organization's leader, got 213 years. "Bowling-score sentences," Arsenault thought, sitting stunned in the front of the courtroom.

News of the verdict spread through the streets and prisons and sent a powerful message to potential cooperators. Lenny was in the holding pens behind Snyder's courtroom when Martinez' sentence was announced, and he spoke to the gang leader immediately after. It was a moment he wouldn't forget.

For years Manhattan DA Robert Morgenthau had been out front in the battle against Manhattan's violent drug gangs: HIU had been his shock troops. But their previous successes had barely won a nod from the media. The Gheri Curl case was different, however—because of its size and the conspiracy format that allowed prosecutors to tell a story, to weave together the gang's many acts of violence and the details of their culture into a rich, gripping narrative. The press seized on images of the gang's uniform permed hairstyles and their identically gold-painted cars, and ran stories throughout the trial, as well as its dramatic conclusion.

Buoyed by the Gheri Curl verdict, pumped up with new resources, HIU seemed possessed by a spirit of unlimited possibilities. Earlier in the year, Morgenthau had asked Arsenault to list the gangs operating in Manhattan, and Arsenault had sat down with Fernando Camacho, Terry Quinn, and Ellen Corcella, a veteran prosecutor who handled the unit's American black and Puerto Rican targets, and literally mapped out the whole of Harlem and the Heights and the Lower East Side, law enforcement's first encyclopedic look at gang activity in the borough—some 150 organizations from small street-corner crews to big supply and retail outfits with multiple outlets and ranges of several blocks. It was a template for action, and Camacho for one was chipping away at the whole—167th Street, 155th, 156th, 159th; the Gheri Curls, Super King Bodega, Diamedis, Los Brothers, La Compania; one investigation bleeding into the next.

In years past the unit trucked along one big case at a time, and that case would be broken down into smaller cases—a gang's leader, his top lieutenants, hit men, managers; one murder here, a double homicide there, an assault, a drug sale. HIU consisted of William Hoyt and maybe one assistant, Arsenault tackling the Jamaicans, and just a handful of detectives spread out among them. Now Arsenault would walk through the unit on a busy morning and there would be seven, eight prosecutors and twice as many police, including the detectives from HIDTA and the precinct cops who were working on joint cases, or who'd come in to interrogate prisoners or just trade information; the offices would be humming, alive with the din of the squad room and the clap of male laughter; six, seven, eight investigations going at a time.

But the Cowboys had become the jewel in HIU's crown. With the Bronx and now Brooklyn on board, and given the size and complexity of the case, not to mention the sheer avalanche of violence, the Cowboy operation dwarfed the Gheri Curl investigation. And that didn't count Cuevas' gang or Ray Polanco, El Feo or Freddy Krueger, or the whole pantheon of drug lords and killers who orbited Lenny's world. Arsenault found himself coming into work with the same enthusiasm and sense of anticipation that he'd felt as a young prosecutor in Bergen County.

But not everyone was so exhilarated.

Despite progress in the case, Dan Rather was becoming increasingly uncomfortable about his role in the investigation. He'd never quite forgiven Arsenault and Quinn for the way he felt they'd foisted HIDTA on him a year ago, a decision that continued to haunt him through the spring. HIDTA's detectives had been instrumental in building a strong surveillance case against the Cowboys; they'd engineered the raid that had netted Louise McBride; and they'd made scattered small buys into the gang's sellers at the Hole and other nearby locations. In May, a HIDTA undercover had worked his way into the graces of Rennie Harris, one of Lenny's top managers, and busted him for a 300-vial sale, enough to charge him with a top felony. But to Rather's thinking, HIDTA had been too cautious in their investigation; Benitez and his CO, Charles Rorke, had never authorized as many buys as Rather had been pushing them to, and it was only thanks to Quinn's intervention that they'd undertaken the Harris bust. By then Rather's communications with Rorke were barely civil.

But it was his relations with Arsenault and Quinn that troubled Rather most. Rather had felt Arsenault to be personally chilly, almost unapproachable, from the start, and his sense of estrangement had deepened with time. Rather got on better with Quinn; the demands of the investigation forced them into close daily contact, and they had a good working relationship for the most part. But Rather viewed Quinn as Arsenault's man, someone he couldn't trust or control.

Rather's resentment toward Quinn flared up in the spring over an incident that he would later term "the single most outrageous act he'd witnessed during his career in law enforcement." Until then he'd felt Quinn had been merely difficult, producing some witnesses when he didn't want to see them, continuing to prepare others after he'd decided not to use them. But now he felt that Quinn was deliberately challenging his authority in a matter of vital importance.

Rather had knowledge that Lenny, then in jail, was calling his lieutenants at the apartment of Blue Eyes—Garry Dugan's Washington Heights informant—and issuing orders to the gang. Rather wanted to wiretap the phone line, feeling that the taped conversations would "kill all the top leaders."

Quinn balked at the idea, however. He reminded Rather of HIU's policy against wiretapping. It was too costly; the unit simply didn't have the manpower. Besides, Quinn pointed out, the case against Lenny was already formidable; the unit's resources could better be used in other ways.

Rather discounted Quinn's objections. He knew that Quinn had never used taps, and felt—as did others in the unit—that he was biased against the technology because he didn't understand how it worked. What's more, Rather felt he should have had the last word. Though HIU's DA's almost always deferred to detectives over tactical issues involving the street, its cases were prosecutor-driven. The DAs shaped the unit's investigations to fit their trial strategy. So Rather was shocked when he learned that Quinn had either directly or indirectly informed Blue Eyes of the proposed tap, effectively sabotaging Rather's plan.

But the situation appears to have been more complicated than that. In addition to his usual objections to using phone taps, Quinn was concerned about Blue Eyes' safety. He says he discussed the matter with Dugan, who convinced him that if the recorded conversations became evidence, they could cost Blue Eyes his life; and that he may have advised Dugan to alert Blue Eyes to the danger he was facing.

Dugan adds another perspective to the events. He clearly recalls telling Rather the plan was fraught with unacceptable risks, and that Rather himself informed Blue Eyes about the wire tap in order to secure his cooperation. In contrast, Rather points out that with a warrant Blue Eyes' consent would have been unnecessary, but Blue Eyes confirms that Rather called him to get him on board. It was only then, Dugan says, that he took it upon himself to apprise Blue Eyes, whom he felt had been insufficiently warned by Rather, of the substantial risks involved.

These kind of arguments are all too common in law enforcement. Strong personalities, highly subjective decisions, and life-and-death stakes are a recipe for disagreement. Indeed all these elements, along with an apparent breakdown in communication, played a part in the current case. Rather felt that the tap was an invaluable investigative tool that could ultimately save lives, and that "under even the highly unlikely worst-case scenario, involving revelation to the gang of the existence and basis of the wiretap," Blue Eyes would not be in jeopardy. "On the contrary, it would protect [Blue Eyes] by creating the impression that [he] was an investigative target." Quinn, Dugan, and Tebbens, who was also party to the discussions, strongly disagreed. They felt the tapes would inevitably become part of discovery, and that the gang— known to kill on the slightest of suspicions—wouldn't require proof to retaliate against Blue Eyes. But regardless of the merits, Rather felt that

Quinn had unilaterally countermanded his decision to use electronic surveillance, and once again apparently good intentions led to bitter feelings among the principals in HIU's investigation.

Much of Rather's frustration at that time may have been rooted in Arsenault's management style. Arsenault treated his assistants as colleagues, giving them wide latitude in their cases, rarely interfering with their day-to-day tactics, unless asked. He also kept a sharp eye on how things were going through daily briefings by Quinn and through his own quiet wanderings about the office—listening in to his detectives' conversations or even riffling through reports on a prosecutor's desk. But Rather interpreted Arsenault's arm's-length approach to supervision as indifference to his case, and had begun to solicit the guidance and support of Trial Division chief Nancy Ryan, with whom he shared a close, personal friendship.

Such an occurrence was not unprecedented. As handpicked professionals, Morgenthau's assistants viewed the chain of command with a good deal less reverence than, say, their counterparts in the police. And as Trial chief Ryan had the authority to take command over any of her division's cases, a prerogative she exercised from time to time in big press cases like the Cowboys. In other instances, she took a personal interest in the attorney handling the case. Ryan had mentored Ellen Corcella's career at the DA's office, for example, and continued to monitor her cases after Corcella joined HIU. In fact, as Arsenault's boss, Ryan was expected to oversee the unit's cases in a general way.

Nonetheless, members of HIU were shocked that a relative newcomer to the unit like Rather would try to short-circuit Arsenault's instructions or that Ryan would interpose herself between Arsenault and an investigation he was actively supervising. What's more, neither Arsenault nor Quinn knew about her growing involvement in the case or her consultations with Rather.

The fact was that Arsenault, so perceptive about the behavior and psychology of suspects in criminal investigations, could be remarkably guileless about what was going on in his own office. He had no idea that Rather was nursing grievances toward him, much less that he'd confided them to Ryan, or that Ryan might be sympathetic to them. In fact, Arsenault regarded Ryan, rightly, as having been HIU's, and indeed his own, greatest champion. It was Ryan who had built up the unit, who had stocked it with her favorite DAs, including Arsenault, and who had guided its progress, and his, through the political thickets on the eighth floor. Ryan was a constant visitor to the unit, and Arsenault stopped in at her eighth-floor office almost daily after his lunchtime run to update her on the latest developments. "Nancy was more than just a friend and supporter of Walter," recalls Barbara Jones, Morgenthau's chief of staff at that time. "She made him."

Thus the stage was set for a blowup between Arsenault and Rather. Rather was likely to perceive any attempt at intervention by Arsenault as arbitrary and ill informed, and Arsenault was just as likely to be galled by Rather's efforts to bring Ryan in to mediate their differences. Moreover, both men were proud, at times uncommunicative, and stubborn in their convictions.

Arsenault got his first inkling that things were not as he expected on one of his post-jog visits to Ryan's office in late spring. Arsenault had been venting some of his concerns in the Cowboy case. Rather, he told Ryan, had at times been unavailable to the witnesses, shutting himself in his office, saying he was too busy to see them when they came to ask him for some favor, or just to talk about the case. Normally this kind of thing wasn't troubling; the witnesses in most of the unit's cases were cooperators, felons and former gang members who were testifying in exchange for leniency. But HIU had no leverage over most of the key witnesses in this case; many of them were victims or bystanders, and many had been threatened or offered bribes not to testify. They were also street people, like the Cruz-Morales family—frightened and thin-skinned, with tenuous connections to the legal system. They needed to be stroked, to have their hands held.

But Ryan's response brought Arsenault up short. She told him that the problem was Terry Quinn, who had a habit of producing witnesses at times that Rather told him were inconvenient. Arsenault, she said, was overreacting and should leave Rather alone. He knew what he was doing. This advice struck Arsenault as odd, and not just because he felt his concern was genuine and needed to be addressed. In the past, Ryan had always chided him because his supervision was too lackadaisical and urged him to get more involved in his assistants' cases. "Suddenly I went from being too detached to being a micro-manager," Arsenault recalls.

Arsenault didn't think too much of the incident at the time. With the case slated to go to the grand jury for indictment at the end of May, there were strategic issues of size and timing that needed to be re-solved. Arsenault wanted to cast as wide a net over the gang as possi-ble, then press the lower-echelon workers to cooperate against the leaders. Accordingly, he wanted to indict 40 to 50 gang members, nearly twice as many as in the Gheri Curl case; Tebbens and Dugan, who between them had spent years compiling dossiers on the Cow-boys and their associates, envisioned an indictment with even more than that.

But Rather seemed intent on narrowing the field to 20 to 30. In fact, unbeknownst to the unit, he'd begun pleading out gang members who'd been arrested on drug charges earlier in the investigation. When the detectives found out later that summer, they were furious and complained to Arsenault.

Even more controversial was the so-called must-haves list. In all its gang cases, HIU tried to arrest the leaders and most violent mem-bers early—in part to get them off the street, but also to prevent them from fleeing on the chance they got spooked by the investigation. This was especially true for Dominican gangs like the Cowboys, because the Dominican Republic, having no extradition treaty with the United States, provides fugitives with a relatively safe haven. Nelson was al-ready in the Dominican Republic, and Lenny and Platano were in jail, but Don Hill was eager to apprehend Fat Danny, a defendant in the

Quad, who had managed to get free on bail and was rumored to be planning to abscond to the Dominican Republic. Hill was fuming that a predicate felon charged with four murders could be on the loose, and had made it a condition of the Bronx's joining HIU's case that they arrest Fat Danny at the earliest opportunity.

Arsenault and Quinn were also eager to nab Pasqualito, though for a different reason. Numerous informants had told Quinn that Pasqualito was extremely dangerous, that he had bragged to them that he would draw down on cops if they tried to arrest him. Quinn knew that Pasqualito had upcoming hearing dates in the Michael Cruz shooting case and wanted to arrest him in court, where he wouldn't be armed.

The problem was that there were no warrants outstanding on either Fat Danny or Pasqualito. So Arsenault and Hill wanted Rather to have the grand jury vote out a piece of the conspiracy indictment, and use it to arrest the two Cowboys.

Rather wasn't keen on the idea. Though he never told Hill he wouldn't arrest Fat Danny at an early date, it had taken until June—well over a year since Rather had begun his investigation—to get the case to the grand jury, and Fat Danny's indictment still seemed weeks away. Rather seemed even less enthusiastic about Pasqualito. He clearly felt that indicting both Fat Danny and Pasqualito would send the rest of the gang into hiding. And neither Rather nor Ryan, who sided with his position, felt that Pasqualito posed as grave a security risk as Quinn did. Sometime later when Quinn voiced his concerns about the dangers of taking Pasqualito in the open, Ryan told the fiery detective, "Why, Terry, I didn't think you were afraid of anything."

SITTING in the back of the van, Pasqualito hadn't seen Carlos work the clavo switches on the dashboard or noticed the hidden compartment open near his feet. When he looked down, he saw a trench full of automatic weapons, enough firepower to storm a small precinct. The large, heavyset man sitting across from him smiled.

"Anything happens," he said, pointing at the guns, "I'm behind you."

It was a warm June night, the last night of spring, and though it was past eleven, Broadway was crowded with people, men in shirt-sleeves and young women in shorts and tank tops. Pasqualito caressed the 9 mm pistol he'd been holding in his lap; he felt nervous and impatient, more so than usual before a hit. Tonight his target was a celebrity. His gallery included notables as well. Sitting beside him, his wheelchair angled toward Pasqualito, was El Feo, and next to El Feo, Freddy Krueger, the most feared killer in the Heights.

"There he is," Carlos said. Craning his neck, Pasqualito saw the Lincoln Town Car parked halfway up the block on their left, its passenger-side door open. Leaning into the door frame was the broad, unmistakable back of Frankie Cuevas.

Moments ago, at Pasqualito's hangout on West 171st Street, one of his men had told him that he'd spotted Cuevas visiting his girlfriend nearby. Jumping at the opportunity, Pasqualito flagged down El Feo and Krueger, who had business on the block, and the three of them set up the hit. Pasqualito armed himself with the 9 mm, donned a wig made of dreadlocks, and together they headed up Broadway in El Feo's van.

Carlos double-parked the van two cars down from the Lincoln, and Pasqualito slid open the side door and jumped down lightly into the street. He noted a white Chevy belonging to Cuevas' lieutenant Roberto Peralta parked behind the Lincoln, but Peralta was standing at the corner with another gang member some fifty feet away. There was nobody between Pasqualito and his target. Suddenly, as he crept up on the tail of the Lincoln and raised his gun in front of him, a young woman sprang out from behind Cuevas' hunched-over frame—a wraithlike figure—and darted around the front of the car. Cuevas' girlfriend, Patricia. Cuevas spun around to see what had spooked her.

Clad in a gray silk shirt, Frankie was huge, with a mountainous chest and fierce mustache. But it was his eyes that drew Pasqualito's gaze. They already seemed dead, frozen with the certain knowledge of what was about to happen. Pasqualito squeezed off the first shot.

Sitting behind the wheel of the Lincoln, Manny Guerrero whirled around a split second after Frankie. He recognized Pasqualito, saw his gun light up, and heard the shot all within the same broken fragment of time. He began searching frantically for the gun that he kept hidden under his seat. But it had slid out of easy reach, and Manny already realized there wasn't time. He heard the pops of gunfire—nine, ten—then, looking up, saw Frankie's body crumpled in the street and Pasqualito staring at him through the open door of the Lincoln.

Casually, almost as if in an afterthought, Pasqualito tossed a final shot into the car, splitting Guerrero's belly. The adrenaline was still coursing through him as he climbed into the back of the van. He let out a yell of jubilation as Carlos peeled out into the street, the side door still open, and when they got to the corner, fired several times into the air. Frankie Cuevas, Lenny's archrival and a legend among the gangs of Washington Heights, was dead, and he, Pasqualito, had killed him.

15

THE BLOWUP

SUMMER 1993

ARSENAULT was standing in front of Quinn's office in an alcove behind the squad room, feeling relaxed for the first time in weeks, when he saw Rather striding toward him, his face clenched, a document in hand. It was the last Monday in June, and he was waiting for Camacho and Dan Brownell, a homicide assistant who'd recently joined HIU. That afternoon the three of them had planned to drive down to the MAGLOCLEN Conference, a federally sponsored gang fighters' convention held each summer in Baltimore. It was a chance for Arsenault to talk shop with far-flung colleagues, showcase his unit's accomplishments for an appreciative audience, and knock back a few drinks in the evenings. But with Rather bearing down on him, he knew his getaway wasn't going to be pleasant.

Tensions had continued to run high between the two men since Rather had convened the special grand jury at the end of May. Even before the start of the proceedings, they sparred over the order of witnesses. Arsenault wanted to lead off with Terry Quinn to explain the nature of violent drug gangs and give jurors an overview of the case. Rather argued for Freddie Sendra, the former Cowboy gang member, now in prison for shooting at police. He felt Sendra could provide a picture of life inside the Cowboys that Quinn could only relate from hearsay. In the end, Rather deferred to Arsenault, but when the unit chief prompted Rather in the first session about another prosecutor's examination, Rather apparently complained to Ryan. According to Arsenault, Ryan told him to get off Rather's back. (Ryan denies saying anything to Arsenault.)

Arsenault had been stunned and felt that his advice was unwelcome at the hearings. Grand juries are the forums in which DAs obtain charges, in the form of indictments, against the targets in their investigations. But they're also a prosecutor's first chance to officially lay out his case, and thus provide a record and template for subsequent trials. How a DA decides to tell his story, from whose point of view, using what witnesses and what evidence, is important in a simple felony; in a big, complex conspiracy case like the Cowboys, it's vital. By admonishing Arsenault, Ryan had weakened one of his main supervisory functions.

But it was the fact of Ryan's intervention that troubled Arsenault more. Ryan had been his political mentor, his protector on the eighth floor. Who could he turn to now? Having to fence with an assistant over a tricky case was bad enough, but a poor relationship with Ryan could have a disastrous impact on the unit.

Through the spring, unit members had cautioned Arsenault about Rather's close relationship with Ryan. Rather had begun quoting

Ryan to Hill and Grifa as the case arbiter, even before Rather's dislike for Arsenault became known. With its long hours and insular culture, the DA's office was a kind of petri dish for gossip, and Arsenault had dismissed the warnings that his role as supervisor was being undercut. But now he was forced to take the problem seriously. He couldn't ignore the fact that the head of the Trial Division, his chief supporter, sided with one of his assistants over routine management issues.

For weeks Arsenault was gloomy, padding through the unit head down, shoulders slumped. "You could see physically he was beat-up," recalls Luke Rettler, the Asian Gang chief, who shared offices with HIU. "He'd drop by my office, plunk down on the sofa, and not say anything. I'd ask him how the case was going, and he'd say, 'Ask Nancy. It's her case now. I don't even get the grand jury minutes on time anymore; they go straight to the eighth floor.' "

But as so often happens in HIU's cases, events in the street soon overtook issues in the courtroom. Cuevas' homicide on June 20 jolted the unit, not only adding a bloody new execution to the case but ratcheting up the pressure on Rather to wrap up his investigation and take down the gang. Arsenault argued he couldn't afford to leave the Cowboys out on the street. Why wasn't he already indicting and arresting the gang's more violent members? Pasqualito himself was no longer an issue. Having executed Cuevas in front of several eyewitnesses, including Cuevas' bodyguard, Manny Guerrero, Pasqualito was rumored to have fled New York to the Dominican Republic, using the passport of one of his lieutenants. But in view of Pasqualito's actions, Don Hill was lobbying more intensively than ever for Fat Danny's arrest. If Pasqualito could kill and flee the country, so could Fat Danny.

Once again Arsenault and Rather were cast on opposite sides of the argument. Arsenault supported Hill's position, both on its merits and because HIU had promised Hill, as part of their deal with the Bronx, to get Fat Danny remanded at the earliest opportunity. What's more, Arsenault knew that Hill was under pressure from Ira Globerman, the Bronx Supreme Court judge handling the Quad, to issue a new indictment that would supersede the previous charges. Until then, the Quad would remain on Globerman's docket, and he would have to keep adjourning the case while the defendants languished in jail. Sooner or later, Hill argued and Arsenault agreed, Globerman was going to lose patience and let them go.

Rather doubted that would happen—after all, the defendants were murder suspects in a big press case—and he continued to conduct the grand jury investigation at a pace that struck Hill as irritatingly deliberate. Moreover, he resisted Hill's efforts to proceed against Fat Danny. On the one hand, Rather felt that Danny wasn't much of a flight risk: if he were intending to abscond, he would already have left. On the other, Rather didn't want to tip his hand to the gang's lawyers by voting out pieces of the indictment early and arresting gang members piecemeal.

Whatever the issues between Rather and Arsenault, their debates had begun to take on a nasty, political edge. Rather was convinced that Arsenault and Quinn were trying to wrest control of the case from him and take credit for work he had already done. But Arsenault had always applauded his assistants, regardless of the role he played in their cases. More important, the Cowboys had become HIU's biggest case. The unit had vast amounts of time and resources, not to mention prestige, invested in its outcome. To many working on the case, the efforts by Rather, a newcomer to the unit, to belittle Arsenault's advice was extraordinary.

Instead, their colleagues felt the disagreements between the two men were personal. Something about Arsenault—his brusqueness, his inscrutability—set Rather off and skewed even their most straightforward dealings. Rather claimed that Arsenault had simply been inaccessible to him, though other prosecutors in the unit had had the opposite experience. Whatever the reason, Rather developed a visceral dislike for his chief; and he seemed to physically recoil when Arsenault was in his presence. "The tension was escalating," Garry Dugan remembers. "If Mark and I were in Dan's office discussing the case and

Walter came in, Rather's attitude and demeanor would change. He didn't want to deal with Walter. If Walter would ask him, say, to change the indictment, it was like putting a knife down his throat."

Hill recalls one incident about that time that brought home to him how far things had gone. Hill had driven up to Columbia-Presbyterian with Rather and several investigators to videotape a Q & A with Manny Guerrero, recovering from the gunshot wound he'd received in the Cuevas shooting. It had been a difficult interview. Guerrero feared what would happen to himself and his family if he cooperated, and Hill had to coax him for twenty minutes—at one point literally holding his hand—before he'd allow Rather to question him. Rather got him to name Pasqualito as Cuevas' assassin, but perhaps in his haste to debrief Guerrero, he failed to have Guerrero identify Pasqualito by stating his real name or by picking him out of a photo array.

Back at the unit, when Arsenault reviewed the tape, he pointed out the oversight to Rather in front of the rest of the team. "This is legally insufficient," he said. "You're going to have to go back up there and do it again."

It was an obvious error, and Hill recognized it right away, admitting that he'd been distracted during the interview. But Rather bristled at Arsenault's criticism. Instead of simply owning up to his mistake, Rather played down its significance, according to Hill, forcing a heated exchange with Arsenault before grudgingly agreeing to redo the interview.

Others in the unit had noticed Rather's stubbornness. He was bright and good-looking with an undeniable charm, and his famous connection imbued him with an aura of glamour, all the more so because he downplayed it. But some colleagues thought it was an act. They felt the office had given him an easy ride, and that he'd exploited his status in subtle ways: taking extra time on an investigation, shying away from the courtroom, getting bumped up to a homicide unit without having tried a homicide. To his detractors—in and out of the unit—he seemed to radiate a sense of entitlement. He didn't take criticism well, he became defensive when challenged, and he had a bluff, arrogant streak that expressed itself at odd times, in marked contrast to his usually friendly, low-key demeanor.

None of that would have mattered, perhaps, had Arsenault been another kind of administrator, had he been more politic or indulgent, or had he reached out more strenuously to Rather at the start of his tenure. But Arsenault, though he was devoted to the unit, rarely socialized outside of work, wasn't demonstrative or tactful, and was quick to anger if he felt ambushed or betrayed, as he clearly did by Rather and Ryan.

Things came to a head on that Monday, June 28, the day Arsenault and other members of the unit were scheduled to leave for the MAGLOCLEN Conference. A few days earlier, Hill, tired of what he viewed as Rather's foot-dragging, had cobbled up a rough draft of an indictment against Fat Danny, the first step in his plan to take down the Cowboy leader early. Hill brought the draft to Arsenault, who approved it, then presented it to Rather. Hill says that Rather told him he was not going to attend the conference, and that they'd work on the indictment together and vote it out during the week when everyone was away.

Rather denies making such a commitment to Hill. In fact, he says he read the indictment over the weekend and hated it. That Monday, furious that Arsenault had authorized Hill's plan without consulting him, Rather decided to confront the unit chief. Brandishing Hill's indictment, he strode up to Arsenault, standing in front of Quinn's office. "Did you authorize this?" Rather asked, thrusting the document at Arsenault.

Arsenault, taken aback at Rather's vehemence, said he did.

"Who the hell are you making deals with out-of-county DAs?" Rather demanded. "Stop fucking up my case."

"It wasn't your case until I gave it to you, and I'll damn well do what I please," Arsenault replied.

"Fine, then you do the case."

"You'll do what I tell you," Arsenault shouted back. "I'm the boss of this unit, and I make the fucking decisions around here." Their voices carried back to the squad room. Dugan recalls wandering into the alcove to use the copying machine next to Quinn's office and hearing the two men arguing over the number of defendants in the proposed indictment. Arsenault wanted more. Rather wanted fewer. But there wasn't much substance to the discussion, and tempers escalated quickly.

"You're not a man," Rather said at one point, goading Arsenault.

"You want to back that up?" The two men glared at each other. Neither was physically imposing. But Rather was an athlete who dined out on tales of his tough Texas youth, and Arsenault had studied martial arts since he was a teenager. Throughout his life he'd surprised friends and colleagues by standing up to bullies in the schoolyard and the office, and he wasn't backing down now.

The men edged closer, locked in mutual animus, avatars of opposite styles and points of view: Arsenault—squat, rumpled, a brilliant, blunt pragmatist who regarded the law with skepticism and bent it to his will; and Rather—starched and aloof, a relentless investigator, whose slow, perfectionist approach to casework clashed with that of his boss.

And then as abruptly and nonsensically as it had started, the fight was over. Rather peeled off, calling over his shoulder that it was Arsenault's case now. Arsenault, after responding that it wasn't, headed down to Baltimore for the conference.

But Rather was shaken by the argument. He still hadn't resolved the Fat Danny issue, and now his role in the case, and indeed the unit, was in jeopardy. He called several confidants, including Nancy Ryan, who advised him to stick to his position on Fat Danny and patch things up with Arsenault as best he could. Later that afternoon, he drove down to the conference with Ryan to clear the air with his boss.

Rather tracked down the unit chief in a bar near the hotel conference site. "We *have* a case," Rather said, offering his hand. Arsenault shook it, and Rather remained at the bar drinking with Arsenault's group. But the two men spoke little to each other the rest of the evening, and didn't discuss the case at all. Whatever trust had existed between them before that morning's blowup had been irreparably shattered, and nothing the two could do could piece it back together again.

MEANWHILE, the investigation lurched forward, and even accelerated as it approached the final takedown. Don Hill was now working regularly at the unit, and was joined by an assistant from the Bronx, Linda Nelson. Lori Grifa had also come over from Brooklyn, bringing the Michael Cruz shooting and Papito murder cases with her, and Dugan and Tebbens had begun working full-time on the Cowboys. After twenty-five years, Dugan had retired from the NYPD and accepted a job offer at HIU; and Ryan had arranged with the PD for Tebbens to be assigned to the DA's office on temporary loan. Paired together, the two detectives spent every day tracking down new suspects and witnesses, expanding the case into uncharted areas.

HIDTA's team had also been busy. First, there was the 300-vial buy one of their undercovers had made from Rennie Harris; then, just weeks later, Eddie Benitez had collared Jose Rios, a Cowboy worker known as "Corky," transporting eight bundles (800 vials) of crack to Beekman Avenue. Corky began cooperating immediately, calling Pasqualito to report the loss of the bundles while HIDTA's detectives listened in.

The investigation seemed to have taken on a life of its own. Nearly every day that summer Rather, Hill, and Grifa sorted through mountains of evidence involving more than fifty gang members and hundreds of illegal acts, at the same time prepping and presenting more than a hundred witnesses—many of them reluctant and unreliable—for the grand jury. It was a gargantuan task, especially since Grifa was maintaining a full caseload back in Brooklyn, and

Rather and Hill were also supervising several other, smaller investigations.

But the Arsenault-Rather situation made everything more difficult than it might have been otherwise. The poison between them leached into the fissures that develop in the course of any complex investigation, imparting a political dimension to the smallest disagreements. The person most affected was Hill, who had negotiated his office's cooperation with Arsenault, and now had to deal increasingly with Nancy Ryan, who seemed to support Rather's decisions at every critical turn.

A typical example was the resolution of the Fat Danny issue. When Hill had shown up at HIU during the week of the MAGLOCLEN Conference expecting to craft an indictment with Rather against Fat Danny, he found that Rather had gone to the conference himself, without leaving Hill so much as a telephone message. Worse, on his return to HIU the following week, Rather told Hill he'd decided not to indict Fat Danny before the takedown. Hill was furious. He knew that Rather had been delaying, that he had reservations about the plan, but Hill had never doubted Rather's intention to honor what Hill thought was HIU's commitment to the Bronx. When pressed, however, all Rather would say was "that's the way Nancy wants it, and that's the way it has to be."

"I don't work for Nancy," Hill said, flushing. "And I don't work for Morgenthau either."

In fact, it was unclear who Hill worked for. His first loyalty was to his bosses in the Bronx, but they were only peripherally involved in the investigation, and Arsenault, whose judgment Hill trusted, was apparently out of the decision-making loop. Otherwise Hill regarded Rather as an equal partner, and resented his using Ryan as a hammer in the disputes between them. In Hill's opinion, she was an outsider to the case, and her intervention not only gave Rather an unfair advantage in their dealings but suggested that the Bronx was a junior partner in the investigation.

Unable to make headway with Rather, Hill stormed out of the unit and went for a walk to try to cool down. He knew that his office had gone too far down the road with HIU to pull out of the case now. But his relations with Rather would suffer from that point on, and for a few precarious moments he considered taking the Quad and trying it back in the Bronx. Lori Grifa recalls working at a desk outside Rather's office with Hill's assistant, Linda Nelson, when Hill strode angrily past. "Well, it's been nice working with you," Nelson said to her.

Grifa had been having her own problems with Rather. Courted assiduously by him for the two Brooklyn Cowboy cases her office controlled, Grifa and her supervisors struck a deal with HIU: they would let Manhattan have their cases, and Manhattan would allow Grifa to present them to the grand jury. But once she settled in at the unit, she became a de facto member. She loved the work she was doing there and developed close relationships with Quinn and Arsenault, who invited her to stay on through the summer and help with the grand jury. Grifa cleared it with her office, but apparently nobody informed Rather. In fact, he was saying goodbye to her after she'd finished her grand jury presentation, when Grifa told him she was staying on. "Like hell you are," he snapped.

"It's already decided," Grifa shot back. "If you don't like it, talk to Walter."

Rather simmered down quickly, and by the summer's end he would even encourage her to continue working with the unit after the grand jury. But the damage had been done, and it was clear to Grifa in the succeeding months that Rather did not want her there. No doubt Rather resented the summary way in which Arsenault had added another prosecutor to his case, even one willing to accept a subordinate role; and he seemed to regard Grifa's good relations with Quinn and Arsenault with mistrust. Whatever his reasons, they added another layer of dissension to the already beleaguered unit.

With the investigation unraveling, Ryan stepped in. But her efforts to ameliorate the tensions were unconvincing, and may even have made things worse. When Arsenault angrily confronted her about countermanding his orders regarding the arrest of Fat Danny, she told him: "You've got to back up your own assistant against out-of-county prosecutors." Then she called Hill down to her office after his blowup with Rather and went back over their reasons for not indicting Fat Danny—mainly that they wanted to protect the secrecy of the grand jury proceedings. But Hill left unpersuaded. In his view, Fat Danny was already under indictment in the Bronx. Recasting the Quad or some other violent act as part of a narcotics conspiracy involving Fat Danny was not going to jeopardize the investigation.

Ryan also called Barry Kluger, the Bronx DA's executive assistant, and made an appointment to see him on July 23, the morning after her conversation with Hill. According to Ryan, it was a courtesy visit, an attempt to explain her decision to her counterpart. The meeting was cordial. Kluger agreed to go along with Ryan's strategy, and even said he'd call Globerman to reassure the judge that an indictment was forthcoming. In exchange, Ryan agreed to a deadline for the takedown—September 14—and promised to beef up the surveillance on Fat Danny. But according to Hill, Ryan had neglected to inform him about the meeting in advance of her coming, further alienating the Bronx prosecutor. (Ryan recalls she informed Hill in advance of the meeting.)

Later that afternoon, Ryan called the main players in the case to the eighth-floor conference room. The meeting dealt with tactical matters—her decision on the Fat Danny issue, expanding the search for Pasqualito, preparations for the now-imminent takedown—but was also Ryan's way of consolidating her control over the case and getting everybody on the same page.

Ryan, however, said nothing explicit about her expanded role in the investigation. Indeed Grifa sensed from her tone—at times scolding and sarcastic—that she was distancing herself from the unit. Even more mysterious was Rather's mood. On what should have been a triumphant occasion for him, the coronation of Ryan as case supervisor, he seemed morose and uncommunicative. Dugan, who liked

Rather and enjoyed working with him, was shocked when he saw Rather outside the conference room before the meeting. "He had several days' growth, his tie was askew," Dugan recalls. "He could barely nod when I said hello. He just sat there head down, staring at the floor, as if he had more important things to think about. He almost needed to be asked into the meeting."

Once there, he was silent. "I poked him several times under the table because I wanted him to back me up on some things I was speaking about, but he didn't respond," Dugan says. "I was amazed. I kept asking him if he was all right, and he just nodded."

Rather seemed to recover his spirits quickly. But the long hours—he often worked through the night at the office—and constant wrangling took its toll. At different times he seemed to be at war not only with Arsenault but also with Quinn, Hill, Grifa, and Rorke; and through the summer he became increasingly uncommunicative. He already spent the bulk of his days outside the unit attending the grand jury proceedings or consulting with Ryan on the eighth floor, and in August, with the grand jury on vacation, he shut himself in his office to write a prosecution memo, a summary of the events of the case. By the end of the summer, he had almost no contact with Arsenault, and at times he would take off without notice. Dugan once spent a day trying to locate him, finally tracking him down through his cell phone to a stream near his home upstate, where he'd gone fly-fishing.

Rather recalls that summer as the best and the worst of times. His schedule was grueling—he admits taking the rare day off when the opportunity arose—and he felt that Arsenault and Quinn had turned the unit against him. But he was proud of the work he was doing with the Cowboys and in his other cases. "I had great investigations popping everywhere," he recalls. "I felt everything I touched was gold. I was doing really good work and I knew it . . . You aspire to those moments when everything comes together . . . I was making tough decisions: Put a pen register [a device for identifying incoming and outgoing call numbers] here—it happens. Buy this guy—boom, it happens."

But his colleagues formed a less rosy assessment of the case. The unit was split into two camps without clear lines of authority, or often even communication. Dugan and Benitez got into the habit of preparing two reports, one for Rather and one for Quinn. At times Hill and Grifa found themselves thrust into the grand jury with a witness they'd had no time to prepare, increasing the probability of mistakes and inconsistencies that could haunt them later at trial or on appeal. And Arsenault was edged out of his oversight role almost completely. As fall approached and Rather was drawing up the final indictment, Grifa had to sneak Arsenault copies of her current drafts, and then present his corrections and recommendations to Rather as her own.

Worst was the mood in the unit. "The morale was deteriorating," Luke Rettler recalls. "Just walking through the office you could feel it. By the end of the summer, everyone was just dragging through to the end. Usually it's the opposite. Everything builds up to the takedown, the crowning moment when you arrest the guys you've been investigating for months or even years, and you bring them in and see them for the first time when they're stunned, when they realize their lives will never be the same, these guys who were just out in the streets killing and selling drugs and living incredibly high.

"But it wasn't like that. The morale was so bad, guys were like, 'Let's just get this over with.' You'd see Walter with his shoulders beaten down. Even Mark and Garry, who are very upbeat guys, were very quiet. They were doing all this hard work and not getting the benefits, worrying about what's going to happen. The focus had changed and there was a real foreboding about once we do this, what's going to happen next?"

16

TAKEDOWN

SEPTEMBER 1993

A MONTH LATER, on the morning of September 14, Mark Tebbens arrested Fat Danny Rincon. Accompanied by six HIU and HIDTA investigators, he swooped down on the Cowboy leader as he exited the Bronx Supreme Court building surrounded by his family and lawyers. "You have the right to remain silent," one of the detectives intoned, as two others struggled to cuff the 300-pound Rincon. "Anything you say may be held against you in a court of law . . ." True to his name, Fat Danny was so broad it took two pairs of linked cuffs to bind his hands behind his back.

It was a cool, clear, sunny day, the first fall-like day of the year. Summer was ending, and so, it seemed, were the Cowboys. Fat Danny was the first arrest of the takedown. If everything went according to plan, the next few hours would be the final hours of freedom for the gang whose reign of terror had lasted more than seven years.

Quinn had been preparing arrest folders in anticipation of the raid since July 1. In addition to the usual pedigrees, the files included information about where subjects hung out, with whom and at what times. Rather's final indictment named 35 defendants. Some, like Lenny and Platano, were already in jail; a few others, who had open warrants, had been arrested ahead of time; and Nelson and Pasqualito were known to have fled to the Dominican Republic. Quinn prioritized the remaining 20-plus gang members still on the street, and began to draw up an attack plan in late August.

September 14 had been selected as the takedown date because it allowed Rather enough time to complete the grand jury, and still ensured that the weather would be warm enough to induce gang members to gather in the street, making them easier targets for Quinn's men. But Hill, always suspicious of Manhattan's penchant for publicity, noted that the date also coincided with the post-Labor Day news cycle, when wealthy, influential New Yorkers return from their summer vacations. In his view, the investigation could have been wrapped up four to six weeks earlier. As it was, Rather barely made it by the fourteenth. He presented the last of 84 witnesses the week before, and on Friday, September 10, the grand jury voted a fifty-eight-count indictment that included nine murders and numerous other violent acts.

Four days later, in a lot behind the Cotton Club on West 125th Street, Quinn assembled his troops—ten HIU investigators, Eddie Benitez' eight-man team, and some twenty additional HIDTA officers drafted for the takedown. He'd already divided them into a dozen or so squads, and now he went over their assignments and the targeted schedule of arrests one last time. There wasn't much to say. Many of the men had been working on the case for more than a year and had made extraordinary emotional investments in its outcome. For months, Benitez had been doing surveillance drive-bys on his own time. Tebbens had been crusading against the Cowboys since arriving in the 40th Precinct four years before. Quinn made sure everyone's radio was tuned to the same wavelength. "Let's get them all," he said.

After the police collared Fat Danny, they radioed teams watching the apartment of Jimmy Montalvo, the top Cowboy manager known as Heavy D. They nabbed Montalvo, known to be a late riser, while he was still in bed. Then the teams went after lower-tier gang members, simultaneously hitting their residences and sales locations. Quinn and Tebbens trolled the streets around Beekman Avenue in a van picking up strays; Tebbens became so excited by the prospect of arresting gang members who had evaded him for so long that he snapped a handgrip he'd been exercising with. By midnight Quinn's men had 28 of the 35 indicted defendants in custody.

Back at HIU, Dugan processed the incoming prisoners, fingerprinting and photographing them, separating the leaders and top managers. The unit had been converted into a miniature precinct house, the interview rooms and prosecutors' offices serving as holding pens. Dugan introduced himself to each new arrival, calmly, straightforwardly explaining the seriousness of the charges against them. "You're not going to be released," he told them. "This is not like what you've experienced in the past." To the lower-level workers, he added: "Now, we're primarily interested in homicides. We know you didn't do any, but we know that you may have knowledge of some." Then he handed them Rather's card. "When you realize you're the only one who can help yourself, have your lawyer call us."

Because the gang members had already been indicted, HIU's investigators were barred from questioning or even taking statements from them without their lawyers present. Rather turned the prohibition to his advantage. He told the defendants that his case was so strong he didn't need their admissions, that he would leave the room if they tried to confess or even speak.

But it was Quinn—gravel-voiced, streetwise—who delivered the most convincing blow to many of the eventual cooperators. He told them they were facing the city's toughest judge, recounted the Gheri Curl trial, and ticked off the 100- and 200-year sentences handed down to the defendants. "My detectives have spent more time investigating cases than you've been alive," he told them. "You're not playing with precinct cops, with rookies. You don't see many men around here without gray hair." Then he repeated the charges against them, and the number of years they could spend in jail if convicted. "Can you handle that?" he said. "If you can, don't call me. Don't make a deal. But if you decide to make a deal, you better get on the train first, or you'll be left on the platform."

All the Cowboys were stunned by their new circumstances, but Fat Danny seemed particularly put out. Cuffed to a chair in Arsenault's office, he pawed Don Hill with his free hand. "You shouldn't have done that," he told him. "You shouldn't have arrested me in front of my family."

In the morning, HIU and HIDTA investigators led the prisoners in a line past reporters and TV cameras to the courtroom to be arraigned—a since-forbidden ritual known as the perp walk. Shortly afterward, Morgenthau held a press conference to announce the indictment and arrests. On the dais with Arsenault, who sat next to Morgenthau, were half a dozen agency and department heads who had never set foot in HIU, who had merely contributed resources or ceded jurisdiction to the investigation. Arsenault was no longer surprised or disconcerted, as he once had been, by their presence; indeed, he knew that those promised chairs, those few minutes in the warm glow of the media, had bought him and his men invaluable cooperation. Arsenault wasn't troubled at all by who was there—success, he knew, has many fathers. But he was deeply troubled by who was missing. Dan Rather was nowhere to be seen.

FROM ARSENAULT'S point of view, Rather had been acting strangely lately. The last few weeks before the takedown he'd been more reclusive than ever. He was rarely in the unit, spending most of his time in the grand jury and on the eighth floor, writing the final indictment in consultation with Ryan. He barely spoke to Arsenault now. He did send him drafts of the indictment, but he didn't confer with him.

Arsenault was taken aback by what he read in the indictment. It left out a number of defendants, as well as several overt acts, including a homicide. But what rankled Arsenault most was the conspiracy charge underlying the indictment. In Arsenault's view, Rather had omitted one of the fundamental charges in the investigation.

There are two types of conspiracy in New York State law. A basic conspiracy charge inheres when two or more persons agree to commit a crime and perform two or more actions in furtherance of that crime. These so-called overt acts do not themselves have to be criminal. The purchase of a flashlight in order to perpetrate a burglary counts as an overt act, even if the buyer didn't steal anything. Convictions for conspiracy to commit a top felony carry a sentence of two to six years. (Individual members of a conspiracy can also be tried and punished for the specific crimes that also serve as overt acts for the conspiracy. Thus Lenny and Platano, for example, were indicted for conspiracy to distribute narcotics *and* for murders and assaults committed in furtherance of that conspiracy.)

The second conspiracy charge must satisfy all the conditions of the first, in addition to one more. If the conspirators are over 18 and involve a minor under the age of 16 in their illegal activities, then the conspiracy itself is charged as a top felony and carries a sentence of eight and a half to twenty-five years. This so-called A-1 or top felony provision of the conspiracy statutes had been a key element in the Cowboy investigation. For years the gang had been employing neighborhood youngsters in their operation as a source of cheap, replaceable labor and because minors aren't liable to the stiff penalties called for under New York's tough drug laws. All three Cruz-Morales brothers, among others, had been recruited by the gang since they were 12 or younger, and HIU's investigators had meticulously documented their involvement in the gang's activities. Charging the Cowboys with an A-1 conspiracy meant that even some of the lowliest street sellers would be facing serious jail time, and were far more likely to make a deal with prosecutors in exchange for their testimony against the gang's leaders and enforcers.

But Rather's indictment made no mention of the A-1 conspiracy, although he says he planned all along to include the higher charge in a superceding indictment, and that Arsenault was aware of the plan. However, Arsenault, who had little contact with Rather, says he had no idea what was going on, and had to ask Lori Grifa to transmit his comments and recommendations to Rather as her own. "It was extraordinary," Grifa recalled later. "I told [Walter], 'You're *his* boss. He works for you.' And he said, 'I know, I know. But what can I do?' "

Grifa was even more surprised a week later, a few days before the takedown. She was sitting with Rather in the unit lunchroom—a small office with a fridge and a coffee machine—when Arsenault stuck his head in and told them they were expected downstairs on the following afternoon to brief Morgenthau and his chief assistant, Barbara Jones, for the upcoming press conference. Arsenault generously included Grifa in the meeting, but, Grifa knew, the summons was intended for Rather. After Arsenault departed, however, Rather said to Grifa, "You know, I would never go to a meeting like that."

Grifa didn't know that at all. In Brooklyn, unit chiefs were absolute monarchs, the first assistant was God; she'd never even been in to see the DA. "There must be some mistake here," she thought at the time.

But there was no mistake. The next day Arsenault stopped at Rather's office on his way down to the eighth floor. Rather had his feet up on his desk. "I'm not going to the meeting," he told Arsenault.

"It's not an invitation," Arsenault said. "The boss wants to see us now."

Rather turned away, and after a moment Arsenault headed

down to Jones's office with Grifa. Jones, Grifa recalls, was furious at Rather's no-show. "Who the fuck does he think he is?" Jones fumed, until a few minutes later Ryan joined them and explained that Rather was too busy to attend. Jones then brought the group into Morgenthau, and Arsenault, having been shoved to the margins of the case, now found himself cast as its spokesman.

But things took an even stranger turn the morning of the press conference. Rather had stayed in the office during the takedown until about 2 A.M., when he left with Grifa to drop her off and then get some sleep. He was back early the next morning showered and shaved in preparation for the conference, or so Arsenault thought. But Rather had another agenda. When Grifa phoned him with a question about the arraignment, Rather refused to take her call and redirected her inquiry to Arsenault. Then shortly before the conference began, Rather disappeared altogether, and Arsenault was slotted into Rather's seat next to Morgenthau.

The conference went off without a hitch. Morgenthau led off with a statement about the pernicious effect of drug gangs on city neighborhoods, Arsenault added some telling details about the size and violent nature of the Cowboys, and the heads of a handful of law enforcement agencies issued statements extolling the cooperative effort that made the takedown possible. It was a seamless performance duly reported by the papers and local news stations. "Cowboys Lassoed" read a typical headline in the *Post*; and other editors too seized on the Wild West imagery—first conceived by Terry Quinn—to tell the saga of the Cowboys' violent rise, and their demise at the hands of a small but determined band of lawmen.

The skirmishes behind the scenes at the DA's office were unreported. The night of the raids, when Arsenault volunteered his assistance, Rather ignored him. He saw the offer, coming so late in the campaign, as a slight or worse, an attempt by Arsenault to ingratiate himself with Rather now that the investigation was about to go public. In Arsenault's view, Rather's unexplained absence from the press conference seemed to augur a puzzling new turn in his conduct of the case. Arsenault was still trying to figure out what it meant, when he learned that Rather had taken off on a fly-fishing trip to Texas. Arsenault was irate. He had wanted to reconvene the grand jury as soon as possible to improve the conspiracy charge. Worse, some of the information he thought he would need for the defendants' arraignments and bail applications was locked in Rather's office.

Rather, not surprisingly, had a very different view of events, stemming from his belief that Ryan, not Arsenault, was his supervisor on the case. There was no mystery about his nonappearance at the press conference or the meeting with Morgenthau, he said. He simply doesn't like publicity, and he wanted his work to speak for itself. Moreover, he didn't trust Arsenault's spin on the investigation. Rather said his so-called vacation, more of a long weekend, had been planned for over a month; the first few days after a takedown are usually quiet, and he needed a rest before the investigation started up again. He was back Monday to do some arraignments, and whatever information Arsenault needed in the meanwhile was easily accessible through Ryan.

Whatever the truth, Rather's actions were odd at the very least. No matter how publicity-shy he may have been, he failed to inform even Ryan he wouldn't attend the press conference until the morning of the event. And however long Rather had been planning his vacation, about which he says he informed his colleagues, Arsenault, Hill, Grifa, and the investigators say it was news to them. In fact, they were shocked he'd leave the day after the takedown: at the time they had no idea when, or if, he'd be returning. Once again the stability of the trial team seemed to be in doubt.

When Rather came back the following Monday, he met with Ryan in her office to discuss his status at the unit. "He asked me if I thought there was any way he could reasonably stay on the case," Ryan recalls. "Naturally he wanted to stay on and try the case, and we discussed the pros and cons of his doing that at length. But in the end we both realized it was going to be a big, difficult case to try, even with everyone pulling in the same direction, and under the circumstances he felt his staying on would hurt the unit's chances of succeeding, and much as I wanted to, I couldn't disagree with him."

However, not everyone in the office felt Rather was eager to go to trial, or believed his reasons for quitting the unit. Luke Rettler, among others, was mystified when Rather stopped by his office to explain his departure. "He gave me three reasons for leaving," Rettler recalls. "He said that he couldn't get along with Walter and didn't want to work with him any longer, that everyone was trying to steal his case, and that he wasn't getting any support. When he said that I just had to laugh. I told him, 'Don't give me that. If you can't get along with Walter—well, that's just something you'll have to deal with. But don't try and tell me that everyone's trying to steal your case. I guarantee you no one wants that monstrosity. And as far as not getting any support, the whole office is working on your case. You've got Dugan and Tebbens, the two best detectives in the world, working for you full-time.' "

In Rettler's opinion, Rather was suffering from cold feet and using his feud with Arsenault as an excuse not to go to trial—and he was not alone in his thinking. Earlier that summer, Dan Brownell, a top prosecutor who'd joined HIU in January, had been chatting with one of Rather's old bureau mates, an assistant who knew Rather's work well, and mentioned that Rather was going to try the Cowboys case. "No, he won't," the assistant remarked somewhat cryptically. Brownell didn't press him at the time, but now in the wake of Rather's departure, he understood what the assistant had been trying to tell him.

In fact, Rather had tried the average amount of cases in his early years, including a tough, politically fraught misdemeanor and a high-profile rape case that he second-seated, and he'd rapidly moved up to the homicide chart. But for one reason or another—he served as a Criminal Court supervisor; he specialized in investigative cases, all of which pled out—he never tried a murder to verdict and never made his mark as a trial lawyer. Often, when lawyers fail to gain sufficient major felony experience, the fear of going to trial becomes increasingly daunting. This is true for any prosecutor, but is especially the case for one like Rather, whose early prominence and perfectionist ethic can create high, even unreasonable expectations. "At some point you've got to just lay it on the line," Rettler says. "But some guys are afraid of getting beat up and you're going to get beat up. There are plenty of lawyers who are going to be better than you when you get started, and the longer you wait, the harder it becomes. You've just got to take the plunge and if you don't do it while you're young, when it's okay to make mistakes, it just gets harder and some guys never get over it."

Privately, Rettler speculated that was happening now. He had hoped that the Cowboy case would be the one that got Rather over the hump, and he told his friend to stop kidding himself about his reasons for leaving the unit. Rather didn't respond. Rettler remembers that after a while he became quiet and detached, and seemed to stop listening. Then he got up, left without a word, and never spoke to Rettler again.

Rather denies he was afraid of going to trial and maintains that his decision to leave HIU was motivated by a desire to return to his previous work in "firearms trafficking on a full-time basis and on the practical impossibility of my continuing to prosecute the Wild Cowboys case with Walter Arsenault as the unit chief."

A day or two later Ryan reassigned Rather as chief of newly created Firearms Trafficking Unit, a program that targets the city's gun sellers, much as HIU targets violent drug gangs. Then she called Arsenault down to her office and told him the case was now his. She recalls that the meeting was perfunctory. Arsenault told her that he couldn't do the case himself but the unit could handle it; and then they discussed candidates to replace Rather, deciding on Dan Brownell.

Arsenault was shocked when Ryan told him Rather was quitting the case. Whatever Rather's and Arsenault's differences, however poorly they got on, the case was the important thing; not seeing it through, short of leaving the office, was an unpardonable sin in Arsenault's view. Moreover, it created a huge headache at the unit. Camacho was bogged down in several investigations, and Arsenault couldn't handle the case and continue to act as supervisor to HIU. True, Brownell was a highly regarded litigator; but he was then in Africa on vacation, and even if he agreed to take the case on his return, it would take him months just to get up to speed. "Oh no, you wanted [this case]," Arsenault says he told Ryan. "Now it's yours."

But even as he said it, Arsenault knew he was just venting. HIU had too much invested in the case to give it up now. Anything short of a resounding triumph would jeopardize the survival of the unit, and at this stage even a victory might not repair the damage to Arsenault's career.

17

BACK ON TRACK

FALL 1993

TALL AND LANKY with broad shoulders, jet-black hair, and finely chiseled features—co-workers compared him to the young Gregory Peck—36-year-old Dan Brownell had a knack for making things look easy. A star runner at Syracuse, he had a long, loping stride so smooth and unhurried that you thought he wasn't really trying or going very fast, until you checked his results. He once clocked a 4:11 mile indoors, and he was still improving when he ruptured his Achilles tendon in his sophomore year. The injury cut short his running career. But years later colleagues, watching him in the courtroom, noted the same poised, effortless style that marked him as an athlete. "He has this relaxed, conversational way with witnesses and juries, as if he were talk-

ing to them in his living room," Luke Rettler said. "But he's so methodical; underneath he's making his points boom-boom-boom, bringing
in the facts always at just the right time. And yet if you're not paying
close attention to what he's doing, it sounds like he's making it up as he
goes along."

Nothing, according to Rettler, could have been less true.
Brownell was a tireless worker who prepared rigorously for every court
appearance and rarely slept on the eve of a trial. But he affected a be-
mused detachment that seemed to shield him from the sweat and
squabble of everyday lawyering, and he had a deft touch and quick dry
wit that enabled him to carve up witnesses or tweak a fellow jurist
without causing offense. Arsenault recalls a time when Leslie Crocker
Snyder, the formidable, and sometimes lecture-prone, Special Narcotics judge who presided over HIU's cases, was hectoring Brownell
during a routine hearing. "Let the record reflect that being in this court
is like trying a case in front of my mother-in-law," Brownell announced. Then while anxious colleagues waited for Snyder's reaction,
Brownell asked the stenographer to read back his statement; he
wanted to send a copy to the Appellate Division, he said. Snyder just
laughed.

"No one else could have gotten away with that," Arsenault
said. "Nobody else would have tried."

Brownell's people skills, as much as his courtroom expertise,
made him the ideal replacement for Rather. Throughout the fall and
winter, his steady, congenial presence served as anchor and magnet for
the disparate, and at times headstrong, personalities involved in the
case. Quinn, Hill, and Grifa—all of whom had been operating on a
need-to-know basis during the last months with Rather—now felt as
though they were back in the loop. "He was an incredible consensus
builder," Grifa recalls. "He built a bridge to HIDTA, got the detectives in
the squad working together, made sure Don and I were part of every
decision, and kept Walter involved in the process, which was maybe
the best thing he did. Walter was just this great resource. He'd done

dozens of these investigations and he had all this experience, which none of the rest of us had; but we'd been afraid to go to him before because there was a sense that somehow we were being disloyal [to Rather] if we did."

Arsenault and Brownell made an odd team. Standing next to each other, they were a study in contrasts—one lean, angular, and polished; the other compact, rumpled, and combative. But their different styles complemented one another, especially when dealing with people outside the unit. Brownell projected a calmness and an affability that worked as a perfect foil to Arsenault's prickly intelligence. He was accessible, where Arsenault was reclusive; politic, where his boss was blunt. And if at times Brownell seemed a little facile, too cool or impersonal in his approach to the case, Arsenault added grit and a spark of passion.

It was as if a great weight had been lifted at HIU. "I didn't appreciate how big a cloud we'd been working under all summer until Dan took over," Grifa recalls. Don Hill began to look forward to coming in to the office for the first time since his flare-up with Rather in June. Even Arsenault seemed to recover some of his old jollity. "I remember one afternoon I took Dan, Don, and Lori out to lunch," Arsenault recalls. "It was nothing special—just some neighborhood Thai place—and I couldn't even tell you the conversation. But we laughed for two hours straight, and I remember thinking: 'This is how it should be. This is how it used to be.' "

But things were not as they had been. The schism between Arsenault and Ryan had deepened in the wake of Rather's departure, and despite positive changes in the Cowboy investigation, Arsenault worried about the future of the unit, as well as his own future. Ryan was a formidable enemy, both personally and institutionally. Arguably the most powerful administrator in the office after Morgenthau, she had, in Arsenault's view, the power to make or break a prosecutor's career. Of course, Arsenault was no ordinary assistant, but he'd seen Ryan reward Rather with a promotion to unit chief, and he wasn't about to wait for the other shoe to drop. "The day I took over the case, Walter stopped by my office to congratulate me," Brownell recalls. "It was a good news–bad news kind of thing. He said he was thrilled we'd be working together and offered to help me any way he could. Then he told me he was planning to leave the office."

Arsenault had been running the case in the wake of Rather's departure. During the past three weeks, he'd rallied Hill and Grifa, re-convened the grand jury, and re-presented the case as an A-1 conspir-acy, increasing the number of defendants and adding another homicide as a substantive act. It had been an invigorating time for him, and he enjoyed working directly with Hill and Grifa. But he knew it was temporary.

Even when running smoothly, the unit now required close su-pervision. Camacho had initiated several large investigations, and he was just one of six prosecutors; and Arsenault was negotiating pleas on two Jamaican homicides left over from the Spangler case, in addition to his lecture work and intelligence-gathering activities. But these days the unit was not running smoothly. Even before the Cowboy case, it had been plagued by factionalism, with rival camps of investigators barely speaking to each other, much less sharing CIs and information. Some old-timers who'd joined HIU under Bill Hoyt resented the new regime, and particularly objected to Quinn's rising profile and take-charge personality. Others clashed as a matter of style. Investigative work is highly subjective, and differences in approach tend to be sharpened by competition and big egos. Most good lawmen have them.

In the past, the rivalries among detectives had been manage-able, at times even healthy. HIU had been small during Hoyt's tenure, and Hoyt ruled over his domain with iron resolve. Then, when the unit expanded after his departure, Ryan installed James McVeety, who had worked with her on the Jade Squad, as chief investigator. Moreover, Ryan and Arsenault had presented a solid front against the forum-shopping and backbiting that flared up from time to time. But once

Ryan and Arsenault began to snipe at each other, conditions deterio-rated, with investigators choosing sides. Worse, McVeety, whose ad-ministrative role already triggered bitter feelings among some detectives—Quinn in particular—was now viewed by Arsenault's allies as Ryan's conduit and spy.

But Arsenault's feud with Ryan had far more troubling impli-cations for the unit. As HIU's champion, Ryan had been a strong wind at Arsenault's back. If he needed more resources or personnel, or if he wanted a case that was mired in one of the trial bureaus, Ryan made it happen. No request was too large or small for her consideration—from installing a shower-changing room in the unit to recruiting the office's best new talent. Now the opposite seemed true. Suddenly, he recalls, cars became unavailable. A request for a $200 easel to present charts in court went unapproved. A promising young assistant, whom Ryan had encouraged to join HIU before the summer, would later be told that a transfer to the unit would damage his career. And every miscue, however innocent, seemed game for reprimand. Camacho, who could do no wrong in the aftermath of the Gheri Curl trial, was called on the carpet several times over procedural issues. McVeety dis-covered improprieties—albeit minuscule ones—in the unit's fiscal re-porting.

Arsenault fell into a funk, recovered, then slipped again. His weight fluctuated wildly, and he began to sleep fitfully. Some after-noons he'd wander into Brownell's office and slump onto the ratty couch, too tired or upset to speak. Brownell would prop him up, coun-sel patience—"This will all blow over. You can't quit now, you can't let them win"—and Arsenault would march back to his office recharged. But then he'd hear rumors being circulated that he'd stolen Rather's case, that the unit was out of control, that he and Quinn engaged in practices that were unethical, if not outright illegal, and it would de-flate him. He'd try not to take things personally, but it was not his na-ture to turn the other cheek. Worse, he saw no way of fighting back. In palmier days, Ryan had shielded him from eighth-floor politics, and at the time he'd been grateful for her protection. Now he just felt isolated.

Arsenault did have a formidable ally in Barbara Jones, Morgenthau's chief assistant. The 46-year-old Jones had been a fixture in local law enforcement since the early 1970s. Originally from California, she'd grown up partly in Egypt—her father, an airlines radio operator, flew the Bombay–Dar-es Salaam–Cairo route—and studied law at Temple in Philadelphia. Prompted by an uncle who was a federal agent, she entered a Justice Department honors program, and was assigned in 1973 to the Organized Crime Strike Force in the U.S. Attorney's office for New York's Southern District.

The only woman on the force, Jones landed in the white-hot center of U.S. law enforcement. The Organized Crime Strike Force—with a dozen or so units across the United States—was part of a program developed under the Justice Department to focus federal resources in law enforcement's war against the Mafia; and Manhattan was home base for the Mafia's top crime families. Louis Freeh, the future FBI chief, was a young agent working on Jones's cases. (The two of them helped put together the so-called Pizza Connection case, which effectively busted the Mafia's main narcotics operation.) Then, in 1983, Rudolph Giuliani took command of the office.

Jones thrived in the atmosphere of pressure and close teamwork. She was made chief of the unit in 1984—the first woman to head a strike force—and by the time she left the office in 1987, it had carried out groundbreaking prosecutions against the Mafia, locking up the heads of four of the five New York families. Jones had personally prosecuted cases against Anthony "Tony Pro" Provenzano, Russell Bufalino, and Frank "Funzi" Tieri, top boss of the Genovese family.

In 1987, Jones accepted an offer from Morgenthau to become his first assistant and run the Manhattan DA's office as his chief of staff. A perfect foil for the famously private Morgenthau, Jones had a warm, outgoing manner and a dedication to public service that eclipsed her personal ambition. Almost unknown outside law enforcement, Jones was the consummate insider. She had dated Al D'Amato in the 1980s; Louis Freeh was her confidant; her best friends were Mary Jo White, the current U.S. Attorney for New York's Southern District, and Venia Mucha, the future governor George Pataki's chief spokesperson.

New York was then entering a golden age of law enforcement. With Giuliani as mayor-elect and William Bratton poised to take over as his Police Commissioner, the city's crime rate would plummet over the next five years and cops would become the heroes of the 1990s. Operating behind the scenes, Jones would play a pivotal role in the process, using her numerous contacts to align Morgenthau's office with the Feds and the police, build bridges to City Hall, and reduce tensions among the fractious elements within the DA's office itself. HIU had been a special project of hers, a reminder of the days when she ran her own task force. She had helped them get federal grant money, and she was especially fond of Arsenault and Quinn. But Jones was a facilitator, not a fighter, still relatively new to the office, still defining her role as the nominal second-in-command. She was not about to confront Ryan over HIU, and Morgenthau was well known for not getting involved in personnel disputes.

Unfortunately, Arsenault made things worse rather than better. Given the raw state of his emotions, he tended to cast any effort at supervision by Ryan in a political light, and he made no attempt to alleviate the tensions between them. That fall, when Ryan visited Arsenault to clear the air, Arsenault ignored her, refusing to respond to her overtures. Too much had passed between them, and Arsenault, never good at disguising his feelings, didn't do so now. Perhaps if Ryan had merely taken the Cowboy case away from Arsenault, he could have reached an understanding with her. But allowing Rather to leave the case and then rewarding him with a promotion was, in Arsenault's view, unpardonable. Since his days in Bergen County, Arsenault had one cardinal rule: Never give up. Short of leaving the office, you always took a prosecution to term, through trial if necessary, even if the odds were stacked heavily against you. In fact, it was more of a personal credo. Just as when as a youngster he competed in karate, he never backed down, never gave up without a fight. After a while no one had wanted to spar with him, because even if he lost he always hurt his opponent. That's the ethic and the image he tried to impress upon the unit, that HIU was relentless, that it never stopped coming until it had locked you up. He couldn't forgive Rather for quitting, however adverse the circumstances seemed, or Ryan for condoning his action.

After the takedown, he asked friends in the U.S. Attorney's office in Boston if they would be interested in his setting up an HIU-style gang unit for them. They indicated they would be and promised to get back to him.

AS THE CASE ground on, Brownell was left with little time to worry over the politics of the unit. As a result of Judge Snyder's busy calendar, he had nearly a year to prepare for the trial—in all likelihood the first of several multidefendant trials—scheduled to begin the day after Labor Day the following September. But given the number of potential defendants and the complexity of the case, that was not a lot of time, even if Brownell had had some familiarity with the Cowboys. Despite his personnel problems, Rather had run a skilled investigation, and his prosecution memo had given Brownell a broad overview of the gang— some of their history, their key players, their most violent crimes. But when Brownell started to break down the case into its provable elements, he became lost in a welter of facts, hearsay, and half-truths. The sheer magnitude of information that he needed to learn— there were nearly 60 felonies, 45 defendants, over 100 witnesses—was overwhelming. Even more troubling, he had no way of weighing the reliability of informants or the culpability of defendants. He had not participated in HIU's eighteen-month investigation; had not acquired a hands-on feel for the gang; had not sat down with their leaders, managers, pitchers, clients, and victims; had not viewed hundreds of hours of surveillance tape; and, perhaps most important, had not developed a real-time appreciation for the cumulative rhythms of their operation: the grind of sales at the Hole, their protracted war with Cuevas, and the periodic violence by which they disciplined their workers and intimidated suspected cooperators.

Brownell read through the thousands of pages of grand jury minutes; debriefed hundreds of informants, cops, and detectives; and watched a year's worth of videotaped drug buys in the Hole and at other Cowboy locations. Then he had Quinn and Arsenault run photos of the defendants by him in the manner of flash cards and quiz him on their roles in the gang, their criminal histories, and personal quirks. "That's typical of Dan," Arsenault says. "He could have just summoned Garry and Mark and said, 'Bring me up to speed.' Instead he decided to bring himself up to speed."

Brownell quickly realized that he needed to streamline the case. Through their arms and drug suppliers, and their shifting alliances with crews like the Cuevas organization, the Cowboys were connected to broad swaths of the city's criminal activity; and HIU's detectives had reached that obsessive stage of the investigation where every facet seemed to open onto a new cast of characters and a new string of murders—bringing with them a level of complexity and detail that no prosecutor, much less a juror, could possibly appreciate or even remember.

Brownell was ruthless. He vetoed new cases, chopped off investigative tendrils, and routinely threw Quinn or Dugan and Tebbens out of his office when his eyes began to glaze over. Earlier that summer, the Feds had expressed an interest in El Feo, and Arsenault had turned over the results of their investigation to Alcohol, Tobacco, and Firearms (ATF) agents working with prosecutors from the U.S. Attorney's office. Now Brownell severed Raymond Polanco from the case, and instructed Dugan to share his voluminous findings about the Brooklyn gun runner with another group of ATF agents.

Brownell figured he already had enough charges to send most of the Cowboy defendants to prison for several lifetimes. And he had plenty of witnesses to help him prove those charges—dozens of cops and detectives who had bought drugs undercover from the gang or investigated past shootings and assaults; victims like Janice Bruington, the woman Stanley Tukes had shot in the back during the Quad; and former gang members like Freddie Sendra, the Cruz-Morales family, and Louise McBride, the Cowboy worker whose apartment was used by the gang as a stash house until HIDTA raided it the previous fall. What Brownell didn't have were current gang members, witnesses with up-to-date knowledge of the Cowboys' operations. None of the gang members corralled in the takedown had approached Brownell about cooperating. Clearly, no one wanted to testify against the gang, and it troubled the prosecutor.

Then, out of nowhere, Brownell and the case got an unbelievable break. Lenny's lawyer, Franklyn Gould, phoned Arsenault in early December to inquire about the possibility of a plea bargain, suggesting that Lenny come up for a Queen-for-a-Day—a free-ranging, off-the-record conversation that allows defendants to tell their stories to prosecutors without fear of self-incrimination. Investigators usually like this format, even if it doesn't lead to a deal, because it enables them to probe a defendant's knowledge of their case; and without a single high-ranking gang member on board, Lenny's cooperation was an enticing prospect. But Arsenault and Quinn were both chary of the gang leader's request. A cagey subject can turn the tables on an unsuspecting interviewer, using his questions to gauge how much he knows and who else is cooperating. Rafi Martinez, the leader of the Gheri Curls, had tried that; and neither Arsenault nor Quinn trusted Lenny's intentions. Arsenault considered turning down Lenny's offer, but decided in the end that it would be unfair to deny him a hearing. Instead he recused himself from the meeting and let Quinn handle the debriefing.

The conference took place just after noon on December 11. Quinn picked up Lenny at the "bridge"—the passageway that links the

Tombs with the Criminal Courts building—and escorted him to HIU in an elevator that connected directly with the unit. None of the other prisoners or even the guards knew about his visit. Once at HIU, Quinn took Lenny to the "cafeteria," where they were joined by Brownell and Gould. The lawyers rehashed the ground rules; nothing Lenny said could be used against him, except to impeach his testimony, should he choose later on to take the stand. Then they excused themselves, leaving the detective and the gang leader alone.

Lenny was dressed in jeans and a form-fitting T-shirt. He was bulked up from working out, and his skin—sallow from his ten months in jail—lent his eyes an inward, brooding intensity. Quinn started off by exploring Lenny's history, his early exploits under Yayo and his entry onto Beekman Avenue. The questions were designed to put Lenny at ease and get him talking about himself. In Quinn's experience, subjects were almost always willing to admit nonviolent felonies. It was their chance to show good faith without implicating themselves in anything too serious, and Quinn had expected Lenny to be frank. But Lenny was not only forthcoming; he seemed to genuinely enjoy talking about his trade, glad for once to have a knowledgeable audience. "This guy wants to make a deal," Quinn thought.

Quinn listened intently, prompting Lenny now and then with questions about this or that incident, reminding him that he already knew much of what Lenny was telling him. But he didn't press Lenny about the violence, letting him author his own biography the first time around. A half hour into the interview, however, Quinn decided to test Lenny's candor. "I know you don't want to talk about it, but now we gotta talk about it," Quinn said. "You know, the thing with the truck on the highway."

The request clearly stung Lenny. Cargill's murder wasn't in the indictment—there wasn't enough evidence to prove it—and Quinn knew it was the kind of act, aberrant and unjustifiable, that the gang leader wouldn't want to admit to. Lenny lowered his head and began jiggling his leg. "Naw," he said. "A lot of people are saying we did that, but I had nothing to do with that."

Quinn could see from his body language that he was lying, and he told him so. He was done playing around. Cargill was the linchpin of any plea bargain, and he wanted Lenny to know that. "It ain't just people been saying that," Quinn told him. "You've been saying that—first you talked about it on 171st Street, then your brother was talking about it. We know what happened. What do you think people talk about when they come in here? What do you think Platano said when he was in New Jersey?"

"Platano said that?" Lenny was dumbfounded.

"Do you think we picked you out of a fucking haystack? You made statements. People pick up on it. If I'm guessing— Look, we talked about all these other things. Did I tell you what you did? Why would I make this up?"

Lenny shook his head.

"You were the shooter. It wasn't anybody else. It was you.

"Look, you can't do this halfway," Quinn went on. "It's all gotta be out on the table. Lying's like being pregnant. You can't be a little bit. You either are or you're not. It can't be a little of this or a little of that. That's not the way it works. You got to do the whole thing, get the whole truth out, or it's the same as nothing at all. You nullify all the good stuff you told me. Now we're back to square one."

Lenny was hunkered low at the table, his legs jumping up and down. "Look at you, you can't hardly contain yourself," Quinn said. "It's time to get this off your chest, make a clean breast of this, so we can move on."

"Naw, it wasn't like that," Lenny said. "It's not the way you're making it out to be."

"Well, then you tell me the way it happened, so I get the truth. 'Cause other people are putting out their stories. You don't want their versions to be the only ones we're hearing."

Lenny stopped rocking, stopped shaking his leg. Quinn knew at that moment that he had him, that Lenny wanted to talk, that he was just looking for an out; Quinn decided to give him one. "I know you're not proud of this, that it's the one shooting you didn't have to do, that had nothing to do with business," Quinn said. "I know this didn't start out being an intentional thing. You'd been drinking, you were fucked up. You didn't use judgment. Maybe you were just trying to shoot the car a little. The road was wavy. You were bouncing up and down."

Lenny leaned in toward Quinn, close enough for the detective to put a hand on his arm. The gang leader had been preparing for this moment for over a month, ever since Gould had visited him in jail after the takedown and laid out the indictment against him. He'd known then, as he knew now, that his only chance of seeing the streets again was to cooperate. But admitting this, a murder without reason, was harder than even he'd imagined. He took a breath and began to speak.

18

BREAKTHROUGH

WINTER–SPRING 1994

WALTER ARSENAULT was struck dumb when Quinn stuck his head out of the cafeteria and told Arsenault that Lenny had just given up Cargill. He'd seen Quinn do some fairly amazing things before, but this was beyond his wildest expectations. Quinn had cracked a two-and-a-half-year-old case that many in the office thought would never be solved. What's more, Arsenault reasoned, if Lenny was willing to admit to Cargill, he was likely to give up the "whole boatload"—Raymond Polanco, El Feo, the mysterious and lethal Freddy Krueger, the people at the Quad, and every gang-sanctioned assault, shooting, and murder dating back to 1986. "Lenny was the Rosetta stone," Arsenault would later say.

But Arsenault had some reservations about Lenny's cooperation. For one thing, he wasn't sure he could sell a plea bargain to Snyder or Bronx DA Rob Johnson, even if he could get Lenny to accept the
serious jail time that would be part of any agreement. Moreover, he
knew if he signed Lenny up, he'd be violating one of the unit's cardinal
rules. In the past, HIU had always flipped a gang's mostly nonviolent
underlings against its leaders, the heavyweights who ordered and
committed the murders. Making a deal with Lenny was reversing that
process. But Arsenault realized that in the case of the Cowboys, many
of the underlings were violent as well.

THE NEW YEAR began well for the investigation. After Lenny's
December visit, the first members of the gang in the indictment to cooperate trickled in. They were mostly lower-level workers, often as
much victims of the gang's capricious violence as perpetrators. Juan
Abarca, a transporter for the gang, flipped in January. One of Pasqualito's recruits, he was so thickheaded and guileless that no juror,
Brownell reasoned, would believe him capable of making up the events
he described. Israel Rios and Martha Molina, the crackhead who had
been beaten into a coma by her manager, were typical among those
who pitched for the Cowboys to support their habit. Molina's brain had
been damaged by the beating, her vision blurry, her speech slurred;
she'd spent years in jail, and Social Services had taken away her kids.
Ordinarily, she would have made a terrible witness, but Brownell
wanted the jury to see firsthand the soul-destroying effects of the drug
that had made the Cowboys rich.

Starting in the early spring, Cowboy workers George Santiago
and Frankie Robles regularly visited the unit from jail. They had both
grown up in the lap of the gang, having resided as children in the Beech
Terrace tenement where Nelson and Lenny first started selling Red-
Top. Santiago was candid and articulate, and could recite the history of
the gang since they moved into the area, as could Robles, who'd been

Pasqualito's sidekick and had worked at almost every level of the organization. Together, along with the others who cooperated, they provided investigators with a rich, detailed picture of gang life on Beekman Avenue and the violent events that punctuated the day-to-day workings of the crack trade.

But once Brownell and the prosecutors started prepping the witnesses in earnest, a host of problems emerged. "There was a lot of trouble with their statements," Brownell recalls. "These were people who were never particularly interested in accuracy in their everyday lives. When they were telling a story, they'd mix in hearsay, and they couldn't remember what they'd actually seen and what someone else had told them. Or they'd just see bits and pieces of something—like the Quad or the Double—and they'd make up the missing parts according to what they thought you wanted to hear, or what they thought must have happened, which was usually wrong."

Language was another complicating factor. They were poor communicators, and in some instances even worse listeners, unable to follow instructions or read simple diagrams. The prosecutors spent long hours with nearly all the witnesses. In addition to the scores of police officers and detectives who needed to be debriefed, Brownell made it a rule to bring in at least one civilian witness a day. He and Hill and Grifa worked through whole mornings and afternoons with the Cruz-Morales kids, Abarca, Molina, and Santiago, going over their testimony, slowing their stories down frame by frame, teasing out the particles of information they had imagined or fabricated. Then, in April, Don Hill had the office build a scale model of the neighborhood, complete with cars and figures representing the gang and their victims. "You can't imagine how a simple little idea like that changed things," Brownell recalls. "There were parts of the Double and the Quad I'd never understood before, or that had seemed flat and sterile when they'd been described to me. Now those crimes just snapped to life for me. It was like watching children relive their memories by playing with dolls."

But the prosecutors could only do so much. They could not, for example, edit out the trail of written statements dating back to the Bronx grand jury in the Quad case in which many of their main witnesses contradicted not only each other but their own later testimony as well. Armed with those statements, any seasoned defense lawyer, Brownell knew, should be able to unhinge even the cleverest, most confident witnesses. And HIU's witnesses were far from ideal. In fact, they were scared at the prospect of simply appearing in a courtroom, much less jousting with attorneys. Brownell had to train them not only to defend their stories against cross-examination but to explain why they varied, sometimes widely, from earlier versions. "There were days when I panicked, when I felt there was no way I can do this," Brownell recalls. "When I read the record, I'd get depressed. But then we'd have a couple of good sessions in a row, and I'd start to think things weren't so bad. There was one rule I learned from running cross-country: When you run uphill, you always look at your feet. I tried not to look too far ahead. I knew I'd go crazy if I worried about things I couldn't control, like whether we were going to be ready in time. What saved me in the end was knowing that every day we did something productive."

ALL THE DETECTIVES were working overtime that winter. Transporting, guarding, and debriefing witnesses and informants took up the brunt of their days. But they were also tracking down fugitives and helping the Feds build parallel cases against Raymond Polanco, El Feo, and El Feo's notorious henchman, Freddy Krueger. Over the years, and especially during the Arsenault–Quinn era, HIU had acquired a macho reputation in the DA's office. Unlike the Trial Division, which was about 50 percent female, the unit was almost exclusively male. Moreover, HIU's prosecutors targeted the city's deadliest killers, worked hand in hand with veteran detectives and undercovers, and cultivated sources among the very gangs they were investigating. Yet because the unit operated so close to the street, they developed a connection to their "clients" that even their colleagues at the defense bar didn't achieve. At times during his Jamaican campaign, Arsenault functioned almost as much like a social worker as he did a prosecutor—walking informants and cooperators through VD clinics, GED programs, job interviews; listening to their troubles day and night; and maintaining avuncular relationships with witnesses long after they'd outlived their usefulness to the unit.

After a rocky start, Tebbens and Dugan had developed a good relationship with Lenny, whom they met with every week or two in preparation for his plea agreement. Convinced that Lenny had ordered the Quad from prison, Tebbens had disbelieved Lenny's steadfast denials, until new information confirmed the gang leader's version of events.

Dugan was also against Lenny at first. Already miffed at Quinn for questioning Lenny about Cargill without him—after all, Dugan had been the principal investigator in the case—Dugan was furious when he learned that Lenny had claimed he hadn't intended to kill Cargill when he shot into the Nissan pickup truck, and that Quinn had let him get away with it. "What the hell did you do that for?" Dugan said to Quinn outside the interview room. "That's the last thing you should have done."

"Well, that's how I got him to fucking come on board," Quinn said. "What the hell difference does it make as long as he admits he's the shooter?" Quinn had a point; Lenny was guilty of murder no matter what he was thinking when he pulled the trigger.

"In my opinion, that's not enough," Dugan said in the low, clipped voice he used when he was angry. "This guy intended to kill him, and he should admit it."

"All right," Quinn said. "You go in and try it."

Dugan spent the rest of the afternoon, and much of their next session, painstakingly extracting every detail of the night of the shooting. In the end, Dugan had not only Lenny's full confession but his grudging respect.

DURING THAT same time, Tebbens and Dugan, along with HIDTA's Eddie Benitez, continued to investigate Pasqualito's whereabouts. They haunted the fugitive's known hangouts—the tenement where his mother still lived on West 171st Street, his girlfriend's luxury apartment in Riverdale, the gang's old headquarters on Cypress Avenue. Despite persistent rumors that he'd fled to the Dominican Republic, all three detectives had heard reports of sightings in town, and because Pasqualito had been born in the States and was a U.S. citizen, they felt that if he were living in the Dominican Republic, they might still arrest him and bring him back. Then, in early March, Blue Eyes—the informant Dugan had cultivated in Pasqualito's old neighborhood—tipped him that the gang leader's mother was planning a trip to the Dominican Republic.

Dugan and Joe Flores, a veteran NYPD detective who'd recently joined HIU, staked out Anna Llaca's apartment, and in the early morning hours of March 7, the day of her scheduled flight, followed her out to La Guardia. When the detectives got to the airport, Flores noted that Llaca's bags at the curbside check-in had been ticketed for San Juan. If Pasqualito were meeting his mother in Puerto Rico, there would be no extradition problems. With no time to check with Quinn, Dugan and Flores decided to board the flight.

The detectives managed to follow Llaca to a modest house that belonged to Pasqualito's wife and daughter in Las Tejas—a rural village in the center of the island—where they set up surveillance. Pasqualito failed to show up. Then, five days later, on the afternoon they were scheduled to return home, the detectives got a call from Tebbens in New York. Thanks to a tip, Tebbens heard that Stacey Scroggins,

Pasqualito's girlfriend and the mother of another of his children, was flying down to the Dominican Republic, and HIDTA had alerted Kevin O'Brien, a DEA agent posted to Santo Domingo, that Pasqualito was coming to the airport to meet her that afternoon.

Late that afternoon, five members of the special airport security force in Santo Domingo confronted Pasqualito in the main terminal building. Despite the police's overwhelming numbers, Pasqualito reached for his gun. Almost anywhere else the agents would have shot Pasqualito dead. But the airport was crowded, so they rushed him instead and wrestled him to the ground before he could get off any shots. Pasqualito was now in police custody in Santo Domingo.

Quinn got on the line. "Take the next flight over there," he told them, "and see what you can do about getting him back."

O'BRIEN MET Dugan and Flores at the airport in Santo Domingo, and introduced them to Julio Cesar Beyonett, a general in charge of the Dominican Republic's security forces. Heavyset with a moon face and straight black hair, the general greeted the visitors from behind a large, clean desk in his office at police headquarters. Like many island officials, whose power derives more from their rank than the law, he exuded an insidious air of courtliness and utter command. His index finger seemed connected by an invisible string to an aide sitting at a small desk at the far end of the room. Whenever Beyonett wanted something—coffee, paperwork—he merely flicked his finger backward and the officer snapped to attention.

After exchanging pleasantries, the general asked the detectives about their business. Dugan explained through Flores—the general didn't speak English—who Pasqualito was, how dangerous he was, and how many men he had killed. Then they submitted documents proving Pasqualito's U.S. citizenship. Finally, Flores announced that while some of Pasqualito's victims were of Dominican descent, all were, like him, American-born. Dugan knew that if Beyonett thought that just one of the deceased was a Dominican national, he would order Pasqualito tried on the spot.

Beyonett listened intently to the detectives, glanced through the files they handed him, then fixed Dugan with a decisive look. "Okay," he said. "I don't want this piece of dirt. He's not a *nacional*, you can have him."

Dugan was stunned. But O'Brien had already warned him: "They'll say yes, even when they mean no. You won't really know you have him until the plane is off the ground." Dugan sat quietly while Beyonett ordered his aide to start the extradition process.

"This will take a few days," he told the detectives. Then he stood to accept their thanks. The meeting was over.

The next day, Dugan and Flores were back in the general's office. They wanted to know if they could get hold of the gun that Pasqualito was arrested with; he might have used it in one of his murders. Accustomed to observing a strict chain of continuity in handling evidence, Dugan was surprised when Beyonett reached into his desk drawer and pulled out the revolver. He handed it to Flores, then flicked his finger and spoke rapidly over his shoulder to his aide, now standing rigidly behind his desk. The police have already distributed the bullets among their troops, he explained to the detectives. His aide would retrieve them. Was there anything else he could do?

There was, Flores said, after thanking the general profusely for his help. A second U.S. fugitive was residing in their country, he said, a Nelson Sepulveda, whose case was similar to Pasqualito's. At that point, the aide, begging the general's pardon, interrupted. He said the police knew of this man, Sepulveda, and the detectives would be advised to speak to the colonel in charge of the sector where Sepulveda was living. The aide said he would arrange a meeting.

The next day, however, someone had leaked the story of Pasqualito's capture to the press, and the country was in an uproar; politicians and pundits were weighing in against extradition to the

United States in any form. After a few minutes of panic, Dugan and Flores decided to proceed as though everything were normal. That morning they met with the colonel who was overseeing Nelson's case—he said he was going forward and counseled patience—and then drove to the airport to pick up Quinn and Tebbens, who'd flown down to help with Pasqualito's release. Then they waited.

Finally on March 31, O'Brien phoned the investigators and told them to meet him at the airport. Beyonett had decided to go ahead with the extradition. At noon, they met with the security force that had captured Pasqualito and presented them with gifts: HIU T-shirts and caps, embossed coffee mugs, and gold-plated DEA pins. A half hour later Pasqualito emerged. He was chained around the arms and legs and surrounded by four Dominican soldiers pointing machine guns at him. When the prisoner spotted Dugan and Tebbens among his captors, he smiled broadly. "Boy, am I glad to see you guys," he said.

HIU'S INVESTIGATORS could not help liking Pasqualito. Although a psychopath, the most precipitously violent of the Cowboys, he had a directness and stand-up quality that was appealing. He was invariably jovial in his encounters with the detectives, and though he'd openly taunted Tebbens, Dugan, and Benitez in the past, he tipped his hat to them now. It was business, as far as he was concerned; he had a job to do, and so did they.

Whatever their feelings toward Pasqualito, the detectives weren't taking any chances with him. They kept him in irons during the plane ride and refused to let him eat or drink. They didn't want him going to the bathroom until after they landed. The gang leader took it in stride. Sandwiched between Dugan and Tebbens, he entertained them with tales about the Dominican corrections system. The last five days he'd been locked in an eight-by-eight cell with a hole dug in the center for a toilet. There was no bed, just a little straw in one corner of the cell, and no food. In the Dominican Republic, a prisoner's relatives provide the food; Pasqualito had none on the island. He hadn't eaten for five days, and he'd been afraid to drink the polluted water. Another few hours, he said, wouldn't make a difference. "I can't wait to get back to Rikers and have me a steak," he told Dugan.

Dugan let Pasqualito talk. He wasn't allowed to question the gang leader, in any case, without his lawyer present. However, at one point, he noted that Pasqualito was sporting a tattoo on his forearm, an image of a skull with snakes crawling in and out of its apertures.

"You like that?" Pasqualito asked.

"Yes."

"I got that the night after I killed Frankie," Pasqualito blurted out.

The detectives had barely deplaned when they received news that trumped their extradition of Pasqualito. Bobby Tarwacki, who'd been waiting on the tarmac with a van to transport Pasqualito, told them, "Walter just got a call from the DR. They've got Nelson."

NELSON SEPULVEDA was neither as large nor as intimidating as his brother. His features had been chiseled with a finer tool, and he seemed distracted much of the time. But the "Whack," as Nelson was known on the street, was the better athlete of the two, a tough, wiry running back on his high school football team with fast hands and a hair-trigger temper. Nobody fucked with Nelson, though it was Lenny, with his cool, businesslike approach to violence, who headed the gang's enforcement wing.

Little of Nelson's sinew was in evidence upon his return from the Dominican Republic, however. Sitting across from Arsenault in the unit chief's office in mid-April, he looked like a man about to give it up. After fifteen years of interviewing potential cooperators, Arsenault could sense, even before they spoke, who was going to sign on and who wasn't. The hard cases like Pasqualito had a defiant glint in their eyes, a bright, steely expression that virtually guaranteed their information would be scant or misleading. Nelson's eyes were dead. He'd left the business behind when he'd absconded to the Dominican Republic more than two years ago, and now he seemed out of it completely. But he'd known that this day might come, and he'd already decided how he'd deal with it. "I'm going to tell you everything you want to know," he said to Arsenault. "But I want you to give me back a little piece of my life."

Nelson didn't seem to want to wrangle; he was determined to make a deal. Moreover, he'd formed a bond with Tebbens, who'd flown down to the Dominican Republic with Dugan to bring him back, and he trusted the detective, as much as his lawyer, to look after his interests.

For his part, Brownell was eager to conclude the negotiations as quickly as possible. Brownell had already decided by then not to use Lenny as a witness. Lenny's leadership position in the gang, his history of violence, and his cold-blooded murder of Cargill would repulse any jury, and might well taint their case by association. Nelson's record was not all that much better than his brother's. In the weeks after his return to the United States, he'd admitted ordering the Quad, though he didn't participate in the actual shooting; killing Anthony Villerbe, the former Corrections worker who, according to Nelson, had tried to pass counterfeit bills to the gang; and committing a host of lesser crimes. But Nelson, unlike his brother, had never been the driving force behind the Cowboys, had never been its true leader, and it showed in their demeanor. Lenny was a boss. No matter how earnestly he cooperated—and his efforts had been substantial—he couldn't shake the air of arrogant command that seemed a natural part of his actions. Nelson, on the other hand, seemed softer, if not exactly remorseful; and with his detailed knowledge of the Quad, he'd emerged in Brownell's plans as a key witness. All that was left was to fix the terms of the sentence. Brownell offered twenty-two years, based on the twenty-five-year sentence they had offered Lenny. The idea was to give both brothers as stiff a penalty as possible, without snuffing out all hope for a life in the future. Arsenault knew there were DAs in the office for whom any plea would be too generous, given Lenny's and Nelson's history. But twenty-two years, with no guarantee of parole, was an effective life sentence, tougher than many similar agreements, and a good deal tougher than the deal shortly to be handed by the Feds to Sammy "the Bull" Gravano. Gravano, a mob informant who admitted killing more than twenty people, served five years for his crimes—a pact that still generates delusions of leniency among potential cooperators.

With Nelson on board, Lenny's cooperation was assured. Ten days later, he accepted the twenty-five-year plea offer, and on May 16 appeared before Leslie Crocker Snyder to make his allocution. A kind of extended guilty plea in which a defendant formally admits to the particulars of his crimes, an allocution is usually an unremarkable affair. The prosecutor does most of the talking; the defendant merely assents that he did such and such a thing on such and such a date. But Lenny's hearing was different. An air of expectancy hung over the tense, packed courtroom, which, though closed to the public, was filled with HIU and HIDTA personnel, prosecutors from Brooklyn and the Bronx, and, most prominently, the Cargill family. They had come to see close up the man who had killed their son and brother; to hear him do penance, or at least confess to his crime; and perhaps without knowing it, to test afresh their reactions to an event that had numbed and diminished their own lives.

After her breakdown and hospitalization in the summer of 1991, Anne Cargill lapsed into a steep, protracted depression. Already abusing pills before her breakdown, she began increasing her dosages and mixing Percodan, Vicodin, Fiorecet, and alcohol. Before long she was hooked, and her life unraveled completely. For years she had done the marketing for her husband's small business. Now she stopped coming into the office altogether, causing sales to drop off sharply. Worse, she isolated herself from her family when they needed her most. Afraid she was becoming suicidal, Innes and their four daughters organized an intervention in June 1993. Anne was furious—she felt her privacy had been invaded—and per her therapist's instructions, the family left her alone. Innes moved into the home of one of his daughters, and the family refused to communicate with her. Forced to confront herself, Anne realized she wanted to live, to grow old and get to know her grandchildren. Three days after the intervention, she checked herself into Four Winds, a rehab facility in nearby Katonah.

Six months later, prodded by his wife, Innes entered AA.

Both Innes and Anne had been clean for months when Arsenault briefed them on the details of their son's murder the evening before Lenny's allocution. Still, seated with two of their daughters in the close atmosphere of HIU's conference room, the Cargills had difficulty grasping Arsenault's description of what had happened. "I felt like I was watching a movie, that I was floating above the room, looking down on the action," Innes Cargill recalled. "It was as close to an out-of-body experience as I've ever had. I had to keep reminding myself: This is my son they're talking about. This is David."

Now, flanked by his lawyers and surrounded by a phalanx of security guards, Lenny stood behind the defense table facing the judge. His hands were cuffed in front of him and his voice, at first, was barely audible. Anne Cargill felt a strange swelling inside her chest. She had expected to feel angry, vengeful, repulsed. Instead, she saw a young man, not much older than her son would have been, shackled and bowed before the bench, his life, his free life at any rate, effectively over. What she felt was pity.

Don Hill led Lenny through his exploits in the Bronx—his activities as the Cowboys' boss and his role in a series of violent shootings, several of them fatal. In one typical instance, he was charged with ordering the death of a rival dealer, who happened to be sitting in a car at the time with his pregnant wife. "On that date, December 30, 1990, were you present in an automobile in the vicinity of Vyse Avenue and 181st Street in the Bronx?" Hill asked him.

"Yes, sir."

"Did you ever have a conversation with another individual at that location by the name of Manuel Lugo?"

"Yes."

"During that conversation did you relay to Manuel Lugo that you wished to engage in a business transaction with him?"

Hill's formal locutions and Lenny's terse replies and matter-of-fact tone had the effect of two alien worlds colliding. But it wasn't until after Hill rested and Brownell elicited the details of David Cargill's murder that the true, anarchic dimensions of Lenny's violence took shape. As Innes Cargill leaned forward in his seat, his face a blur of incomprehension, Brownell questioned Lenny about the night of the shooting. "You were in a car at the time?" Brownell asked.

"Yes."

"What type of car?"

"A Buick Regal."

"Who was driving that car?"

"Raymond."

Two weeks before the Cargill incident, Lenny had bought a dozen Uzi 9 mm automatics from Raymond at $2,500 per—guns he'd been stockpiling in preparation for a war with Yellow-Top, the same guns the Cowboys would later use in the Quad. One had been defective, and he'd given it back to Raymond to repair. Now Raymond was returning it to him outside the Palladium.

It was 3 A.M. Lenny was wasted. He'd been drinking kamikazes and rum punches, whatever they'd put in front of him, until closing; and he'd been smoking blunts, the cigar-sized joints that were the Cowboys' drug of choice. Platano and Nelson had been with him, and were waiting for him now in Platano's BMW to drive to an after-hours club in the Bronx. But he told them to go ahead; he'd follow them in Raymond's car.

That was his first mistake. His second was going up the West Side. Normally he would have taken the East River Drive to the Bronx, but Platano wanted to check out the Limelight and some other nightspots, so they drove up Sixth Avenue, then cut over to the highway. Raymond was at the wheel, trying to keep up with Platano, who was threading traffic at speeds up to 70 mph.

"Can you tell us what kind of vehicle David Cargill was driving that night?" Brownell asked him.

"A red [pickup]," Lenny answered.

"And where was the first time that you saw that red [pickup] he was driving that night?"

"On Fifty-seventh Street."

"Fifty-seventh and where?"

"The West Side Highway."

They were heading north on the highway, following Platano onto the ramp leading to the elevated portion of the road. Cargill's pickup truck was traveling west on 57th Street and had run a red light at the intersection with the highway, cutting Platano's BMW off on the ramp, nearly forcing him into the divider.

"That fucking guy's crazy," Platano said. Polanco had pulled the Regal abreast of the BMW, and Platano was yelling at Lenny through their open windows. "He almost hit me. Give me the fucking gun, I'm going to light him up."

Lenny looked down the stretch of dark highway. He saw the pickup's taillights winking in the distance, and on his left a few scattered pairs of oncoming headlights, and a single black ribbon of river and night. "I'll take care of it," Lenny said.

"So Platano drives off," Lenny told the court, "and Raymond passed me the Uzi and said, 'Go test that out,' because I was in the transaction of buying an Uzi."

"This was an Uzi you wanted to make sure was working?" Snyder asked.

"Yes."

"So you decided to test it out by shooting the guy who almost hit your friend's car?"

"Yes."

"What did you do with the Uzi?"

Lenny had retrieved the gun from a clavo secreted behind the center console in the rear seat, and locked a cartridge into the chamber. Meanwhile, Polanco had gunned the Buick and had almost pulled even with the pickup. "Light him up, light him up," he yelled at Lenny, nudging the car forward.

Lenny aimed at Cargill's door, just below the driver-side window, and squeezed the trigger. Nothing happened.

"So I told him, 'This gun is no good,' and then he took it back and I held the steering wheel as he slowed down, and then he did something to it. I don't know what he did to it, and he passed it back to me. He took back the steering wheel and he drove up to it again, and it misfired, and so we tried it again, the same procedure."

The second time the gun jammed, Lenny cursed Polanco. What if this happened in a shoot-out? He'd be dead. Polanco took the Uzi from Lenny, ejected the jammed cartridge and slid another one into the chamber, while Lenny guided the wheel. Then he handed the gun back to Lenny, and floored the accelerator.

The car lurched forward, pinning Lenny briefly to the back of his seat. Then Polanco whipped the Buick into the left lane, hugging the guardrail through a lazy curve. The speedometer was topping 100 when they let out onto a long straight stretch of road. Lenny saw the loops of vibrating lights atop the George Washington Bridge, the BMW's taillights dancing a hundred yards ahead in the far right lane, and closer in, like a slow-moving target in the middle of the road, the boxy silhouette of Cargill's pickup. "Now, try it now," he heard Polanco's hoarse voice urging him above the noise of the engine and the wind gusting through the open window.

The gun exploded to life, the magazine emptying out in one drunken gasp. Lenny saw the plumelike pattern of bullet holes in the door of the pickup as the Uzi's recoil drove the short barrel upward. The last few bullets crashed through the pickup's window, and Lenny saw the profile of his victim for the first time, a young white male slumped over at the neck. It was over in a second or two. The Buick picked up speed, and behind it, the pickup slowed precipitously, lurching left and right, before heading off onto the exit grid at 158th Street.

The courtroom was silent after Lenny finished his testimony—a hushed, stunned silence like a ringing in the ear. Then Judge Snyder, tight-lipped, unable to hide her anger or disgust, reviewed the salient terms of Lenny's cooperation agreement, before retreating abruptly to her chambers.

Back at the unit a half hour later, the prosecutors were still barely speaking to each other. There were no words to characterize what they'd just heard; even irony, the gallows humor that coated their stomachs against the acid reality of the streets, failed to mitigate the horror of David Cargill's murder. Finally Brownell called Hill and Grifa into his office and began going over the schedule for the rest of the afternoon. There was, he knew, no time to mull over, much less digest, the meaning of what was already past. They had a trial coming up—eight defendants, all killers like Lenny—and just three months left to prepare.

19

THE TRIAL BEGINS

THE COWBOY conspiracy trial, which began on September 20, 1994, promised to be a prolonged, raucous affair. There were nine defendants in all, Platano, Pasqualito, and Fat Danny among them. They would wait until later to try or plead out the others who weren't facing murder charges. Just the logistics—coordinating them, their lawyers, their special needs and objections—were daunting. Actually laying out their individual cases for a jury, defining their roles within the gang and their relationship to one another, seemed at times like an impossible task. But the prosecution's case was so large and unwieldy—at one time there were nearly 200 candidates on their witness list, many of them in jail or in hiding—both Arsenault and Brownell felt they had only one shot at a trial, and they wanted to include all the defendants indicted for murder.

Arsenault and Brownell were also keenly aware of the stakes of the trial. They needed a total victory to ensure that none of the Cowboys' violent enforcers returned to the streets, where they could retaliate against the witnesses. Moreover, seeing their mates get stiff sentences would help persuade the remaining gang members to accept reasonable plea bargains. Most important, though, was the effect the outcome would have on future cases. "The credibility of the unit was at risk," Arsenault recalls. "We'd built up a reputation over the years with Hoyt and Ellen Corcella, with the Spanglers and the Gheri Curls and all the other gangs we'd done. We were pretty well known on the street, and I knew that if we got beaten by the Cowboys, that would be well known too. Plus our professional and ethical reputations were on the line. In big conspiracy cases like the Cowboys, the defense always tries to attack the integrity of the cops and prosecutors at trial. It's the only way they can refute the evidence we present. Finally, there was the additional burden of having three offices try the case. That kind of cooperative effort was unprecedented in my experience, and it was important to show that it could work."

Arsenault was also feeling pressure from inside his own office. As his rift with Nancy Ryan deepened, Arsenault relied increasingly on Barbara Jones, Morgenthau's chief assistant, to act as his liaison with the eighth floor. In fact, the unit had taken some steps toward autonomy. In the spring, Jones had replaced James McVeety and a handful of detectives thought to be allied with Ryan, and installed Quinn as chief investigator. And Arsenault, having decided to stay with HIU, had withdrawn his offer to the Boston U.S. Attorney's office. But he still felt he was one mistake away from a debacle.

Arsenault's suspicions were confirmed to him in an incident that occurred as the trial got under way. A few days into jury selection, Morgenthau's public affairs officer asked Arsenault to talk to a local reporter on background about the Cowboys. Ethically, government prosecutors are enjoined from commenting publicly about ongoing investigations. In fact, DAs routinely grant "for background only" interviews to the media in high-profile cases, if only to counter the spin of media-cozy defense counsels. In this instance, however, the reporter not only twisted Arsenault's general comments about gangs to make it sound like he was talking specifically about the Cowboys, but attributed off-the-record quotes to the unit chief. Not surprisingly, the article triggered vigorous protests from the Cowboys' defense lawyers. According to Arsenault and other knowledgeable sources, it also prompted a visit from Nancy Ryan to the judge, censuring Arsenault for his indiscretion, a meeting Ryan denies. Arsenault, who was called before Snyder that same morning and formally reprimanded, accepted his fate with equanimity; it was, he felt, the cost of doing business. But when he learned that his own supervisor not only had failed to make clear the true circumstances behind his actions but had actually criticized him, he snapped. It was clear to him now that Ryan would take every opportunity to attack the unit. By noon, he'd tendered his resignation.

The following Monday, DA Robert Morgenthau summoned him to his office.

BY THE 1990S Morgenthau was far and away New York's preeminent lawman. His connections to the power elite, combined with his nearly thirty years as a top prosecutor, had made him an outsized figure in enforcement circles, a kingmaker. Dozens of former associates had ascended to the bench; still others occupied sensitive positions in state and local government. But Morgenthau's authority stemmed from his political skills. Despite a clear lack of charisma, he was a master at getting his message across to the press—he enjoyed particularly good relations with the *Times*—and he was a ruthless behind-the-scenes operator.

He was less hands-on in the administration of his own office.

Apart from a few big investigations that claimed his close attention, he rarely bothered himself about the legal maneuverings of a particular case. Most line assistants met Morgenthau twice during their tenures, once when they joined the office and then again when they left, and he held himself aloof from internal politics. This attitude of benign disinterest—as a top aide said, he ruled the office the way the viceroys once ruled India, rarely taking sides between factions, or firing, or even censuring his lawyers—enabled him to rise above the squabbles and professional jealousies that constantly rose among the ranks. Most assistants regarded him, when they regarded him at all, as a sort of paterfamilias, the kindly old gent who signed their paychecks, encouraged them to do the right thing, and protected them from the excesses of the press and the evils of political influence.

The less salutary effect of this was the Balkanization of the office, as bureau chiefs and unit chiefs cultivated fiefdoms, and division heads and eighth-floor executives forged alliances or battled over territory like medieval princes. It was the very issue that had brought about Arsenault's resignation.

Morgenthau was waiting for him at his conference table at the far end of his gymnasium-sized office. He was deceptively frail-looking with wavy white hair and a beakish nose, his eyes were watery behind thick glasses, and he had a prissy, headmasterish mouth, dour and disapproving in repose. In fact, he was surprisingly spry for a man in his seventies, his handshake was firm, and he had one of those rich, laminated New York voices—hints of his German-Jewish ancestry and Yankee upbringing audible beneath the asphalt rasp of Manhattan. "Sit down," he told Arsenault.

Arsenault walked past Morgenthau's desk piled high with papers and a wall full of photographs of famous people, feeling the same mixture of awe and anticipation he always felt when meeting with the boss. He got along well with Morgenthau, though there wasn't much interaction between them. Morgenthau was less a lawyer or an administrator than a politician; he dealt in the realm of the possible, what he could do for HIU or what the unit could do for him and, by extension, the office and the city. This afternoon, Morgenthau had a gift for Arsenault.

"I just had lunch with [Police Chief] Bratton," Morgenthau told Arsenault, after he'd sat down. "He asked me what we needed, and one of the things I asked for was help for HIU. And now you have four new detectives."

Morgenthau was clearly pleased with his offering, and normally Arsenault would have been also. "That's great news," he told Morgenthau. "But didn't Barbara tell you that I'm leaving?"

"Oh, that," Morgenthau said, waving him off. "I know all about that. That's been taken care of."

"Well, how?"

Morgenthau shushed him with an impatient look. "Barbara will explain it to you later," he said. "You're not going to go anywhere."

AFTER THE MEETING, Jones told Arsenault that Morgenthau had taken HIU out of the Trial Division, away from Nancy Ryan. From now on he would report directly to Jones. Heading back upstairs, Arsenault felt a measure of vindication and relief, and no little excitement at gaining four more detectives. But he knew in his heart that the long-term fate of the unit still depended on the outcome of the Cowboy trial.

Arsenault kept Brownell in the dark about the backstage maneuverings. There was no point in distracting him; he had enough on his mind. In addition to the usual case of nervousness before trial, Brownell was concerned about his witnesses. He felt confident that he had more than enough evidence to convict, but nearly all that evidence was in the form of testimony from witnesses whose criminal backgrounds impeached their credibility before they opened their mouths. What's more, their poor communication skills, their fear of testifying, and in many cases their hair-trigger tempers made them liable to self-destruct under cross-examination. Cynthia Williams, a gang member with a history of violence and mental instability, and a key witness in the Brooklyn murder of drug dealer Juan "Papito" Francisco, had physically attacked Lori Grifa during a recent prep session. And Grifa's taunts were nothing compared to what Williams was likely to face on the stand.

Brownell's strategy was to bury the jury in evidence, "to throw as much stuff out there as we could and see what sticks." But there was a danger in this approach: If the defense could discredit enough witnesses, they would taint the rest of the prosecution's case by association. In a nine-month trial the jury was not likely to remember the welter of detail that the DAs presented as much as they would the high points, the moments of emotion. In the end, Brownell felt, they would judge with their hearts, not their heads. If the defense could persuade just one juror that there was reasonable doubt, the defense would win; and as Brownell knew, a hung jury was the equivalent of an acquittal. There was little hope, he realized, of going through another nine-month trial.

At times, he wondered whether he was going to get through the trial as it was. Just gathering a jury pool took two weeks. Snyder packed the potential candidates in her courtroom 100 to 150 at a time, explained to them the nature and projected length of the trial, then cleared the courtroom and fielded excuses one by one. Most candidates pled work obligations or financial hardship—jurors are paid only a modest stipend. Others had physical disabilities, had been victims of a crime, were biased against the police, had an extreme aversion to violence, or had one of a myriad other reasons why they couldn't spend the better part of a year in Snyder's court. John Kennedy, Jr., who showed up in the first panel of jurors, was deemed a public figure, whose presence in the courtroom would distract from the proceedings. Women who were pregnant or who might become pregnant were also excused.

Snyder was usually tough on dropouts—jury duty, in her mind, was an obligation, not a right or a privilege—but even she recognized the turbulent effects of a nine-month trial, and by the end of each tedious session, only a handful of candidates remained in the pool—mostly government workers, elderly retirees, and unemployed persons. Brownell was not happy about the mix. In his experience, retirees didn't like to spend weeks, much less months, in a courtroom, and were liable to lose interest in a prolonged case like the Cowboys, or worse, begin to resent the government officials whom they were likely to blame for keeping them there. The unemployed, especially the chronically unemployed, were even worse. There was usually a reason for their status—poor concentration, antisocial attitudes, mistrust for authority.

In the end, the prosecutors managed to get a jury—twelve regulars and eight alternates—that was a broadly diverse mix of working New Yorkers: office workers, a schoolteacher, a postal employee, an electrical engineer; evenly split among men and women, blacks, Hispanics, and whites. The group was somewhat younger than Brownell would have liked—mostly in their late twenties and thirties—but they were all employed, and many of them lived in neighborhoods where crime in general and drug dealing in particular were a problem. What rankled Brownell, however, was the time and effort involved in the process. It had taken weeks just to get to voir dire—the process by which litigators question candidates and select a final jury. Meanwhile, the defendants refused to waive their right to be present during the entire selection process, even though one of them slept through most of the proceedings, and whole days were lost when Corrections failed to produce all nine prisoners. Then the defense mounted a Batson challenge, claiming that the prosecutors were using their vetoes in a pattern that suggested a racial bias. (It's an open secret that prosecutors don't like to impanel young black women, feeling that they have unusual difficulty condemning young black men to long prison terms.) The challenge was defeated, but time wore on. By the time the lawyers were ready to give opening arguments in mid-October, a month and a half had elapsed since hearings had begun, enough time to try several serious felonies from start to finish. "We had decided Don [Hill] would do the opening, and it was a good thing," Brownell recalls. "I remember walking into court that first day and feeling completely worn out, and then realizing: We still haven't started yet."

PART 51, Leslie Crocker Snyder's Special Narcotics Court, was a relic from the 1940s, a vast square church of a room, calculated to cow even the righteous. A broad center aisle cut through seven long rows of spectator pews, divided the gated arena known as the well between defense and prosecution, and ran up to the elevated, altarlike bench from which Snyder presided—with queenly control—over the proceedings. On her right sat her bailiff; on her left, the jury; and behind her, soaring to the triple-height ceiling, a lacquered wood panel proclaimed the court's trust in God.

But nothing about the court's physical plant was as intimidating as the judge herself. Decked out in her robes, with classic good looks and a mane of streaked blond hair, Leslie Snyder, 52, cut a glamorous figure, which, when combined with her obvious intelligence—she'd graduated first in her class at law school—and imperious tone, made her a mesmerizing and at times exasperating presence in her courtroom.

She also cut a broad swath through the criminal justice system generally. Among the first female prosecutors at the Manhattan DA's office—she'd joined the office in 1968 under Morgenthau's predecessor, Frank Hogan—and the first woman to try serious felonies, she founded Manhattan's groundbreaking Sex Crimes Prosecution Bureau, and later pioneered legislation that modernized New York State's rape law. A formidable trial attorney, she was appointed to the bench by New York mayor Ed Koch in 1983, and quickly established a reputation as a tough, rigorous judge willing to hand out heavy sentences to violent offenders—something of an anomaly in New York's famously liberal courts. Known as a prosecutor's judge, she was feared and in some cases disliked by the state defense bar, but even her critics conceded that she knew the law and was as likely to censor an unprepared prosecutor as a lawyer for the defense.

THE COWBOYS launched the first strike in their defense before the trial began. That fall a prison informant told Tebbens that Pasqualito and Fat Danny had put out murder contracts on Snyder, Brownell, and Tebbens. Apparently, Pasqualito had bribed a guard to use his cell phone, contacted an associate from his old Washington Heights neighborhood named Daniel Cabon, and told him to arrange the hits with El Feo and Freddy Krueger. The price on Snyder's head was $25,000. Brownell and Tebbens went for $10,000 apiece.

The scheme sounded far-fetched. But knowing the gangsters involved, HIU didn't take any chances. They contacted the police, who assigned round-the-clock protection for Snyder, and they moved Brownell to a "safe house" apartment in Battery Park City. Police officers escorted him to and from court; he was instructed not to return home or venture out into the city.

Meanwhile, the unit's detectives took aggressive action to preempt the contracts. Dugan had run across Cabon—who dealt drugs in the Heights—several times during his investigation of the Cowboys' Manhattan connections. Dugan directed HIU's undercovers to Cabon's selling location, where they bought crack from him and arrested him. Later, under questioning, Cabon admitted his drug activities, but refused to give up Pasqualito or Fat Danny, and disavowed any knowledge of a murder plot.

HIU went after El Feo and Freddy Krueger as well. They prevailed on Laurie Horne, the ATF agent who'd taken over El Feo's case, to expedite his arrest, and on December 12, Horne, along with Terry Quinn and HIU investigator Jose Flores, nabbed the gang leader at the Hilton Hotel where he'd been holing up in Miami. Meanwhile, Dugan tracked Krueger to his girlfriend's apartment in the

Heights, but missed him by hours, before learning that he'd absconded to the Dominican Republic. A Dominican national, Krueger would not be as easy to extradite as Pasqualito or Nelson. But as long as he remained in the Dominican Republic, he posed no threat to the judge.

D O N   H I L L   began his opening on October 18. He felt a surge of relief at finally delivering the statement he'd been preparing for weeks, in some ways for years.

Opening statements, by law, may not be argumentative and, by convention, should not be overly dramatic. Their purpose is to establish what the prosecution intends to prove, and how it intends to prove it. Anything else, in theory, is extraneous. In practice, however, the opening is the prosecution's first real crack at the jury, and it sets the tone for the rest of the trial. Moreover, Hill could not talk about the Cowboys' exploits without feeling, and he wasn't about to try.

Hill spent the afternoon session—about two hours—talking about the Quad. For him it was the gang's most heinous crime, perpetrated at the apogee of their power—an act of pure arrogance and brutality, the best example of what happens when the law allows a cancer of violence to metastasize freely. It was a crime that Hill had lived with for nearly two and a half years. He was conversant with every detail, and barely referred to his notes.

Standing at the rail of the jury box, he let his eyes range over the jurors' faces, and turned away only to point out the defendant whose deeds he was describing. He rarely raised his voice, and was careful not to dwell on the gruesome aspects of the crime. His purpose was simply to humanize the victims. They were not heroes, he said. They were not all good citizens. They were just ordinary people going about their business, and even if that business was buying crack, they didn't deserve to be butchered for it.

It was the first time Hill had told his story to an audience, and as he enumerated the dozens of smaller crimes that culminated in the four cold-blooded homicides—the competing crack sales between the Cowboys and Yellow-Top, the purchase of the firearms from Raymond Polanco, the distribution of the guns to the shooters in the hallway of 348 Beekman just hours before the Quad, the planning of the murders on the rooftop of No. 348, and the brazen shooting into the alleyway— Hill noted with a shock of recognition the utter horror and revulsion mirrored in the gaze of the jurors.

Hill concluded his opening statement the next morning by tracing the origins of the gang at Beech Terrace, then moving forward in time, delineating the development of their conspiracy, and sketching in the violent incidents leading up to the Quad and beyond. With each shooting and stabbing he described, he could sense the growing incredulity of the jurors. By the end, he'd laid out a rough itinerary for the prosecution's case. He'd also sounded its theme: For many years, while building an empire through greed and ruthlessness, the Cowboys had been a law unto themselves. Now it was time for the real law to judge them.

The defense's openings were brief, and mostly of the "prosecution has offered no evidence yet to prove their claims" variety. But two strategies emerged: First, the lawyers noted that the prosecution's case was big and confusing, and like the street itself, full of ambiguities, inconsistencies, discontinuity, and irrationality. Clearly, the defense intended to take advantage of that confusion to argue against the prosecution's contention that there was an organized conspiracy. Yes, their clients dealt drugs—most of the lawyers were prepared to admit that. And yes, their clients knew one another, many of them since childhood. But they were in business for themselves. The idea that there was a rigid hierarchy, or any kind of complex set of agreements or protocols among them, was absurd.

The second theme was adumbrated in the opening by Pasqualito's lawyer, a fierce and sometimes strident advocate named Valerie Van Leer-Greenberg. The government's civilian witnesses, she said, were scum, no better, and in many instances worse, than the defendants; and they were unreliable, and had been paid and manipulated by the prosecution.

But the prosecution's biggest challenge had nothing to do with the defense's arguments. With nine defendants, a pared-down witness list that still hovered around 100, and dozens of charges in the indictment, including ten homicides, Brownell feared that jurors wouldn't be able to remember, much less keep straight, the abundance of detail he needed to elicit over the next six to nine months just to make his case legally sufficient. Worse, he and his colleagues risked alienating the jurors, losing their attention and sympathy.

HIU had devised several tactics to counteract the length and complexity of a multidefendant conspiracy trial like the Cowboys trial. The simplest was the use of visual aids—a photo array of the gang's hierarchy, a chart listing the main charges (the Quad, the Double, etc.), and the model of the Beekman Avenue neighborhood that the prosecutors had used to prep their witnesses. Every time the jurors entered the courtroom, they would be faced with the same menu of violence, the same gallery of mug shots matching the defendants' faces; and whenever they could, the prosecutors intended to refer witnesses to the displays, underscoring the who, what, and where of their testimony.

HIU's chief strategy, however, was simply to tell the Cowboys' story, to use narrative and dramatic techniques to depict their seven-year reign of terror over a neighborhood. As obvious a tactic as that may seem, many prosecutors balk at the notion that they're also entertainers, preferring to argue their cases in a dry, legalistic fashion, relying on the judge's instructions and the jurors' own good sense to lead them to the correct verdict. But Arsenault and Brownell weren't taking any chances. They wanted the jurors on the edge of their seats as much as possible, and they arranged the order of the witnesses to grab the jury's attention early on and build tension throughout the trial, focusing first on the Quad, as Hill did in his opening, and closing with Pasqualito's assassination of Frankie Cuevas.

The prosecution's first witness was Salustiano Sanabria, an emergency medical technician who arrived on Beekman Avenue just moments after the Quad. Sanabria described the carnage and chaotic crowd scene, much like the opening shot in a crime film.

After Tebbens and Benitez testified, Brownell called Freddie Sendra, the former Cowboy manager, to give an insider's view of the gang. Brownell quizzed him about the gang's origins and its early years on Beekman Avenue. Sendra, who joined Red-Top as a shift manager in mid-1988 after a two-year-stint in jail for auto theft, identified Platano, Pasqualito, and Fat Danny as charter members and bosses under Lenny and Nelson. Then, prompted by Brownell, he described the way the organization operated from the time Lenny purchased raw cocaine from a wholesaler in upper Manhattan.

Drugs, money, guns—Brownell debriefed Sendra about the salient features of gang life among the Cowboys. He even grilled the former manager about target practices the gang held on the rooftops overlooking St. Mary's Park, seeing who could come closest to the pedestrians without hitting them. But Brownell was also interested in getting Sendra to talk about another subject: the children whom the Cowboys employed to help out in the business, and whose participation in the gang's activities, if proved, would turn their conspiracy into a top felony with penalties equal to that of a murder conviction. "Well, Mr. Sendra, what were the ages of some of the people that were used?" Brownell asked.

"Ten-, eleven-, twelve-year-olds."

"What were they used for?"

"We used to have them do runs for us, bring over the bundles, and go to the store for us."

"Now, you say 'we.' Who are you referring to?"

"Me, Lenny, Nelson, Fat Danny, Platano, Hector . . ."

"Did you know the names of all the ten-, eleven-, twelve-year-olds that transported in this manner?"

"Just one."

"And what was the one name that you did know?"

"Little Louie . . ."

"How many other people of the age of ten, eleven, and twelve were used to perform this function?"

"About six to eight."

"And where were those children from?"

"Right there on Beekman Avenue."

"And how are they obtained to do this?"

"We just used to pay them, you know, buy them things, get them whatever they wanted, you know . . . Buy them ice cream if they wanted, toys from the store, whatever they wanted . . ."

"Was there any particular reason why ten-, eleven-, twelve-year-olds were used rather than people that were the ages of the pitchers or the managers, older people?"

"Less likely for them to get stopped by a cop."

Brownell finished his direct examination of Sendra on the afternoon of November 2, one and a half days after he began. Cross-examination took three times that long, and was relentless. Platano's lawyer, Robert Soloway, a short, balding bullet of a man with an intense, rapid-fire delivery, took the first shot at Sendra, and not only rehashed his criminal record but targeted his pleas and parole applications—the many lies and broken promises he'd made to judges and other justice officials since Sendra's introduction to the system, when he was 15 years old.

Brownell had tried to cover Sendra's illegal acts in his direct, so Sendra wouldn't appear to be trying to hide anything from the jury. And Sendra, at times during his testimony, seemed to be *too* candid, as though he took pleasure in recollecting his past exploits. But Sendra's lifelong habit of lawlessness made him an easy target for defense lawyers; even when they pursued other lines of questioning, they kept stumbling on instances of criminal conduct.

Ridiculing Sendra's attempts at finding legal work, Soloway established that Sendra had quit his job with a sanitation company because he didn't have a driver's license. Why, Soloway asked, didn't you simply "go down to the DMV here on Worth Street a couple of blocks away, [stand] on line for a few hours," and get one?

"I would have went to the DMV, I would have gotten rearrested," Sendra replied.

"You would have gotten rearrested, and you would have gotten rearrested because you had other . . . you had a parole warrant out on you at that time?"

"No, I owe close to thirteen thousand dollars to the DMV."

"Okay, you owe thirteen thousand dollars. What's that for?" Soloway asked, fumbling for a reason.

"Driving with no license," Sendra said.

But Soloway was unable to deliver the knockout blow to Sendra's credibility he'd been hoping for. Even though he got the former Cowboy to admit he'd fudged the truth in the past in order to obtain a favorable plea bargain, Soloway couldn't show how Sendra's current testimony had earned him much benefit. In fact, Sendra had decided to cooperate, after keeping quiet for two years, because he'd felt betrayed by the Cowboys. All that he'd asked from the prosecutors was a letter to the parole board stating that he'd cooperated with the DA's office and a few dollars for his commissary account. Soloway made as much as he could out of that request, but it was Pasqualito's lawyer, Valerie Van Leer-Greenberg, who inflicted the most damage. "And you have told these ladies and gentlemen that the two considerations and two benefits conferred upon you are letters that would be written to a parole board?" she asked Sendra during cross the following day.

"Yes."

"Sir, isn't it a fact you were excluded from the indictment that these men [are] on trial for?" Van Leer-Greenberg asked, gesturing at the defendants.

"Yes."

"That these forty people were indicted for?"

"Yes."

"Isn't it a further fact that they were indicted for conspiracy in the first degree, right?"

"I don't know exactly what the charge . . . how, what the degree it was or anything."

"But you are not part of that indictment. You are not being prosecuted, is that right?"

"Yes."

"You are free from the chains of that indictment, are you not?"

"Yes."

"Is that not a benefit, sir, that you are deriving from being here and testifying today, and giving testimony in this trial?"

Brownell watched stone-faced. The cross had already gone on too long, as one lawyer after another dissected Sendra's life, and not politely. But there was nothing he could do. Sendra was the first of the former gang members to take the stand, and Brownell knew that the defense would take their best shots at him, and that Snyder would give them more latitude than she would later, when their rap about unscrupulous prosecutors and disingenuous snitches became stale. Meanwhile, he tried to stay cool and not object too strenuously.

On the morning of November 9, a week after he'd taken the stand, Sendra was finally excused. For three days, the defense had beaten up on him and scored points against him repeatedly. But he'd never once lost his temper, and at times his steadfastly calm demeanor had made the defense seem shrill. Brownell judged that much of his testimony would hold up, and that some of the damaged bits might even be redeemed by corroboration and argument. "The thing about a trial like this," Brownell would later recall, "is that you start out with all this evidence you've got to get in, and it's like this huge weight on your shoulders. But then as you get through each witness, if they don't get too banged up, it's like one more thing you don't have to think about again. The load just keeps getting lighter, like sand draining out of an hourglass. Freddie was a difficult witness because the defense just savaged him, and there was nothing we could do but sit there and let him take it. But when he held up and it was over, it was a huge relief. He was a big piece of our case, and now we didn't have to worry about that anymore."

20

THE TURNING POINT

FREDDIE SENDRA'S testimony was one of the trial's early turning points. The prosecution had led with one of their least sympathetic witnesses, and the defense had come at him with everything they had. That they failed to break him, despite landing several heavy blows, took some authority away from their later crosses, which at times seemed shrill or tendentious. Even then, the lawyers' skills were less at issue than their clients' blatantly violent behavior and the grit and preparedness and last-ditch courage of the witnesses. Typical among them was Janice Bruington, the sole surviving gunshot victim of the Quad.

Bruington, who followed Sendra in the witness box, was hardly an exemplar of virtue or probity. A fortyish welfare mother of four, she'd been drinking and using hard drugs since she was a teenager, and looked like she had. Her face was haggard and there was a feral gleam in her eyes, like an animal for whom survival is a daily concern.

But like many of the hard cases along Beekman Avenue, she possessed a well of pluck and humanity not told in the box score of her life. Quizzed by Hill, she sketched her history in Mott Haven—moving with her children to Beekman Avenue from Harlem in 1982, entering a methadone program, and struggling for four years to stay clean before succumbing to crack, bought mainly from the Cowboys. Even then, she said, she worked odd jobs to help support her family, and moved them back to Manhattan in November 1991, when the neighborhood became too dangerous. "When I first moved there, it wasn't that bad; then it got worse," she said.

"And when you say that conditions got worse, how did they get worse?" Hill asked her.

"They just got worse. You couldn't sit outside. You had to learn to duck from bullets."

But Bruington said she returned to Beekman Avenue on December 16, the night of the Quad, to pick up her son, who was visiting his pregnant girlfriend. She had just turned onto Beekman and was crossing the alley where Yellow-Top sold three-dollar crack, she told the court, when she saw Stanley Tukes shoot Anthony Green. She had known them both as youngsters.

"After you saw Stanley shoot Anthony Green, what did you do then?" Hill asked.

"I turned to run."

"Did you do or say anything before you—"

"I screamed. I turned around and I got shot," Bruington said. She recalled the sting of the bullet as it ripped through her, indicating where it caught her in the back and exited her right shoulder. She then hit the pavement and rolled under a car, she said, pretending to be dead as the shooting continued. From her vantage point, she was able to pick out Platano and Fat Danny, as well as Tukes, running from the alley with guns in their hands.

Eventually Bruington found her way to Salustiano Sanabria's ambulance, where she heard the dying Anthony Green tell his brother Chubby that "Stanley shot me." But Bruington kept her mouth shut. Her travails, she knew, were just beginning.

A lifelong addict with little education and no employment record, Bruington should have been an easy mark for the defense. Even her proximity to Yellow-Top's sales location on the night of the Quad added to the doubts about her reliability as a witness. Moreover, for nearly a year after the incident she'd told the police that she couldn't identify her assailant, much less any of the other shooters; and the circumstances surrounding her eventual cooperation were murky. She told the court she'd been in constant fear for her life and for the lives of her children, that she'd gone into hiding and didn't want to become involved. It was only when Platano contacted her through her son, and offered to "take care of her" if she agreed not to testify, that she felt she was being set up and applied to the DA for protection. Even then, she'd held back salient details about the shooting from Hill and Tebbens.

Thanks largely to Tebbens' assurances, Bruington had eventually filled out her story, including details about Platano that had not been part of the original record; and the defense homed in on the inconsistencies between her earlier and later statements. Platano's lawyer, Robert Soloway, in particular, questioned Bruington on a deposition she'd given to Don Hill in which she seemed to change her mind about seeing his client among the shooters. "Do you remember there was a break in the stenographic recorded statement that you spoke?" Soloway asked.

"They stopped for a while and went out," Bruington said. "I went to the bathroom. I went over there, talked to my son. Me and my son sat down. I talked to my son. Me and my son had to talk."

"Did you talk also, in addition to your son, with Detective Tebbens?"

"Nobody else, no, but my son . . ."

"What did you talk about with your son at that time?"

"My son told me, 'Mommy, don't be scared. Tell the truth.' He said, 'Be honest,' you know. 'You survived, you lived,' you know. 'They don't know where you're at, so tell the truth.' "

"Your son told you to tell the truth?"

"Yes."

"And did Assistant District Attorney Hill and Detective Tebbens also tell you to tell the truth?"

"Yes."

"And this was after you had said that you [saw] Platano and Fat Danny, and they did not have weapons that you could see, is that right?"

"Yes."

Soloway had been driving at Bruington for some time, questioning her in a brusque, staccato style; and she'd been holding her own. But now her face had taken on a quizzical expression, at once plaintive and defiant.

"You then went back into the room and the stenographically recorded statement . . . ," Soloway started to ask. "Sorry, is there something misstated?"

Bruington's face had crumpled. "Because you're saying, you know— You're acting the way you're saying, you know—" she said, her throat constricting. "Okay, like I admit to the first [part], I admit to the whole thing, that I wouldn't get involved because I didn't want, you know—

"But when I sat down, I felt my son said, 'Mommy, listen, you know, tell the truth.' Nobody forced me to tell the truth. I'm telling the truth on my own, because I'm tired. I want to get on with my life. I'm scared to go this place, that place. I want to get on with my life. I've no life. For so many years. I need a life now."

The courtroom was briefly silent. Bruington lowered her head and covered her face with her hands, crying silently, unexpectedly. Soloway had penetrated her street-hardened facade, but instead of finding lies and distortions, he'd hit upon her terror and despair at living almost three years under the threat of death, the fear each time the phone rang or she left her apartment, the fear inspired by the defendants sitting just a few strides from the witness stand. "Mrs. Bruington—" Soloway started again, but Snyder cut him off.

"This is a good time to break for lunch," she said, summoning from the jurors, no less than from Bruington herself, an audible sigh of relief.

AS THE TRIAL entered its third month, it took on a life of its own, subsuming the lives of the participants, binding them to its rhythms of preparation, examination, and analysis. More than his office at HIU, certainly more than the furnished apartment where he holed up for the trial, Snyder's courtroom had become Brownell's world. He knew the grain and placement of every piece of furniture; the look and feel of the room at different times and in different weathers, the way the wan north light filtered through the double-height windows over the jury box on November afternoons, paler even than the icy fluorescent trays hanging from the ceiling; and he knew with an unwanted familiarity the quirks and habits of his colleagues. Hill, low-keyed and laconic in the office, had become the team's pit bull, snarling and snapping at Soloway or Van Leer-Greenberg at sidebars. Grifa possessed excess nervous energy that she funneled through a series of tics—toe tapping, leg pumping, pen clicking. Brownell and Hill would remove any hard implements from her place at the prosecution table before the start of each session.

Snyder was a huge pain, Brownell recalls. A former trial attorney, she couldn't stop herself from instructing the lawyers on their presentation; that she was nearly always right only made it worse. She apparently felt Brownell was too mechanical in his examinations, and frequently suggested at sidebar that someone ought to check whether he had a pulse.

The defendants also made their presence known. Daniel Gonzalez slept through long stretches of testimony, and Stanley Tukes and Platano looked sullen much of the time. But Pasqualito was predictably animated, shaking his head when he disagreed with a statement, and staring down witnesses he didn't like; and Fat Danny, so meek up at HIU after his arrest, was the rowdiest of the group, acting out in front of his pals and taunting the prosecutors whenever the opportunity arose. He got into it so often with Grifa—calling her a "stupid bitch," or making some sexual innuendo—that either Brownell or Hill had to interpose himself between them at the prosecutors' table.

TO THE DETECTIVES and assistants used to seeing a scruffy teenager in jeans and a tank top, 17-year-old Iris Cruz looked like an angel sitting in the witness box. She had always been a cute kid with pale skin, saucer eyes, and a cascade of straight black hair. But with Lori Grifa's help, she'd cobbled together an outfit—a white blouse, a knee-length skirt, and the good black shoes she shared with her two older sisters—that transformed her into a demure young lady.

But the transformation, sudden though it was, was hardly disingenuous. Of the many civilian witnesses who had testified or were scheduled to testify, Little Iris, as she was known, was the one true innocent. She'd been 14 when Pasqualito threatened her and her family at gunpoint and drove them on their two-and-a-half-year odyssey through the city's shelters and a series of apartment motels upstate. She'd never had a chance to get involved in the drug-infested world that had employed her brothers when they were no more than 10, or many of the older girls in the neighborhood. And thanks to her refugee-like existence and interventions by Tebbens and Dugan, she'd managed to steer clear of drugs and boyfriend trouble since then.

Still, Iris had seen plenty in her short, turbulent life. The Cowboys had been a constant presence in the building where she lived, congregating in the stairwell and on the stoop, operating the Hole twenty-four hours a day, seven days a week, since as far back as she could remember. Most of her family, at one time or another, had worked for the gang. Michael, her closest sibling, used to leave the apartment at 8 P.M. and stay out all night in his capacity first as a lookout, then as a pitcher. Her neighbors—Fat Iris, Louise McBride, the hapless Baker sisters—looked out for her after a fashion, cautioning her to stay in school. But they did so handling drugs and guns for Red-Top in front of her. Fat Iris once even enlisted her to help tap vials, for which she paid her $300. Little Iris was 12 at the time.

Lenny, Nelson, and Platano had keys to Iris' apartment. They used to pay her mother $50 to cook for them, and they used her living room like a clubhouse, kicking back after work, openly discussing their business, and bragging about their exploits with women. Iris' introduction to the mysteries of sex consisted of the "trains"—serial intercourse—that the gang members pulled on the "club women" they brought back to the neighborhood, or on customers desperate for crack. Iris remembers one they locked in the basement for two days, remembers hearing her screams at night and seeing the blood in the hallway the morning after she disappeared.

When she was a little older, Platano used to pin Iris against the wall when she passed him in the stairwell and tell her he was going to make her his girlfriend. "There can't be no virgins on the block," he'd say to her. Iris' first boyfriend was a Cowboy lookout and pitcher named Manny. She used to cut school and hang out with him on the roof, help him watch for cops. But after just a few weeks, she saw him having sex with his boss, Myra, an older woman addicted to crack. (Myra later died of AIDS; Manny disappeared from the neighborhood.)

But what stood out most was the violence. At times it seemed that everyone along Beekman—workers, crackheads, small-time hustlers—were scamming each other, and Cowboy enforcers administered public beatings on what seemed a daily basis. Not that Iris had a great deal of sympathy for the skells whom Red-Top brought to the neighborhood. She'd lost count of the times she'd been mugged in St. Mary's Park, including the day that Louise McBride's son shot and killed Fat Iris' husband in the elevator of Iris' building. Even worse were the shootings and deadly assaults. Iris had been too young to remember the Double, but she'd had a ringside seat for the Quad, and of course she'd watched while Pasqualito had pistol-whipped her brother Tito into unconsciousness, then threatened to kill her and her family.

Clearly the ghosts of those visions still haunted her. When she entered the courtroom and looked at the defendants, even before she could be sworn in, she broke down in tears. But she regained her composure quickly, and once on the stand, seemed to gain courage, even gazing at her onetime tormentors with frank indignation. For all her shyness and apparent fragility, she possessed the tensile strength of a survivor.

Grifa spent the first few hours roughing out the contours of Iris' childhood among the Cowboys—their imperial hold over the neighborhood, their insidious influence on her siblings, and their ruthless persecution of her family. Then Grifa took Iris back to the night of December 16, 1991. Almost at once her confidence began to falter, and she started to shake.

Iris told the court that she'd gone to the corner store with her sister Ita at about 10 P.M. to buy candy. She remembered seeing Daniel Gonzalez talking to a stranger, and Weeky, the owner; but she'd talked to no one, and left shortly after with Ita. On the way home, she passed Anthony Green in the alleyway behind the candy store; the skinny 17-year-old was selling crack to a woman in a green jacket, and Iris noted the exchange. She knew Green from school—they were classmates—and she said "hi and bye" to him, then hurried off to catch up with Ita.

"What was it like that night? What was the weather like?" Grifa asked her.

"It was cold, quiet," Iris said. "It was the quietest on Beekman I ever knew."

Back home, Iris and Ita stopped on the second floor, which let out onto the Hole, to look for their brother Michael. He was supposed to be pitching that evening. But when the elevator doors opened, Iris said, she was startled by what she saw. "I saw a gun, you know. That's the first thing I saw. A gun. So when I saw— I'm shaking," she said.

"Relax," Grifa told her. "What color was the gun?"

"Black."

"What shape was it? Show us with your hands."

Iris indicated twelve to eighteen inches.

"When you saw it, where was it?" Snyder asked her.

"It was like Platano was holding it like that."

"Platano had the gun in his hand?"

"Yes."

Little by little, always focusing on the details, Grifa had Iris describe the scene she'd stumbled into on the second-floor landing. There were at least a half dozen men there, all of them armed, all of them checking or loading their guns. Platano was attaching a banana-shaped clip that also served as a handle onto his piece, and Stanley Tukes was locking a straight clip onto his. Iris also remembered a tall, burly Hispanic whom HIU detectives were certain was Freddy Krueger, and whom she called X-Man because he was wearing a Malcolm X jacket with a big white X on the back. Iris said she'd asked Platano where her brother was. He told her he was upstairs, and she and Ita went back to their apartment.

Moments later Iris heard the first volley of shots. "There was like fireworks going off, a whole bunch of them," she said. "But it was like one of them was going *ta-ta-ta* real fast. Some of them were going slower."

"How did the slower one sound?" Grifa asked.

"Like *pow-pow-pow*. I ran to the living-room window. I don't remember where I was at. But I wasn't in the living room, so I was running to the living room. You know, because there's a gate in my window, I have to put my hand— I had to stick my body out. When I stuck my body out, the first thing I saw: a black car, four-door, tinted windows."

"Where was the black car?"

"In front of the building."

Grifa asked her to fill in some details, then wanted to know what she saw next. "I saw a white car, four-door, tinted windows."

"How far down the block was the white car?"

"Right in front of the alleyway."

"Is that the same alley where you talked to Anthony?"

"Yes."

Grifa backtracked a bit. She wanted to know whether during the time Iris ran from inside her house to the living-room window the noises from the shots had stopped.

"No, they didn't," Iris said. "They were still going on."

"When you stuck your head out of the window and saw the black car, did you still hear the noises?"

"Yes, and then you saw spots, like white flashes. When I was looking toward the car, you saw white flashes."

"Is that the car on the left?"

"Yes."

"By the alley?"

"Yes."

"What's the next thing that you saw?"

"I saw Platano and Stanley, they were shooting like toward the alleyway."

Grifa then asked some questions about their precise position with respect to each other, the alleyway, and Anthony Green. "Who was [Anthony] closer to? Platano or Stanley?"

"Platano."

"Platano. What did you see happen to Anthony?"

"He was jumping, like when you're shaking, like if you have an asthma attack and you're just shaking." Iris stood up at Grifa's request and made a trembling motion with her body to demonstrate what she saw.

"Was his whole body moving like that?" Grifa asked.

"Yes."

"In addition to shaking like that, was he moving in any direction?"

"He was more . . . he was not so close to the building, he just kept on moving back."

"And then what happened?"

"So the building was like holding him up. So he just like hanged with the building while they're shooting."

"Did he put his arms out?"

"Yes. He had his arms straight out, and he's shaking."

"Then what happened to him? Did you see?"

"He was just shaking, and then I saw a lady. She fell."

"And you saw a lady fall. I want to talk about Anthony for one more minute. What happened to Anthony after the shooting stopped?"

"He fell to the floor."

Grifa drew Iris out on some more details—the lighting conditions, the names and positions of other shooters. Iris was able to identify defendants Daniel Gonzalez, Fat Danny, and Rennie Harris, as well as the X-Man. She said they'd all had guns, and the guns had "lights coming out of them."

After the shooting stopped, Iris ran down to the street. "Did you take the elevator or the stairs?" Grifa asked.

"The stairs," Iris said.

"Where did you go?"

"To the alleyway."

"What did you do?"

"I saw Anthony on the floor. He was still alive. He was bleeding. So I put my arm around his neck to carry—"

"You held his head?"

"Yes."

"What else did you do?"

"[I held] his hand. He was saying, 'Don't let me die.' He kept on repeating it. I was there, and then I looked to see if the girl was alive. And she wasn't. She was just there, and she had this— a red— sorry, a yellow thing in her hand, a top, like Yellow-Top. And I was looking to see if she was alive or saying something. She wasn't.

"So the next thing they pushed me away."

"Who?"

"This black guy."

"What did he do to Anthony, if anything?" Grifa asked.

"He was holding him, shaking, you know."

"Where did you go after you were pushed away by the black guy?"

"Across the street," Iris said.

"Now, did you see the black guy doing anything with Anthony?"

"Yes, he was crying."

Iris ended her direct testimony on November 30, a day and a half after she'd begun. Her recollections about the gang and her clear evocation of the Quad had significantly advanced HIU's case, even though she'd broken little new ground. By the time she testified, Janice Bruington had already supplied the jury with a close-up view of the Quad; Chubby Green had recounted his brother's dying moments, his brother's repeated statements that Stanley Tukes, his old boyhood pal, had shot him; and Fat Iris, who followed Green on the stand, had offered a far more detailed picture of the Cowboys' Beekman Avenue operation than Little Iris.

But there was an unavoidable sense—at least among the prosecutors—that these other witnesses had conspired in their fates. Bruington was a crack addict who'd been a regular customer of both Red-Top and Yellow-Top. Chubby Green had been a dealer himself, and was currently serving time in prison for crack sales. Fat Iris had worked for the Cowboys, and her common-law husband, English, had been a Red-Top manager before he was shot and killed. Little Iris, however, was neither a user nor a dealer, and her story of growing up among the Cowboys revealed the true nature of the gang's impact on the people of Beekman Avenue. From a purely legal viewpoint, she was just another corroborating witness. But the subtext of her testimony—the virtual slaughter of her childhood—left a sickening feeling in its wake.

As the evidence mounted, the defense's options began to shrink. Most of the Cowboys' lawyers had conceded that their clients sold drugs, but strenuously denied that they had been part of an organized conspiracy, or any of the violent acts attributed to the conspiracy. At bottom the lawyers had two lines of attack. One approach focused on the confusing conditions at the crime scenes. The Quad, in particular, had been chaotic. The lighting had been spotty at best; most of the participants had worn hoods and/or masks; and the action had been frenzied, with a number of different incidents occurring simultaneously.

All the defense lawyers scored points bringing to light the eyewitnesses' uncertainties and inconsistencies in describing not only the Quad but also the Double and other violent acts. They also had some success impeaching the credibility of the witnesses, especially cooperators like Freddie Sendra. But this ad hominem strategy, attacking the witnesses' character, was proving less effective than questioning their testimony, and in some instances—as with Janice Bruington—was actually hurting the defense's cause. The reasons why were several. Clearly, the thousands of hours the prosecution had spent preparing the witnesses, making sure they testified only to what they saw or knew to be fact, were paying off. Clearly, too, most witnesses were testifying out of conviction; once they got over their initial fears, their demeanor conveyed their anger and the sadness of their lives. The Cowboys' reign had been so brutal and arrogant that many of the cooperators who'd served the gang had at some level been victimized. No one—not the canniest litigator—could bait or bully them more than the defendants already had.

Nevertheless, some of the defense lawyers continued to try.

Valerie Van Leer-Greenberg, Pasqualito's lawyer, was a passionate advocate who seemed genuinely fond of her client. In her opening statement, she noted that Pasqualito's nickname translated to Little Christmas, an image so at odds with his reputation in the street that Brownell had to literally clench his teeth to keep from laughing. Conversely, any witness who impugned her client was subject to Van Leer-Greenberg's wrath on cross; and those attacks, couched in a shrill voice and sanctimonious manner, provided the trial with several ludicrous moments. During her cross of Little Iris, for example, Van Leer-Greenberg tried to poke holes in her description of the incident in which Pasqualito came to her home with Frankie Robles and threatened to kill her family. "The day that [Pasqualito] came into the apartment with your grandmother and [your niece] Daisy in the hallway—remember testifying to that?" Van Leer-Greenberg asked her.

"Yes," Iris answered.

"Is that the day after your brother-in-law purchased—bought cribs?"

"Yes."

"What's his name? Edwin or—"

"Edgar."

"Did he bring the cribs to your home?"

"Yes."

"And Daisy is three years old, right?"

"Yes."

"And you testified that [Pasqualito] knocked on the door, right?"

"Yes."

"And your mother knew it was [Pasqualito] before she let him in, right?"

"Yes."

Having established that Iris' brother-in-law had bought cribs with the drug money he'd stolen from Pasqualito, and brought them to the apartment, Van Leer-Greenberg was now ready to spring her trap. "And no one bothered to take the three-year-old—this three-year-old is standing in front of you or behind you?"

"In front of me," Iris replied as Grifa objected.

"I can't believe you're asking this question," Snyder said to Van Leer-Greenberg. "In other words, we're now asking her if they were stupid enough to leave a three-year-old in the hall?"

"I'm asking her: Isn't it a fact that you left a three-year-old child—I would never denigrate anyone—in the hallway, when you had four bedrooms with cribs in them that the child could have been placed in, out of any type of danger?"

Grifa objected again.

"Sustained," Snyder said.

"We couldn't," Iris answered anyway.

"Did you move the child at all out of the hallway?" Van Leer-Greenberg persisted.

"No."

Grifa objected a third time.

Snyder had had enough. "Just one minute," she said to Van Leer-Greenberg. "In other words, your question basically is that the child would never have been in danger if someone had the foresight to move the child into another room, because the person coming in might threaten the child with death—is that your question? Are you serious about that question?"

"Absolutely serious."

"Sustained," Snyder said.

"And isn't it a further fact," Van Leer-Greenberg continued, her voice rising, "that [Pasqualito] never touched your grandmother, never harmed her, never insulted her, never said anything to her?"

"Miss Van Leer-Greenberg, don't yell," Snyder interrupted. "You're speaking to a seventeen-year-old witness. You can have vigorous cross. I don't want a witness yelled at or denigrated."

Van Leer-Greenberg apologized and continued in a quieter tone, but she'd already reduced Iris to tears, and in what must have seemed to them one of the more bizarre cases of blaming-the-victim, raised snickers from her co-counsel at the defense table.

IRIS WAS FOLLOWED on the stand by her brothers Joey and Michael. Small, cross-eyed, with a widow's peak of short black hair, 16-year-old Joey Morales bore an uncanny resemblance to the TV character Eddie Munster. Neither cute nor clever, he nevertheless offered a worm's-eye view of the gang, having toiled in the lower ranks of the organization since he was 12. Moreover, he'd witnessed the Double and the Quad, and because he was a minor throughout his tenure at Red-Top, he was able to implicate nearly all the defendants in an A-1 conspiracy.

But Michael provided the drama. His knowledge of the gang was far more extensive than Joey's, and of course he knew what it was like to be caught in the Cowboys' crosshairs. A whippet-thin, smart-alecky street kid when Tebbens first met him in a Brooklyn shelter in the spring of 1992, Michael had matured into a bright, personable 19-year-old. He hadn't lost his cocky manner, but he'd gone back to school—he was in his senior year—and the previous summer he'd worked for the Department of Transportation as a rail cleaner. More important, he'd steered clear of drugs.

That had not always been the case, Brownell quickly pointed out. In fact, Michael's extensive knowledge of the Cowboys was directly related to his extensive experience as a Red-Top worker. He'd even been arrested—once for assaulting a vagrant crack dealer with a golf club, on orders from Stanley Tukes; and a second time when undercover police raided the Hole in February 1992. Platano bailed him out on the latter occasion, then offered to let him keep the bail money—$1,500—in exchange for his silence.

Brownell debriefed Michael about his employment history—

his introduction to the gang as a 13-year-old (he transported drugs around the neighborhood in a book bag and was paid twenty to thirty dollars per trip), his later duties as a pitcher and lookout, the names of his bosses and co-workers. Brownell then directed Michael's attention to September 3, 1989, the night of the Double. Michael, then 14, recalled that he'd been visiting a girlfriend on Cypress Avenue when he heard gunfire. Looking down from her apartment into the street, he saw Lenny, Pasqualito, and Victor Mercedes surrounding a green sedan and shooting repeatedly and at close range into the front of the car. Later, he said, he ran downstairs and examined the victim's bullet-ridden body before the police arrived.

After drawing out a few more details, Brownell skipped to the Quad. Michael said he'd been on the rooftop of 348 Beekman on that night, working as a lookout for the Hole. He told the court he'd overheard a brief conversation on his walkie-talkie between Platano and Fat Danny in which Fat Danny said, "They're here." Right after, Michael said, Platano ordered him to go down to the Hole and close the spot.

Michael got to the second-floor landing moments before his sisters, and stumbled onto the shooters, who'd assembled there before heading over to the alley. Standing by the entrance to the Hole, he was able to pick out Platano, Tukes, Rennie Harris, and the X-Man among the group in the hallway. Then while Michael waited for the pitcher to make a last sale, Fat Danny arrived in the elevator laden with firearms—the same guns Little Iris had testified she'd seen Platano, Tukes, and the others in the process of loading. Michael said he'd collected the cash from the pitcher, sent her home, then departed to the stash apartment next door to deposit the money. By the time he got back to No. 348, he said, he heard a volley of shots and saw Platano and Tukes firing into the alley at the other end of the block. This time, in an odd reversal of form, Michael didn't hang around for the shooting to end, but ran around the corner to his girlfriend's apartment and holed up there until much later that night. Apparently, he'd lost his curiosity about, much less his appetite for, carnage in the two years since the Double. He just wanted to be somewhere safe.

But Michael had run out of safe places. Within months of the Quad, he'd been busted for drug sales in the Hole, then driven out of the neighborhood by Pasqualito's death threats. Michael and his family entered the city's shelter system, moving several times as a precaution; still the Cowboys pursued them, and caught up with Michael in August as he sat parked in his stepfather's car on a darkened street in Brooklyn. "Did something happen to you the summer you left Beekman Avenue?" Brownell asked him.

"Yes."

"What happened to you?"

"I got shot in my face," Michael said.

As the jurors edged forward, Brownell elicited details of the incident: how Michael looked out the window, prompted by his brother-in-law Edgar, who was sitting beside him in the front seat; how Michael saw a blue four-door sedan that he recognized from the old neighborhood parked alongside him. "And when you looked up and saw the blue car, what, if anything, did you see?" Brownell asked him.

"Lenny."

"Where did you see Lenny?"

"In the passenger's side on the front."

"And what, if anything, was Lenny doing?"

"He had his hand out with a gun in his hand," Michael said.

"About how far away were you from Lenny when you saw him with the gun in his hand?"

"A couple of feet."

"And do you know whether or not he was actually firing the gun?" Brownell asked.

"Yes."

"How do you know that?"

"Because I heard shots," Michael said.

"What direction was the gun pointed in? This is the gun that Lenny had when you heard shots."

"In my direction."

"Did you see anybody else?"

"Yes."

"Who else did you see?"

"Pasqualito."

"And where did you see Pasqualito?"

"In the driver's side."

"And what did you see Pasqualito doing?"

"He got out the car, opened the door and put his hands on top of the hood, and started firing."

Brownell asked a series of further questions about the positions of the two shooters, then inquired whether Michael actually got hit.

"Yes," Michael said.

"Did you realize at first that you had been hit?"

"No."

"Why don't you tell us what happened."

"Right after the bullets, I seen blood. So I thought my brother-in-law got shot."

"Where exactly did you see the blood?"

"All over the car."

"Was there a lot of blood or was there a little blood in different spots?"

"There was a little blood in different spots."

"Okay . . . Did you determine where the blood, in fact, was coming from?"

"Yes."

"Was it from your brother-in-law?"

"No."

"Where was it?"

"From my face and the back of my ear."

"Do you know whether or not the bullet stayed in your face or whether it went through some other place?"

"It went through."

"Do you know where it came out?"

"Yes."

"Where?"

"Behind my right ear."

With the completion of Michael Cruz's testimony on December 15, one day short of the third anniversary of the Quad, the prosecution had laid the foundation for their case. They'd depicted the Cowboy conspiracy—its history and inner workings—from a dizzying array of perspectives, and furnished close-up, if somewhat fragmented, accounts of the gang's most shocking crimes: the Quad and the Double. Moreover, their witnesses had stamped a human face onto the corruption and suffering caused by the Cowboys. Janice Bruington, Chubby Green, Fat Iris, Little Iris, and her brothers Joey and Michael had all been subject to the gang's bullying and threats, had all been forced to give up their homes and go into hiding. Chubby had lost a brother; Fat Iris, her husband. Bruington and Michael Cruz had actually been the targets for Cowboy bullets.

Now, with the holidays approaching and the trial grinding to a halt, it was time to regroup. Grifa and her husband had bought a house in New Jersey, and she took advantage of the break to move her things in from Brooklyn. Hill spent a few quiet days over Christmas with his family. Brownell got up to Syracuse to visit his parents. But mainly they went back to work, bringing in witnesses that needed to be prepped, analyzing where they were, plotting strategy—doing the things they wouldn't have time for once the trial got started again after the new year. "In a way it was harder being out of court because we didn't have that structure every day," Grifa recalls. "That's where Dan was so good, motivating himself. He started going over the transcript, outlining the main points of each witness's testimony. He never let up. He just had this amazing self-discipline."

The others worked hard too, not so much long hours—Hill, for instance, tried to leave each night by six to spend time with his children—but with remarkable intensity. Neither Hill nor Grifa could remember taking a meal together outside the office. Often there simply wasn't time. But they also shared a feeling, never articulated then, that if they let up—even for just an hour or two—they might never recapture the focus that had sustained them over the past fifteen months. Civilian life had become a memory. At one point that winter, Grifa discovered three paychecks in her wallet. But it hardly mattered, she realized; she couldn't remember the last time she'd been shopping.

Both Brownell and Arsenault had had to caution Grifa to cut back on her hours, advice Brownell might well have taken himself. Brownell, who knew the importance of pacing from his days as a distance runner, had made a rule when he took over the case never to work more than six days a week. But as the trial wore on, it became impossible to escape, even if he was only thinking about it. Something of an insomniac at ordinary times, he was unable to sleep more than a few hours—a condition not helped by the unfamiliar surroundings of his safe-house apartment. Often he'd rise in the middle of the night and take the subway to his apartment uptown so he could sleep in his own bed, much to the consternation of the police officers charged with bringing him to court the next day. Sometimes he'd simply head to the office. "It was still dark most mornings when I'd arrive downtown," Grifa recalls. "That meant I was actually getting up around five o'clock—four-thirty when I started commuting from New Jersey. I know it was really early because I always got the first parking spot in the station, the one closest to the train tracks. But I never got to the office before Dan."

21

VERDICT

BEGINNING in January, the prosecutors called a series of mid- to high-level gang members who had agreed to cooperate, including Frankie Robles and George Santiago. Both Robles and Santiago had grown up on Beech Terrace in the building where Red-Top had their first spot, and had literally come of age in the organization, starting out as errand boys and moving up through the ranks to become top managers. Examining them was a long, arduous process, due to their wealth of knowledge about the gang, and much of their testimony was dry and technical, concerned with the minutiae of the Cowboys' drug operations—the functions of the different jobs, who reported to whom, personnel problems. But by the end of February, the prosecutors had amassed an extraordinary amount of testimonial evidence establishing the Cowboy conspiracy and linking the defendants to that conspiracy and the vicious acts committed in furtherance of it.

The jury also learned firsthand about two more homicides. In the so-called Rooftop murder, perhaps the most senseless crime charged in the indictment, the defendant, Linwood Collins, a manager for Orange-Top, shot and killed Oscar Alvarez, a 33-year-old crackhead in May 1991. In fact, Collins had been looking for Alvarez' best friend, a pitcher known as Shrimpo, who had run off during his shift with a bundle of crack and about $250 in cash. But Collins couldn't find Shrimpo, and when he came upon Alvarez smoking crack on the rooftop of 600 141st Street, he threatened to throw Alvarez off if he didn't disclose the whereabouts of his friend. According to Sero Rodriguez, a gang member who was with Collins at the time, Alvarez told Collins he didn't know where Shrimpo was and offered to pay Collins back for the missing drugs and cash. Not satisfied with Alvarez' response, Collins emptied his revolver, killing the hapless young man.

Some two years later, the Cowboys committed another senseless murder. According to witnesses, Fat Danny spotted a man parked by a phone booth on Jackson Avenue in the Bronx whom he believed had shot and paralyzed El Feo. Aware that El Feo had put out a $10,000 contract on his assailant, Fat Danny ordered one of his workers, Rob Lopez, to go to the phone booth, as if he were making a call, and shoot the driver of the car. After the deed had been done, Fat Danny drove to 171st Street in the Heights and bragged to Pasqualito and other gang members that "My son got one." Several days later, Fat Danny learned he'd ordered the execution of the wrong man.

But the highlight of the winter session was Brownell's examination of Nelson Sepulveda. Brownell had saved him for the latter part of the trial, despite his extensive knowledge of the Quad; the prosecutor knew the jury would be flagging by then, and he wanted to regain their attention. He succeeded. Grifa recalls that the jurors were literally at the edge of their seats. And the electricity between Nelson and the defendants was such that despite beefed-up security—Nelson alone had two guards flanking the witness box—Snyder felt the need to caution the lawyers to keep an eye on their clients. "There's a tremendous amount of tension in this courtroom," she said during a sidebar. "I want all of you to be careful. I don't know if anything is going to happen here. I have no reason to think anything is going to happen here. I am feeling a great deal of tension and I am looking at the defendants, and I am not getting any good feeling."

Nelson had hardly seemed threatening at first. Of medium height with a wiry frame, deep-set eyes, and dark curly hair, he'd entered the courtroom without incident, and when, after taking the stand, he spilled the glass of water a court officer handed him, he apologized so profusely, it seemed hard to imagine him as the ruthless leader of a drug gang. Moreover, he had an unfocused quality—not exactly shyness, or any kind of nervousness—but a way of seeming only half present. As Brownell later put it, he was spacey.

But Brownell knew it was a mistake to underestimate Nelson. Expelled from high school for punching out a dean when he was 18, he could snap back in your face on the springs of his tightly wound temper, then "chill" just as quickly, without reflection or remorse. Once he began testifying, and let his eyes roam over his former associates with a kind of languid arrogance, there seemed little doubt that he had been their boss.

Brownell led Nelson through a summary of his early career—his apprenticeship under Yayo and Capo, his move to Beech Terrace—paying particular attention to his recruitment of his brother. "When did [Lenny] start to work with you on Beech Terrace?" Brownell asked.

"When the spot wasn't going nowhere, you know, under my leadership. Nothing was happening," Nelson said.

"When you say nothing was happening, what did you mean by that?"

"No sales."

That changed quickly under Lenny, Nelson said. "How much money a week was that particular spot making—and I mean on Beech Terrace—around 1987?" Brownell asked him.

"It was making like thirty thousand dollars."

"A week?"

"A week," Nelson said.

"How much of that would you get approximately?"

"Two or three thousand."

"And how much would Lenny get?"

"Four or five."

"Why would Lenny get more than you?"

"He was the brains. You know, everybody respected him, you know. He was the brains, you know. He practically took over, like." Nelson then traced the Cowboys' dramatic rise through the 1980s, and their expansion as friends from the old neighborhood came to the Bronx looking for work—Pasqualito, Victor Mercedes, Fat Danny, Platano, Freddie Sendra, Tezo—and as the gang absorbed tough young kids from the Beekman Avenue area—Rennie Harris, Stanley Tukes, and Linwood Collins.

One of Red-Top's first workers was Miguel Castillo, a professional baseball prospect, who was killed in a rip-off by dealers who hung out around Marcey Place in the Bronx. Nelson related how the Cowboys drove by their spot and sprayed them with bullets on two occasions, and then gunned down the leader of the crew and his top lieutenant when they wandered inadvertently onto Cowboy turf. But Nelson wasn't present for the Double, as the incident became known, and the victims, murderers themselves, were hardly sympathetic.

But Nelson's description of the events leading up to the Quad had an altogether different, chilling effect. Those events began, Nelson said, when Lenny went to jail on a gun charge in August 1991 and

Nelson took over the gang's operations. "During that time when you were in charge, during the fall and winter of 1991, did anything happen in the spot?" Brownell asked him.

"Yes."

"What happened?"

"The sales was going down," Nelson said.

"When you say the sales was going down, what are you referring to?"

"We wasn't selling as much as before."

"Do you know why that was the case?"

"Yellow-Top was selling treys."

"When you say Yellow-Top was selling treys, what's a trey?"

"A crack for three dollars."

"How much was Red-Top being sold for at the Hole?"

"Five dollars."

Nelson said he had conversations with Platano, Tezo, and Fat Danny, whose Orange-Top sites were also suffering, about the competition. They agreed, he told the court, that something had to be done.

"Because of Yellow-Top, and the fact that they were cutting into the business at Beekman Avenue, did that affect the amount of money you were paying your own workers?" Brownell asked.

"Yes."

"In what way?"

"I had to pay them less," Nelson said.

"When you say you had to pay them less, who are you referring to?"

"To the managers."

"Who were the managers at that particular time?"

"My cousin Mask, Linwood, Rennie, Platano, everybody else."

"Did they ever say anything about the fact that their pay was cut?"

"Yeah."

"Who said anything to you?"

"All of them."

"What did they say?"

"They said if my brother wasn't locked up that . . . If my brother was out, they would still be getting paid."

Nelson explained that managers normally making $700 to $800 were being paid $400 to $500, and that they were pressuring him to act.

"After some of the managers had their conversations with you about the fact that they were being paid less, did you take further steps with regard to Yellow-Top?" Brownell asked.

"Yes."

"What did you do?"

"I went and spoke to El Feo about it," Nelson said.

"And what, if anything, did you say to El Feo when you went to speak to him?"

"I told him if he could lend me his people . . ."

Van Leer-Greenberg objected, citing the inadmissibility of a hearsay conversation, and after a sidebar Brownell resumed his examination. "Mr. Sepulveda, did you in fact have a conversation with this individual known as El Feo?"

"Yes."

"As a result of this conversation, were you able to elicit the help of anyone concerning the problem with Yellow-Top?"

"Yes."

"And who is he—who did you get?"

"Freddy."

"Who is Freddy?"

"They call him Freddy Krueger; he's a hit man."

Nelson said that he also spoke to Reuben Perez, a marijuana dealer allied to the gang, and got him to provide a car—a white Cadillac—for the hit. First, however, he had Stanley Tukes and Platano deliver a message to Yellow-Top to stop selling.

"What is it you had them do?" Brownell asked.

"I had them go over there and beat up their workers, stick them up."

"Is this something that you actually saw?"

"No."

"Then how is it you know that this is what they did?"

"I used to ask Stanley, 'What did you do?' He say, 'Yo, I took their money.' "

Nelson then said he visited his brother in prison to talk about the problem. But Brownell didn't ask him, and Nelson didn't divulge, the substance of their conversation. In fact, Lenny had counseled Nelson to hold off taking action, he would tend to the problem when he got out in the spring. But Nelson ignored his advice.

"Did there come a time when you took definite actions against Yellow-Top?" Brownell asked.

"Yes."

"What is it you did?"

"I put a hit on them," Nelson said.

Nelson then described his preparations on December 16: having Fat Danny drive Perez' white Cadillac to the Bronx that day; parking his own blue Monte Carlo near the basketball courts on Cypress, a safe distance away from the alley where Yellow-Top conducted their sales; and transporting a knapsack full of guns from his home to Brenda's, an apartment the gang used as a stash house on the fourth floor of 352 Beekman. "Where had you gotten those handguns from?" Brownell asked him.

"From the kid."

"What's his name?"

"Raymond [Polanco]," Nelson said.

Later, Nelson said, he cased the neighborhood with Freddy Krueger, Platano, and Tezo, then met with still more gang members— including Stanley Tukes and Rennie Harris—on the roof overlooking

Yellow-Top's alleyway. "What were you doing, Mr. Sepulveda?" Brownell asked.

"You, personally," Snyder cautioned him.

"I was looking down, looking for Gerard [Heard, Yellow-Top's owner], and talking to Platano and Freddy."

"When you say you were looking for Gerard, where exactly were you looking at that time?"

"Looking down to the street."

"Did you see anyone in the street?"

"Yes."

"Who did you see?"

"I saw Amp there on the street."

"Who's Amp?"

"The manager. The fellow that was downstairs."

"I'm sorry, manager of—"

"Of Yellow-Top."

"Where exactly was Amp when you saw him at that time?" Brownell asked.

"In front of the alleyway."

"Did you see anyone else on the street at that particular time?"

"Yes."

"Who?"

"I saw Gerard talking to him."

"And was this the same Gerard that you had been looking for earlier in the evening, or someone else?"

"Same one," Nelson said.

"You said you were talking to Platano and Freddy. Is that correct?"

"Yes."

"And what was the conversation about at that time?"

"I was talking to them about how I wanted to do it."

"What were you telling them about it?"

"I was telling them that I wanted a couple of guys from the back, a couple of guys from the front."

"When you say in the back and in the front, what are you referring to?"

"Guys on the street in front of the alleyway and behind the alleyway."

"And was there any response by either Freddy or Platano or both at that time?"

"Yes."

"What was the response?"

"Freddy told me we couldn't do it like that."

"Who said that?"

"Freddy."

"You said you had some guns in a knapsack. Is that correct?" Brownell asked.

"Yes."

"Were they with you at that particular time?"

"Yes," Nelson said.

"Where were they?"

"On me. On my shoulder."

"Did there come a time when you left the roof?"

"Yes."

"About how long had you been up on the roof before you left?"

"About twenty, twenty-five minutes."

"And was there any particular reason why you left the roof at that time?"

"Yes."

"Was that because someone had seen the police?"

"Yes."

Nelson said he went back to Brenda's with Freddy and Platano, and waited about twenty minutes before returning to the roof. This time Fat Danny and Daniel Gonzalez had joined the group. "And was there any conversation when you were up on the roof the second time?" Brownell asked.

"Yes."

"What was the conversation about?"

"Freddy told me to leave it up to him, for him to do the job," Nelson said.

"How long were you on the roof the second time?"

"A good twenty minutes—twenty, fifteen minutes."

"Did there come a time when you left?"

"Yes."

"Did you leave with someone else or by yourself?"

"By myself."

"Were you the first to leave of the group that was up there the second time?"

"Yes."

"Where were the guns when you left?"

"I handed them over to Platano," Nelson said.

"And were the guns still in the knapsack or in some other fashion?"

"In the knapsack."

"When you gave the guns to Platano, describe exactly what you did."

"I just said, 'Platano, I leave it in your hands. I call you tomorrow. Here, here's the guns.' "

Nelson returned to Brenda's building across the rooftops and exited down the stairs, stopping on the first-floor landing to transfer the day's receipts from his jacket to his pants pockets. "And after you stuffed the money in the pockets of your clothes, what else, if anything, did you do?" Brownell asked.

"Started rolling a blunt."

"When you say a blunt, what do you mean?"

"A marijuana cigarette," Nelson said.

"And where did you do that?"

"In the building."

"And which building are you referring to?"

"Brenda's building."

"Did there come a time when you actually heard shots?" Brownell asked.

"Yes."

"How long, how much time has passed between when you left the guns with Platano on the roof and when you heard shots?"

Nelson estimated a half hour. "Where were you when you actually heard shots?" Brownell asked him.

"In the basement."

"When you say the basement, what are you referring to?"

"The basement of the last building toward St. Mary's."

"Is that the same building you have been referring to as Brenda's building?"

"Yes."

"Then, when you heard the shots, can you describe for us exactly what you heard?"

"I heard a lot of shots."

"Were you able to count them?"

"No."

"Did you see anybody shooting that particular night?"

"No."

"What, if anything, did you do when you heard the shots?"

"I proceeded across the park to go to my car."

"Where was your car at that particular time?"

"On Cypress."

"How was it you still happened to be on Beekman Avenue, the end of Beekman Avenue, when the shots were heard?" Brownell asked.

"I wanted to hear the shots."

"Why?"

"I wanted to be sure that the job was done."

"And once the job was done, and you walked across to your car, what did you do?"

"I went home."

Nelson's examination continued for another hour. He related how he kidded Platano the next day that he'd made the front page of the papers, how they'd disposed of the used guns in the Hudson, tossing them off the jogger's track on the George Washington Bridge. And he told the jury how a few weeks later he and Stanley Tukes had summarily executed a customer—a former Corrections officer named Anthony Villerbe—whom Nelson suspected of paying with counterfeit bills. But once he'd described his actions on the night of the Quad—coolly surveying his targets from the rooftop overlooking the alleyway; smoking a blunt in the basement of Brenda's building and listening for the first sounds of slaughter—the rest of Nelson's testimony smacked of anticlimax.

THE LAST MONTH of the trial was the toughest, an exercise in endurance. Don Hill picked up a flu bug that laid him up for a week and persisted through March. Grifa managed to struggle through the days all right, but returned home most nights too tired to eat, falling asleep on the couch with her clothes on. At least she slept. Brownell barely slept *or* ate in the weeks before his summation. He developed dark half-dollar-sized circles under his eyes, and he looked haggard and emaciated. Grifa joked that she could fit three fingers in the space between his neck and his shirt collar, but it came out sounding like a simple statement of fact, no stranger or more remarkable than the facts the prosecutors were eliciting daily in court.

After Nelson, they called Martha Molina, a 23-year-old poster girl for the evils of crack. With a confirmed IQ of 75, and the voice and manner of a child, Molina recited the sad poetry of her life on Beekman Avenue. Born fatherless, she began smoking marijuana when she was eight, graduated to crack at 11, and sold drugs and then her body to pay for her habit. The Cowboys weren't responsible for her condition, of course, but they showed no sympathy for her deficits and exploited her at every turn. They sold her a steady supply of crack, hired her as a pitcher and a lookout, and generally mocked her as the village idiot. Once, when her manager mistakenly thought she'd shorted him on the count—cheated him on the receipts—he slammed a brick in her face. A few weeks later, at the age of 20, she suffered a stroke and lapsed into a monthlong coma, waking with blurred eyesight and chunks of her memory missing. However, she did remember being on the roof with Oscar Alvarez the night that Linwood Collins shot him—Collins told her before he left, "The only reason I don't kill you is I know your brother"—and she recalled being in Yellow-Top's spot when the Cowboys opened fire the night of the Quad. She escaped through a tear in the chain-link fence at the rear of the alley.

The prosecutors also presented two more murders, Pasqualito's public executions of Papito, the Brooklyn dealer who'd impeded the Cowboys' start-up operation in Brighton Beach, and of Frankie Cuevas. Among the eyewitnesses who testified was Manny Guerrero, the bodyguard whom Pasqualito shot in the stomach after he killed Cuevas. The stare the two old enemies exchanged, while Snyder fielded a phone call, spoke more eloquently about their violent history than anything Guerrero said on the stand.

But nothing seemed to shock the jury anymore. Perhaps the sheer volume of evidence had desensitized them. It had certainly fatigued them. Mercifully, the defense produced few witnesses, preferring to make their case through rebuttal and summation. It was time to close.

The defense summed up over five days in mid-April. Faced with a surfeit of damning testimony, they cited the lack of objective evidence—murder weapons, car registrations, telephone logs—linking their clients to the violent acts charged in the indictment. Then they went after the witnesses, attacking their character, drug use, mental competence, and, especially, their motives. All nine lawyers highlighted the benefits the prosecution's witnesses received for fingering the defendants: reduced sentences, early paroles, cash, and relocation expenses.

Brownell addressed these points at the start of his summation, using the arguments he'd first broached during jury selection. Yes, many prosecution witnesses were less than upstanding citizens; but one would hardly expect to find upstanding citizens hanging out with drug dealers, much less in a position to witness their crack deals and murders. Yes, many witnesses received benefits; but one could hardly expect them to risk their lives testifying without some inducement, if only the promise of protection. Moreover, Brownell pointed out, cooperation agreements were structured so that the surest way for witnesses to lose their benefits was to perjure themselves.

But the main weakness in the defense's contentions, Brownell asserted, was their common assumption of a vast counterconspiracy, an almost unimaginably cynical plan by the many DAs, detectives, and police officers involved in the case to thwart and manipulate testimony. How else could so many witnesses—civilian and police—corroborate each other on so many vital points? Either they had to be telling the truth or a substantial portion of New York law enforcement was part of an intricate scheme to orchestrate their lies.

How intricate? Brownell spent the next day and a half analyzing the prosecution's case for the jury. It was, by any measure, a tour de force. The trial had run nearly six months (not including hearings and jury selection), featured more than sixty witnesses, and generated over 25,000 pages of transcript. An inveterate list maker, Brownell had outlined all 25,000-plus pages of testimony. Then he'd broken down the indictment's various charges into their provable elements, and cross-referenced them with the witnesses' statements. Now, as he ranged over the Cowboys' major crimes, piecing together bits of testimony from different witnesses, he built strikingly coherent pictures of each act, each defendant's record.

Taming so much material had required a daunting mastery of

detail; communicating the results cost a debilitating physical effort. By the second day, Brownell's voice had petered to a reed-thin whisper. At times he seemed light on his feet, grasping the jury-box railing for support, letting the dense accumulations of evidence serve as his ballast. One could impeach the credibility of almost any witness, Brownell had conceded earlier. But when he superimposed the recollections of Michael and Little Iris Cruz onto Nelson's testimony about the Quad, and then added the observations of Janice Bruington and other eyewitnesses with no connection to each other—well, it was impossible to ignore the uncanny way their stories dovetailed and overlapped.

AT 5 P.M. on May 15, the jury-room buzzer sounded in Snyder's court, as it had every working day for the past two weeks, a signal of frustration, a grating on the nerves. Brownell stood up from his perch in the jury box and began gathering his papers. It was quitting time. Another day shot. All around him lawyers were making similar leave-taking gestures. Only Lori Grifa kept still in her seat. Something about the way the buzzer had sounded—longer, more emphatic. She reached out with a staying hand to Brownell. "We have a verdict," she said.

Brownell gave her an annoyed look. The jury had been deliberating for fifteen days—longer than any jury in any of the prosecutors' memories—and had given no sign they were close to a resolution. In fact, they'd recently asked if they could render a partial verdict, just one of the many troubling notes they'd sent to the judge. In another, a juror asked: "If the children under 16, Little Iris, Joey Morales, etc., were used in any capacity in the drug organization, and their parents knew what they were doing and did not object, call the police, protest, etc., can the defendants be held accountable under conspiracy one?" (Snyder answered with a resounding yes.)

Trying to divine a jury's mind-set from their requests for materials or guidance is like trying to read the future in tea leaves. Predictions are invariably subjective, more a reflection of those making them than the evidence at hand. Brownell and Hill, prudent by nature, felt that the length of the deliberations and the tenor of the notes indicated that some jurors were looking for reasons to acquit. Grifa saw the glass as half full. In her view, the jury knew they were about to send the defendants to prison for the rest of their lives and wanted to cross their t's. But few at HIU shared Grifa's optimism. They knew it took only one recalcitrant juror to block a verdict, and it didn't help anyone's state of mind when, a few days earlier, Snyder asked Brownell if he was prepared to retry the Quad independently in the event of a hung jury.

It didn't help either that Snyder insisted the lawyers wait in the courtroom during deliberations. She didn't want to have to round up twelve attorneys when the jury did reach a verdict, and she also wanted them present to help her respond to the jury's questions. So Brownell and his fellow litigants haunted the gallery and jury box like die-hard fans during a rain delay. They read newspapers, worked at crossword puzzles, and when Snyder repaired to her chambers, catnapped or played poker at the defense table. At other times they perused the trial transcripts, trying to anticipate questions from the jury, succeeding more often in raising questions of their own.

"We have a verdict." For a moment Brownell continued shuffling papers, unable to digest the meaning of the remark. Then he stopped. This time the speaker had been Rocco DeSantis, Snyder's clerk, who'd just returned from the jury room. Brownell sat down. All he could think was: It's finally over.

It was still another hour before the jurors filed into the courtroom. It had taken that long to assemble security, bring in the prisoners, alert the press. Meanwhile the pews filled up, jammed to capacity with reporters, cameramen, family and friends of the defendants, and personnel from HIDTA and HIU—Eddie Benitez, Tebbens, Dugan, Arsenault, Quinn. Then, shortly after 4:30 P.M., Snyder brought in the jury; the jury foreperson, a small Hispanic woman dressed in a business suit, stood facing the bench; and DeSantis read the first charge. "How say you to the first count under Indictment 10614 of 1993 charging the defendant Daniel Rincon with the crime of conspiracy in the first degree, guilty or not guilty?" he asked.

"Guilty," the foreperson said.

"How say you as to the thirteenth count under Indictment 10614 of 1993 charging the defendant Daniel Rincon with the crime of murder in the second degree, guilty or not guilty?"

"Guilty."

"How say you as to the fourteenth count under Indictment 10614 of 1993 charging the defendant Daniel Rincon with the crime of murder in the second degree, guilty or not guilty?"

"Guilty."

The verdict was an overwhelming victory for the prosecution. All but two counts resulted in convictions, and the two that didn't—the Rooftop murder and Michael Cruz's Brooklyn shooting—hung at 11–1 for. From all the security in the courtroom—there must have been thirty white-shirted officers milling about the well—Brownell had guessed the verdict. There are few secrets at 100 Centre Street. But as the clerk scrolled down the list of counts, and the jury foreperson chanted guilty 10, 15, 20, 27 times, all three prosecutors experienced an overpowering sense of vindication.

EPILOGUE

ON JUNE 27, the parties to the Cowboy trial met one final time in Snyder's packed courtroom for sentencing. Several defendants spoke first, most of them protesting their innocence. One, Rennie Harris, showed remorse, apologizing to Anthony Green's parents for his part in the Quad. Finally, after the prosecutors voiced their sentencing recommendations, Judge Snyder delivered *her* judgment: "You have no values," she said, glaring at the defendants who had mocked her throughout the trial. "You have no morality. You have no respect for the law. Your lives were simple. You had only one law. If someone got in your way, kill them. Well, I intend to make the rest of your lives very simple.

"A tired neighborhood was almost brought to its knees in fear and hopelessness thanks to your reign of terror, and we can only count the visible victims. Who knows how many others exist? You thought you were above the law. You think you're above the law. No wonder. You were let out on bail all the time in the past, and you committed more crimes, and you were still let out on bail. You scared the witnesses off. You laughed in the faces of the police and the criminal justice system. No one could touch you. You could get away with virtually everything.

"But now we know this: you are not above the law. Because the witnesses in this case did their job. They came forward and spoke truthfully despite threats, intimidation, and shootings. The police did their job, especially Detective Mark Tebbens, bravely and courageously and with absolute perseverance, because it took years. The District Attorney's offices of New York County, the Bronx, and Brooklyn came together to do their job. And the men and the women on the jury did their job.

"Now I have to do my job. Let this sentence be a measure to every other vicious and violent drug gang terrorizing our streets. You will be brought to justice and you will be removed from society forever. This is my job and that is what I am going to do here."

Surrounded by double rows of police, already shackled hand and foot, the nine Cowboy defendants heard their sentences read out in a silence broken only by the anguished cries of their families and girlfriends. Linwood Collins received 20 years; Rennie Harris, $48^{1}/_{3}$ years; Tezo, 50 years; Victor Mercedes, $66^{2}/_{3}$ years; Pasqualito, $116^{2}/_{3}$ years; Platano, $133^{1}/_{3}$ years; Stanley Tukes, $133^{1}/_{3}$ years; Daniel Gonzalez, $141^{2}/_{3}$ years; Fat Danny, $158^{1}/_{3}$ years.

No doubt, the steep sentences sent a message to other gangs on the street. It clearly sent a message to the remaining defendants in the case, all of whom pled to state time before the end of the year.

Nor did HIU rest on its laurels. In the four years following the

Cowboy verdict, the unit successfully prosecuted more than twenty new cases, including major initiatives in Manhattan Valley, the Lower East Side, central Harlem, and midtown. During that time, HIU locked up over 500 gang members and solved more than 50 homicides.

Meanwhile, New York City's crime rate plummeted to levels not seen since the early 1960s. There's been much debate over the reasons for the decline. Certainly, the city's administration deserves the lion's share of the credit. Between January 1994, when Rudolph Giuliani became mayor, and April 1996, when his Police Commissioner, William Bratton, resigned, New York's homicide rate declined 50 percent, a figure that far exceeded the national average, as well as expectations based on non-police-related phenomena (i.e., demographic changes, the peaking of the crack epidemic, and the organization of the crack trade). But reductions in Manhattan's murder rate began earlier than 1994 and were greater than in other boroughs, a difference that Morgenthau, writing in a *Times* op-ed piece, attributed in large part to HIU.

Precinct statistics yield an even clearer example of the unit's effectiveness. After the Cowboy takedown in September 1993, the murder rate in the Four-Oh, the gang's base of operations, dropped sharply, far more than the citywide average. There was an even more dramatic contraction in Manhattan Valley after an HIU initiative there the following year. A small Hispanic neighborhood nestled between Columbia University and the Upper West Side, the Valley had become a war zone in the early 1990s. At least three major crack gangs were vying for supremacy and there were shootings virtually every week. In 1993 alone, there were twenty-six drug-related homicides in the tiny precinct, including the murders of two innocent bystanders. The police had not only lost control of the streets but were themselves targets of the mindless violence. In early 1994, HIU launched a campaign against the gangs. By the year's end, the number of murders had dropped to twelve, and in 1995, after HIU took out its third gang, the Natural Born Killers, there was only one gang-related homicide.

Yet despite its proven success, HIU has not been replicated by local New York law enforcement, although its initiatives have been adopted in other cities around the world. Both Don Hill and Lori Grifa lobbied their offices to set up HIU-style units in the wake of the Cowboy trial—without success. Moreover, HIU's experiment in sweeping citywide investigations ended with the Cowboys.

Their official statements notwithstanding, the Bronx was not happy with Manhattan's handling of the case. Not only did they resent the way Ryan and Rather dealt with Fat Danny's arrest, but they took exception to the stipulations in Lenny's plea agreement, which they felt—mistakenly, as it turned out—jeopardized convictions in another Bronx case. And even though the HIU-led investigation scuttled the Cowboys—arguably the Bronx's most violent and resilient street gang—it failed to shed much luster on the Bronx DA's office. The Cowboys were tried in Manhattan, the case press conferences took place in Morgenthau's office, and the papers and local news reports gave the lion's share of the credit for the gang's demise to HIU and Morgenthau.

Once again, the twin issues of turf and credit—law enforcement's Scylla and Charybdis—raised their monstrous heads, effectively barring future cooperation between Manhattan and the Bronx. They also took their toll on the professional lives of the individuals involved. Don Hill's career would suffer from his close association with the case. Never part of the Bronx's inner circle, Hill found himself even more estranged after his two-year sojourn in Manhattan; and despite his tilts with Ryan and Rather, he was perceived by his bosses as having divided loyalties. On his return to the Bronx, his proposal to set up a gang unit was summarily turned down, and feeling increasingly isolated from the centers of power, he resigned from the Bronx in March 1997 to start his own practice—a small-town law office near his home in Darien, Connecticut.

Back in Brooklyn, Lori Grifa did get permission to try gang cases and managed to run a successful investigation against a heroin outfit in the Williamsburg section of Brooklyn. But she received no support—not one ADA or investigator was assigned to help her—and she left her office in 1996 to join the litigation department of a New Jersey–based real estate firm.

Mark Tebbens' career may have taken the biggest hit. Throughout the investigation, he'd batted back and forth between postings—the Four-Oh squad, HIDTA, the Bronx DA's squad, the Major Case squad—landing finally at HIU, where he was viewed as an orphan, an NYPD detective without an NYPD boss or protector. Nor was he surprised by his predicament. The day Tebbens transferred to HIU to work full-time on the Cowboys, Quinn had warned him: "This is a once-in-a-career type of case. But it will cause you problems. The Department won't like it, and you will not get promoted."

Quinn had been right. Though several detectives peripherally associated with the investigation were promoted to grade, Tebbens, the acknowledged hero of the case, was not. But he had no regrets. He'd achieved what he'd set out to do almost six years before the verdict—clean the Cowboys off Beekman Avenue—and watching the defendants as the verdict was read, seeing the surprise on their faces, and the recognition, as they bowed their heads, that this was finally it, he'd felt it was worth it. Tebbens stayed on at HIU for another eighteen months, and worked on the Manhattan Valley investigation before transferring to the Cold Case squad. He remains a detective third grade, the lowest rank in the division.

Others fared better in the aftermath of the case. Dan Rather continues to head the Firearms Trafficking Unit at the Manhattan DA's office, where Nancy Ryan is beginning her fourteenth year as chief of the Trial Division.

Barbara Jones was appointed to the federal bench in 1998.

Robert Morgenthau was elected to his sixth term as New York County's DA in 1997.

Leslie Crocker Snyder remains a state Supreme Court judge, and is often mentioned as a possible successor to Morgenthau.

Fernando Camacho retired to private practice in 1995 and was appointed Criminal Court judge in 1999.

Garry Dugan, who joined HIU midway through the case, considers the Cowboy investigation to be the capstone of his twenty-five-year career on the force. For once it seemed that every shard of evidence he'd dug up—license plate numbers, phone records, rap sheets, informant interviews—had proved useful. The trial alone had closed out ten homicides. Lenny and Nelson had pled to another four. And HIU's investigation had enabled police to solve an additional twenty-three murders. Dugan remains a senior investigator with HIU.

Dan Brownell also regards the Cowboy case as the peak of his career as a prosecutor. Though he was made deputy chief of HIU shortly after the Cowboy verdict in 1995, and has tried numerous homicides since then, he's never had another case with the scope and importance of the Cowboys.

Terry Quinn and Walter Arsenault recall the Cowboy case with mixed emotions. Its investigation and prosecution defined HIU's approach to future cases, and its impact on the street and in law enforcement circles established HIU as arguably the world's preeminent gang unit. But it also cost them their mentor and friend, Nancy Ryan. Ryan's Asian Gang unit had provided the model for HIU, and she had built the unit into a powerful force, one capable of taking on the Cowboys in the first place. Moreover, she had brought Arsenault to HIU and promoted him to be its chief.

Quinn, Arsenault, and Brownell continue to make cases at HIU.

Meanwhile, the Cowboy case has spawned several major investigations. In December 1994, the Feds arrested Jose Reyes, a.k.a. El Feo, Lenny's erstwhile ally and supplier. Using Lenny as their star witness, prosecutors from New York's Southern District convicted Reyes on racketeering charges in July 1996, and he was sentenced to life without parole. Raymond Polanco, the Cowboys' gun supplier, was also convicted of racketeering and murder charges by U.S. Attorneys from the city's Eastern District, and sentenced to life in April 1997. Both Garry Dugan and Lenny testified for the prosecution. Then, in June 1997, Dominican police arrested Freddy Krueger in his island hideout and returned him to the United States, where he pled guilty to fourteen murders and was sentenced to 50 years in prison. HIU played a pivotal role in all three prosecutions.

Finally, on March 2, 1999, Lenny and Nelson themselves appeared before Leslie Crocker Snyder for sentencing. Apart from HIU and David Cargill's parents, the courtroom was empty of spectators. Reporters, had they known about them, would have considered the proceedings routine. Lenny's and Nelson's plea agreements—25 years to life and 22 years to life, respectively—had been public information since the trial four years ago. Besides, the media were focused on the city's plummeting crime rate. The Cowboys were old news.

But for the DAs and detectives in attendance, the event was far from ordinary. Before Snyder pronounced sentencing, Anne Cargill addressed the court, reading into the record a simple but eloquent account of her family's ordeal. "We came to this country thirty-five years ago with twenty-five dollars and two children under two," she said. "And we had all the hopes of any immigrants. And many of our dreams have come true.

"But on that day, May 19, 1991—I will never forget it—our only son didn't come home.

"And these things, I just didn't believe these things happen to people like us. We obeyed the laws, did what we were supposed to do. All our children have college degrees. And what more could we do?"

Anne Cargill talked about her son, his goodness and his foibles, and the devastation his murder wreaked upon his sisters, his father, and herself. "It's not so violently painful now," she said. "But the first two years, I was an absolute basket case. There wasn't a day I didn't cry my heart out."

And the pain never went away completely. "I had a terrible time a year ago when I went to his best friend's wedding and his best friend danced with his mom. I'll never get to do this. I'll never get to know who my son would have married. I'll never get to see my grandchildren by him.

"And because of one senseless act."

Anne Cargill said she wanted Lenny to know what he had done to her and her family, but there was no rancor in her voice. "We have gone on, thank God," she told the court. "We now have eleven grandchildren. We have done things the right way . . . And the United States has been good to us. But I'm awfully glad that people like Nelson and Lenny are not going to be roaming our streets anymore."

A few minutes later, Nelson stood at the defendants' table and apologized for himself and his brother. "You know," he said, "I was the first one to find this jungle out there, the Bronx, dragging my brother with me, put him through a lot of things that, you know, that an older brother should know [better]."

He glanced back to the Cargills. "I'm sorry to everybody there for the casualty, for this mindless war, trying to make all the money we could, all the wrong ways, all the wrong reasons," he told them.

He apologized, too, to his co-defendants. "We plucked guys out of school and showed them money, and out of churches, just to be around.

"It's sad, you know, to have to be before you right now, say these things there," he finished. "My family had a lot of promise for me and I just let them down, let everybody down. Sorry."

Sitting at the prosecutors' table, Dan Brownell was surprised by Nelson's speech; he had not tried to make excuses or shift the blame. But he was even more surprised when moments later Lenny rose to make amends. Lenny wasn't expected to speak. "I had all the opportunity in the world to take advantage in this great country, and I just couldn't," the former gang leader said in a choked voice. "Can't express, but I'm sorry to cause the family [pain]. Hope everybody in the court-room can forgive me, find it in their heart to forgive me. Sorry."

And so the Cowboy saga ended, not with a bang, but with a whimper. Watching from the jury box, Walter Arsenault felt a sense of closure—not only of the case but of an era. "The Cowboys were the last of the big shoot-'em-up gangs," he said afterward outside the court-room. "When Lenny and Nelson went away, it put a punctuation point on the end of the Wild West syndrome in New York City."

But it was Lori Grifa who had perhaps best captured what the Cowboy case meant. Nearly seven years earlier, on a sunny afternoon shortly after the takedown in September 1993, she'd driven up to Beek-man Avenue with Mark Tebbens to view the block firsthand. The alley-way where four men and women had died in a hail of Cowboy bullets was vacant when they got there. So was the one adjoining No. 348, where tens of thousands of dollars' worth of drugs changed hands every day. Only a blister of rock poking through the cement and a red paint stain evoked the carnage that once emanated from the Hole.

Two hundred yards south, crack dealers still hawked their goods in the doorways along 141st Street. But on Beekman Avenue, the only sounds came from children playing in the street. Grifa had gone up to the roof of No. 348, where lookouts once scouted for police. It was a glorious fall day, the kind you sometimes get in New York when the seasons change, the air clear and fresh, yet warm against the skin. She watched for a moment or two while two girls drew a hopscotch grid on the pavement six stories down, and farther up the block, a group of youngsters tossed a football around. She reflected that she would never again do anything that would mean as much as what she was doing then, that at 31 her best work was behind her.

But that thought passed quickly. She descended to the street, as the people in the neighborhood gathered around Tebbens, touching him like he was some kind of miracle worker, a healer or a saint. It was a heartening image—the tall, muscular detective in the foreground, and behind him children running pass patterns on the street that for years had seen only crack vials and bullets. And it was an image not lost on the residents. A local man, a super who'd serviced several Cowboy strongholds, walked up to Tebbens and Grifa and shook each of their hands. "That's the first time I've seen children playing here in five years," he said.